FIRE
in the Fireplace:

Contemporary Charismatic Renewal

Charles E. Hummel

InterVarsity Press
Downers Grove
Illinois 60515

InterVarsity Press is the book-publishing division of Inter-Varsity Christian Fellowship, a student movement active on campus at hundreds of universities, colleges and schools of nursing. For information about local and regional activities, write IVCF, 233 Langdon St., Madison, WI 53703.

Distributed in Canada through InterVarsity Press, 1875 Leslie St., Unit 10, Don Mills, Ontario M3B 2M5, Canada.

Unless otherwise indicated, all New Testament quotations are from the New International Version, copyright © New York International Bible Society, 1973, used by permission. All Old Testament quotations are from the Revised Standard Version of the Bible, copyrighted 1946, 1952, © 1971, 1973 by the Division of Christian Education of the National Council of Churches of Christ, and used by permission.

ISBN 0-87784-742-8
Library of Congress Catalog Card Number: 77-006031

Printed in the United States of America

21	20	19	18	17	16	15	14	13	12	11	10	9	8	7	6	5	4
96	95	94	93	92	91	90	89	88	87	86	85	84	83	82	81		

To Anne and Wylie

I am grateful for the life and witness of many in the charismatic renewal through whom I have experienced new dimensions in the grace of our Lord Jesus Christ, the love of God and the fellowship of the Holy Spirit.

Counsel and criticism from Earle Ellis, Gordon Fee, Donald Freeman, Everett Fullam, Robert Geehan, Russell Hitt, Clark Pinnock, John Randall and Roger Stronstad are greatly appreciated.

Special thanks to Anna-Lisa Madeira for help in preparation of the manuscript.

Part One:
The Spreading Flame

Part Two:

The Spirit in Luke/Acts

Part Three:
The Spirit in Paul's Letters

Part Four:
Contemporary Issues

Part One:
The Spreading Flame

1
The Fireplace and the Fire

During the Cambodian crisis of 1970 students staged a demonstration at the University of California in Los Angeles. Thousands thronged the approaches to the administration building. Placards bobbed up and down. In the distance, amidst a variety of political slogans, one sign featured four words: "Jesus Yes, Christianity No!"

Why did one student parade this sign? What did he want to communicate? At the very least he was affirming something positive about Jesus while rejecting the establishment called Christianity. Many people today share this ambiguity. They are repelled by the organized church with its programs and seeming irrelevance to the problems of society. Yet somehow they cannot escape the magnetic influence of Jesus Christ.

In a sense this student was right. Much that passes for Christianity in our culture is not Christian. But this is not what Jesus intended. He promised his disciples, "I will build my church" (Mt. 16:18). In the decades following his resurrection the Christian community grew rapidly. Patterns of organization developed. Apostles inspired by the Holy Spirit wrote Gospels and letters which became the New Testament. Throughout the centuries Jesus Christ has been proclaimed by and known through his church. Yet many people like this student at UCLA are not attracted to the established churches.

In recent years students have challenged many institutional structures. They reject systems which dehumanize people frantically struggling to grasp products offering the "good life." As one said bitterly, "I've come to see that even if I do win the rat race, I'm still a rat." In 1970 Harvard senior Mark Gerzon wrote *The Whole World Is Watching*. He noted: "Society has highly praised financial and occupational betterment as the main goal in life, but the young people realize that the only valid purpose of striving for these goals would be to live a fuller life."[1]

Disillusioned with contemporary structures and goals, a counterculture developed its own means to a fuller life. Some pursued self-realization through drugs, alcohol and other kinds of trips. Others went back to nature or into Yoga, Zen or transcendental meditation. Spiritism thrived, while astrology became a new religion.

Into this topsy-turvy scene came the Jesus Movement attracting thousands of young people. In fact, people of all ages suddenly became interested in Jesus. Pasolini's *Gospel According to Saint Matthew* arrested the attention of the film world; *Godspell*, using the text of the Gospels, swept the United States and Europe. Yet people did not turn in large numbers to the churches, where it might have been expected they would discover the full life which Jesus promised (Jn. 10:10). What had gone wrong? Where had the institutional church lost out?

Organization and Life   We find a clue in a comment by Samuel Shoemaker when he was rector of Calvary Episcopal Church in Pittsburgh. Following World War 2 he had a remarkable ministry among college and university students. Many whom I met as I traveled for Inter-Varsity Christian Fellowship in the Northeast during the 1950s had been changed by God through his influence.

In 1952 Shoemaker was the main speaker for Religion-in-Life Week at the University of Pittsburgh. Representatives from a wide variety of denominations—Baptist and Presbyterian, Episcopal and Roman Catholic—were invited to share their faith. Student response was surprisingly good for what had cynically become known as "Nod-to-God Week."

During his address at a closing dinner for speakers and student leaders, Shoemaker surprised us by remarking, "Some have likened the Episcopal Church to the fireplace and the Methodist Church to the fire." After pausing for laughter at his own expense, he continued, "You'll have to admit, however, that the best place for a fire is in the fireplace, and not out in the middle of the floor!" He did not talk about denominational differences, but dealt with a problem that has plagued all churches: the relationship between the organization and the life it is supposed to encourage.

Every organism requires some degree of organization to channel its energy and fulfill its mission. So it is natural for the church to develop confessions of faith, services of worship and programs of activity. Imperceptibly, however, the inner life tends to wane even though the outward form persists. Throughout church history the flame in many organizational fireplaces has flickered and died. Though the fireplace was designed initially to foster a blaze, accumulations of soot eventually clogged the flue and smothered the fire.

The history of human organizations shows this sequence: man, movement, method, monument. A dynamic leader rises to meet the needs of the hour. A following of committed disciples develop a movement with distinctive patterns of activity. Then a second generation of leadership emerges. As the years go by, methods become inflexible and movement often becomes monument. The fireplace may be magnificent, but sometimes only smoldering embers remain.

Eventually another generation, feeling the cold, tries to rekindle the fire. Unfortunately, it does not burn well; the flue is clogged and the hearth no longer fosters a blaze. Yet the custodians of the fireplace often resist the cleaning or painful remodeling which is now necessary. Perhaps they have grown comfortable in customs and secure in traditions which have assumed divine authority. Change, with its risk and discomfort, is resisted.

So the kindlers of the flame are tempted—or even forced—to move their fire out into the middle of the floor. Then, one of two things is likely to happen. Either the fire rages out of control, or its isolated coals die down for lack of a proper hearth. Samuel Shoemaker was right: the best place for a fire is in the fireplace. But it should be cleaned and, if necessary, remodeled.

In recent years the Lord of the church has fanned smoldering embers and lighted new fires in many fireplaces. Spiritual renewal has appeared in a variety of forms. The most significant, in terms of its beginning, its movement across denominational boundaries and its continuing growth, is the charismatic renewal. Like others in the history of the church, it has arrived in a shape as unexpected as it was unplanned, and as controversial as it is powerful. No wonder it stirs reactions ranging from enthusiastic welcome to perplexity to violent rejection.

A Strategic Approach   My first encounter with this renewal and other events that followed have led to a profound change in my view of the Holy Spirit's activity in the life of the church today. Events I never expected to witness opened new windows into Scripture. Study of crucial New Testament passages has given me a greater appreciation of the nature and purpose of spiritual gifts in the body of Christ.

During my college years I realized that Christians are not the only people with presuppositions; the scientist, the historian, the economist all operate on basic assumptions. Since none of us is completely objective in approaching any subject, we should honestly admit this fact and try to recognize our assumptions.

This principle hit home in my graduate studies which introduced me to theological traditions other than the one in which

I was raised. It was disconcerting to discover that over the years I had not studied Scripture as objectively as I had thought. Like others, I had viewed its teaching through a lens colored by an inherited theological system, midtwentieth-century American culture and my personal experience. So I resolved to be more open in the future to the discovery of biblical truth I might have misunderstood or overlooked.

I have come to appreciate the significance of our Lord's criticism of the Sadducees: "You are in error because you do not know the Scriptures or the power of God" (Mt. 22:29). The Bible's teaching directs our actions and helps us interpret our experiences. Likewise God's power in our lives opens new windows of understanding his Word. This dynamic interaction develops a deepening relationship with God, who teaches us through the Scriptures we read and the events we experience. The book of Job, for example, gives clues to the meaning of suffering. But we do not really understand this message —in fact, we hardly take it seriously—until we suffer. Our initial knowledge may come from the Bible, but deeper understanding comes only as we put teaching into practice. This principle has shaped my understanding of the charismatic renewal which has developed over the last decade.

By its very nature the current charismatic renewal is difficult to describe. Springing up spontaneously across the full spectrum of churches, from Protestant to Roman Catholic to Greek Orthodox, its teaching and practice assume varied forms. Reports are not only different but sometimes contradictory, depending on where it is observed and what the viewer is looking for.

One difficulty lies in the fact that the renewal is not a movement, such as those led by Francis of Assisi, Martin Luther and John Wesley. It cannot be traced to one outstanding leader and his followers with the stamp of their doctrinal and organizational convictions. Nor is it like the modern ecumenical movement which was initiated by theological scholars and church leaders.

Rather, the charismatic renewal started as a pattern of events in the lives of a wide variety of Christians. This pattern comes to focus in the exercise of the full range of spiritual gifts (*charisms*) for strengthening the body of Christ in worship, evangelism and service. At the heart of this renewal, amidst its diversity of ecclesiastical and cultural expression, is the doctrine and experience of the gracious gifts of the Holy Spirit.

The following pages view the charismatic renewal in historical and biblical perspective. The approach has been guided by the stages of my own understanding: encounter with contemporary events, reading of history, study of Scripture and struggle with thorny theological issues. The biblical study is by no means a complete account of the Spirit's activity in the church. Rather, it concentrates on two New Testament writings of crucial importance for the charismatic renewal: Luke-Acts and 1 Corinthians.

In my study I have tried to be objective in the sense of "being open to the nature of the subject with a willingness to accept what the evidence demonstrated, even though it challenged long cherished beliefs."[2] I remembered the Bereans who listened to the Apostle Paul's message and then "examined the Scriptures every day to see if what Paul said was true" (Acts 17:11).

This book evaluates the charismatic renewal on the basis of participation as well as study. From its beginning the basis of Christian communication has been personal witness (1 Jn. 1:1). A Christian witness reports an experience of God's redeeming activity so that others may share in it. Like a road sign that does not call attention to itself, a witness points to the path for travel. This book is intended to be a witness and a helpful sign for those who may desire to travel with an open mind along new paths of thought and action in the direction of charismatic renewal.

2
A Secular University

A Saturday morning with the family in autumn 1962 was interrupted by the imperious ring of the telephone. The call came from Inter-Varsity Christian Fellowship regional director Stan Rock in New England to my home in the Chicago suburbs. While emergency phone calls from field staff were not a new experience for me, I was hardly prepared for his question. "What's the official Inter-Varsity policy on speaking in tongues?" When my surprise subsided, I told him we had never given it a thought, much less formulated a policy.

Stan explained that a delegation of students from Yale University wanted to share recent events on that campus. They thought the New England Fall Conference would be an ideal occasion for discussing the gifts of the Spirit and requested that the scheduled topic be set aside. Stan considered the situation serious enough to check with me, the field director.

I prayed for wisdom and suggested a solution. They should keep the planned program and yet be open to any unscheduled teaching God might have, without giving IVCF endorsement of the Yale students' position. The speaker should carry through with the announced Bible study in 1 Peter. Afterward there would be ample opportunity for discussing spiritual gifts at an optional afternoon session. This course of action would give freedom for all interested students to consider the subject without making the discussion an integral part of the weekend program. I was grateful to God for this decision which was vindicated by the events that followed.

The speaker, Dr. Douglas Feaver, Professor of Greek at Lehigh University, and faculty advisor to the Yale Christian Fellowship until his departure in 1956, proceeded along this line. He was surprised at the way the Yale students accepted him and his message with its warning against excesses and advice to test all experience in the light of Scripture. The YCF students were grateful for the openness of the Inter-Varsity staff and for the opportunity to share their recent experiences. About a third of the conference attended the optional session while the others enjoyed a variety of recreational activities. The Yale students reported the remarkable new way the Holy Spirit had begun to work in their lives. After supper the conference program continued according to schedule.

At one point in the conference the Yale students held a prayer meeting for others seeking the gifts of the Spirit. Dr. Feaver reported that this was the first time he had heard praying in tongues in an orderly fashion. He had to admit to himself that the phenomenon could not be summarily dismissed as "ecstatic-babble." Both conference leaders and students followed the Apostle Paul's instruction: "Do not forbid speaking in tongues. But everything should be done in a fitting and orderly way" (1 Cor. 14:39-40).

Late that autumn (1962) Stan Rock visited the Yale campus to see for himself what was going on. He was impressed by the spiritual vitality of the students and reported that the chapter was being transformed in more dynamic worship, effective witness and greater love among the members.

Charismatic Renewal This unplanned turn of events had begun when three student leaders returned to Yale that September. During the summer each unexpectedly had encountered charismatic fellowships in distant parts of the country. Robert Morris, the outgoing chapter president, worked in Detroit. He experienced a deepening hunger for God as he met with a group led by the Dean of the Episcopal Cathedral. There for the first time he witnessed the gifts of the Spirit such as prophecy and praying in tongues, although he did not then become a participant.

David Wills, a graduate student, had contact with a similar group in California. They impressed him deeply with their joy in the Lord, love for each other and power in witness.

Steven Wolfe worked for the government in Baltimore where he worshiped in a Lutheran Church whose pastor, a former Roman Catholic, was involved in the charismatic renewal. There he joined a group of Christians for Bible study, worship, prayer and exercise of spiritual gifts.

A fourth student, David Fisher, arrived in New Haven to begin his year at Yale as a Danforth Fellow. A graduate of Stanford, where he worked with Inter-Varsity, he had studied the preceding year at Princeton Seminary. There he had met with several Pentecostals and an Episcopal group who were manifesting a variety of spiritual gifts.

During the first few days of school David Fisher met the other three. They began to share these events of the summer, wondering about their significance. Each of them had a growing spiritual hunger; they sensed that God had brought them together this first week for a definite purpose.

Bob Morris discovered *Trinity* magazine. Published by the Blessed Trinity Society, it was founded in the spring of 1961 by Jean Stone, a member of St. Mark's Episcopal Church in Van Nuys, California. This quarterly circled the globe with its articles about the charismatic renewal. Its message, beamed particularly toward the historic denominations, urged a restoration of the Holy Spirit to his place of power in the life of the church.

Bob wrote to Mrs. Stone reporting that a number of students at Yale sensed a lack in their Christian lives which hindered their witness and fellowship with each other. He said, "We want the infilling so that we can join in this wonderful revival God is sending in His church. We do not know what sort of trouble the Holy Spirit's denouement on the campus would bring, but we are willing to risk it. . . . Please send someone to us as soon as possible."[1] The students wanted to learn more about these new experiences and their implications for Christian living and witness to the Lord Jesus Christ.

Jean Stone acted immediately. She contacted Harald Bredesen, minister of the First Reformed Church of Mount Vernon, New York, who soon arrived on the Yale campus to speak to the students. After several hours of discussing the gifts of the Spirit with these four students, Bredesen prayed with them. Three began to pray in tongues. Later that evening he addressed a larger group with whom he also prayed afterward.

During the next few weeks these students met regularly for study of the Scripture and prayer. They experienced ripening fruit of the Spirit, especially love for others and joy in the Lord. They found their prayer life, both individual and corporate, enriched by praying in tongues. From the start these meetings were not an official part of the Yale Christian Fellowship program. Rather, they were an informal fellowship attended by some YCF members and others, including a Lutheran and two Roman Catholics.

The students began to wonder how widely they should witness to their new experience. During one of the worship meetings a sophomore gave a word of prophecy: "You shall be my witnesses and carry this word to others." The group received this as a word from God instructing them to share their experiences with the denominational chaplains. David Fisher volunteered to communicate with the university chaplain since he worked closely with him. Most of the chaplains were interested. The university chaplain, who in past years had been a severe critic of the Yale Christian Fellowship, seemed quite receptive.

During the autumn several other prophetic utterances were received by the group and applied to their lives. One condemned them for their tendency toward spiritual pride, whereupon they confessed this sin. Another urged them to move out more freely in evangelism, sharing the good news of Jesus Christ. As a result they became more active in their evangelistic efforts, which had lagged the preceding year.

Members of the group also began praying for each other with regard to minor illnesses and received specific answers in the form of restored health. In November one of the chaplains became seriously ill and was taken to the hospital. The charismatic group prayed for him consistently for nine days. When the chaplain's condition became so critical that an operation was scheduled, the students held a twenty-four-hour prayer vigil. The following day the hospital released him.

Within a period of a few months these students had manifested a variety of spiritual gifts, including healing, prophecy, word of wisdom and speaking in tongues. These gifts built up the Christian fellowship and made it a more effective witness on the campus.

A Visit to Yale   On January 22, 1963 I arrived in New Haven with a mixture of anticipation and old memories. Although the downtown area had been renovated, the Yale campus was just as I had known it twenty years earlier as an undergraduate.

The Yale Christian Fellowship was started in 1943 when another concerned Christian student and I met for prayer three times a week. We started a Monday evening Bible study under the leadership of John Brobeck, a Medical School student. During the years following graduation I prayed for the YCF and as a staff worker with Inter-Varsity Christian Fellowship occasionally visited the campus to counsel with the chapter president. But with the passing of student generations the chapter had come on lean times.

As I now entered the Yale campus, I was grateful that the

YCF was once again on the move, although I was apprehensive about this strange business of speaking in tongues. I had been taught that the extraordinary gifts of the Spirit were given only in the first century to establish the early church. In my theological studies most doctrines were critically discussed, but this one was hardly considered. Now my theological belief was being challenged by reported events, producing a tension between an openness to perceive what might be a new work of God and a resolve to guard against any false enthusiasm or fanaticism.

Stan Rock and I met with half a dozen students to hear them share how the Holy Spirit was working in their lives. One was David Miller, a freshman who had recently become a Christian. The students were very open to our questions. This was the first time I had talked with anyone who had experienced these gifts of the Spirit, including speaking in tongues.

The students were not sure of the nature of the "language," but were convinced of its value in their prayer life. Sometimes it sounded like a soft Middle Eastern dialect, sometimes Oriental and other times European. There was no correlation between their words and thoughts. Bob Morris said this kind of praying formed a kind of "background music" enabling him to pray more intensely. Each witnessed to the fact that this "praying in the Spirit" made relationship with God more meaningful. In group fellowship it brought a greater sense of unity and more effective intercession.

The students had not thought through the implications of these unusual spiritual gifts for the local church. There was no available teaching since the churches they attended did not exercise them. But they were rejoicing in their discovery of the truth of 1 Corinthians 12 that they were members of one body and that they should expect manifestations of a variety of spiritual gifts to build up this body. In a new way they were realizing their unity with each other in Jesus Christ.

These events caused them to study the Bible more diligently and gain greater ethical sensitivity. From all Stan and I could see, both the exercise of these spiritual gifts and their results were quite biblical, although contrary to our own theological convictions.

That evening Charles Troutman, the Inter-Varsity general director, arrived on campus to begin a tour of chapters in New England. The next day a second discussion with the students covered much of the same ground. Charles asked several perceptive questions arising from his wider knowledge of charismatic phenomena. Stan Rock related how his participation in this fellowship on a December visit had profound meaning for him in deepening his relationship to the Lord Jesus Christ. Several students who had not taken part in the earlier discussion gave a similar witness.

The next day I visited the university chaplain, with whom I had become acquainted on my visits over the years. For the first time he spoke appreciatively of the YCF leadership. He told me they were active in their own denominational groups and also in campus organizations. Several were deacons of Battell Chapel, positions of distinction. Three had been elected to Phi Beta Kappa, and one would be a Woodrow Wilson Fellow during the following year. The chaplain expressed deep appreciation for the students' prayer which he felt was instrumental in his healing.

I left the campus with praise for the Lord's work in the YCF and its broadening influence on the campus. I also went away with questions which were to pursue me for several years. What was the significance of this experience for the continuing life and witness of the Yale Christian Fellowship? What was God saying to me and others on the Inter-Varsity staff for our own Christian lives? What was the significance of this pattern of prophecy, praying in tongues and healing for the church as a whole?

Inter-Varsity Policy During 1962-63 the Spirit of God moved in a similar fashion in other Inter-Varsity chapters including Penn State, Kent State in Ohio, Indiana University and Purdue. Many students experienced a deepening relationship with Jesus Christ as the Spirit manifested a variety of gifts for building up the body and empowering witness. At the same time controversy arose as some students questioned the validity of these experiences which they believed God intended only for the early church. Reports of these events in IVCF chapters came to Chicago headquarters and stimulated a discussion of national policy on this issue.

Most IVCF leaders had a theological bias against the movement, yet we wanted to welcome any new work God might be doing. How could we deny the significance of the fact that many were exercising these unusual gifts according to biblical teaching and with beneficial results to students' lives? Since our Basis of Faith did not speak to this doctrinal issue, should there not be freedom for diversity of opinion just as with other doctrines, such as baptism and eschatology, on which Christians within the Fellowship differed?

Our discussion yielded neither biblical nor organizational grounds for discouraging this renewal. We were impressed by the example of Gamaliel. He and his fellow Pharisees were confronted by Peter's claim that the divisive rabbi whom they had killed was now exalted by God as the Leader and Savior of Israel. While his colleagues wanted to suppress the new movement, Gamaliel urged restraint. After all, it was possible that their own interpretation of Scripture could be wrong, that this controversial teacher might indeed be the Messiah. Gamaliel declared: "If their purpose or activity is of human origin, it will fail. But if it is from God, you will not be able to stop these men; you will only find yourselves fighting against God" (Acts 5:38-39).

In April 1963 General Director Charles Troutman wrote a memorandum to all IVCF staff concerning the involvement of IVCF in the charismatic renewal. He noted that "increasingly and inevitably Inter-Varsity is being drawn into one of the modern expressions of a healing-tongues-prophecy movement. Some members of the IVCF have come under the influence of this movement and are occasionally exercising charismatic gifts."[2] He requested earnest prayer that no response on our part would jeopardize the task of university evangelism. He emphasized the interdenominational character of IVCF and its primary task of reaching students for Christ. Some doctrines are important but not essential to this task. "Over the years our policy has been deliberately to set aside as the non-essentials to our task such matters as the mode of baptism, the essential nature of the Lord's supper, and speaking in tongues."[3]

Troutman noted that the current movement differed significantly from the groups which traditionally have been identified with the exercise of these gifts. His memorandum stressed their biblical nature, the fact that some of them appear also in non-Christian religions and the need according to the New Testament to distinguish between true and false spirits. He stated:

> *If this is a movement of God for all His children—even though it may be abused—then we want to be part of it. If this is not a movement of God, we want to help those of our brethren who have become enmeshed. If there is a misplaced emphasis, we want to bring a balance. We must in no way hinder the Spirit of God from working in individuals as He wills.* [4]

He concluded with a number of practical suggestions for the field staff.

This memorandum by Charles Troutman guided the organization during the following years. It showed the willingness of the fireplace to adjust to a new fire.

The Following Years   In September 1963 the new academic year started well for the Yale Christian Fellowship. But eventually the issue of certain gifts became controversial. Two of the YCF leaders urged that the chapter constitution be altered to require charismatic experience as a qualification for office. The executive committee rejected this stipulation by a three-to-two vote. They recognized the chapter's basic commitment to both the historic Christian doctrines expressed in the Inter-Varsity Basis of Faith and the freedom of its members to "agree to disagree" on secondary doctrines. For a year the unity of the fellowship was preserved as both regular chapter programs and the activities of the charismatic fellowship continued. Yet there was no adequate fireplace for the fire; none of the local churches was prepared to guide and nurture this flickering flame with the mature counsel it so much needed.

By September 1964, many of the first leaders of the charismatic renewal in the YCF had graduated, leaving a few students to carry on. Stan Rock had departed for further theological study. During this year an off-campus advisor persuaded the "charismatic" students to separate from the YCF. As a result both groups suffered. The corporate witness to Jesus Christ was weakened; by the end of the academic year it had become ineffective.

At the local level these events at Yale demonstrated the need for mature counsel by the churches to guide young Christians in new spiritual experiences. This brief renewal also stood as a witness in a schedule-oriented, production-minded church to the power and sovereignty of the Holy Spirit who cannot be programmed. Like the wind, the Spirit blows when and where and how long he wills to achieve God's purpose.

In the following years I often reflected on this occurrence at Yale, unplanned by a committee or even one individual, unorganized in standard church fashion and not completely understood at the time by those involved. During the last two centuries a new work of God in the lives of students has often led to revitalization of the church at large.[5] I wondered how the exercise of spiritual gifts such as healing, prophecy and speaking in tongues would function in a local church. How could they flourish freely within its structure? What would be the reaction of the congregation and its leadership, and how would these gifts build up the body of Christ? Five years after the renewal at Yale died out, I found answers to some of these questions in an unexpected place.

3
A Christian Community

During the spring of 1970 I heard reports of charismatic renewal in Rhode Island. We had moved to the state five years earlier when I became president of Barrington College. I was aware that a renewal had begun in the Roman Catholic Church. Meetings at the University of Michigan were attracting several hundred students and faculty each week. Now a Word of God community had formed in Providence.

Some of our friends had visited the community and were impressed by its vitality and joy. Visitors were warmly welcomed. Worship and praise found expression in new hymns and choruses. Members witnessed to a powerful working of the Spirit in their lives. I decided to visit this charismatic community to see for myself how it functioned.

Charismatic Fellowship In October, shortly after the start of the autumn semester, we found a free Thursday evening. Though early, we had difficulty finding a parking place. We made our way to the basement of the Holy Ghost Church where about four hundred chairs were arranged in concentric circles. Although it was not yet eight o'clock, most of these seats were already filled. We spotted several empty chairs in the outside circle near the door (where I thought it would be safest to sit just in case we wanted a speedy exit). To my surprise they were being reserved by an elderly lady. Reserved seats at a prayer meeting—this was new.

Eventually we were seated and began to look around at the crowd. I was immediately struck by the wide variety of people: old women with shawls and young men in leather jackets; priests and nuns and ministers; businessmen in suits alongside tradesmen in coveralls; blacks and whites; faculty types wearing sport jackets, students with jeans and hippies in garb defying description. What a cross section of society! Never before had I seen such a variety of people together in one room for a religious service.

Yet this represented the diversity a Christian "congregation" should have. Our Lord moved decisively across the social, economic, racial and religious barriers of his time. The Apostle Paul declared, "There is neither Jew nor Greek, slave nor free, male nor female, for you are all one in Christ Jesus" (Gal. 3:28). But I had always assumed that he meant the church universal since this reality is rare in a local congregation.

My reflection was interrupted by the voice of a young priest sitting near the center of the group. Father John Randall welcomed all who were present, especially first-time visitors. He said, "Some of you may not understand what is going on, but would you please hold your questions until later? This is not a time for discussion. For the next two hours we will worship and witness as the risen Lord directs the meeting through the Holy Spirit who will be free to manifest his gifts according to his sovereign will. Afterwards there will be several optional groups, one of which will explain to newcomers the nature of this fellowship." Then he sat down.

After a few moments of silence two guitars began a hymn new to our ears: "We see the Lord. He is high and lifted up, and his train fills the temple." Most of the people seemed to know this chorus and sang with great joy and enthusiasm. The rest of us did our best to pick up the words and melody. Several other songs followed—mostly words of Scripture set to music. As they ended, someone stood and read a psalm of praise. The guitars responded with several songs of praise, most of them from the Psalms.

Then a young man stood and testified for the first time in his life to the saving power of Jesus Christ. That week through a series of difficult events he had come to the end of his rope and the beginning of spiritual life. As he concluded many exclaimed, "Praise God" and "Thank you, Lord."

One by one individuals read from the Bible, suggested a song or prayed. Others witnessed to conversion, victory over sin, special healing, wisdom in a difficult situation, new love for neighbors or increased joy in the Lord. Occasionally the guitars picked up the theme and led the singing of an appropriate chorus.

Once during the meeting there was a pronouncement given in tongues which seemed quite natural and in order. After a moment of silence John Randall quietly said, "Lord, speak to us." Shortly someone gave an interpretation which sounded like a message from the Old Testament, an assuring word of God's love and promise to guide our service for him. The message seemed in keeping with the theme of the meeting and was an encouragement to me personally.

The meeting proceeded at a steady, unhurried pace, unplanned in advance and apparently unfolded by the Holy Spirit. There was a dynamic sense of movement as together we experienced its development. I had come into the Word of God community that night with curiosity about its activity and concern over my own problems. Both gave way to worship and praise as I was lifted out of my self-centeredness to rejoice in God my Savior. The two hours passed so quickly that I was surprised when a glance at my watch showed ten o'clock.

Father Randall concluded with a few announcements. Visitors who wanted to learn more about the Word of God community were invited to meet in a side room. Participants in a six-week study course on "Life in the Spirit" would assemble in the kitchen. Those desiring special prayer were to go upstairs to the sanctuary. A book table was available in the foyer.

As people moved in several directions according to their particular interest, we headed for the car with gratitude and amazement. My memory went back eight years to the small group of students on the Yale campus. How different it had been, and yet how very much the same in the quality of experience: love and joy, worship and praise, boldness of witness to the Lord Jesus Christ and exercise of unusual gifts of the Spirit.

During the autumn I returned several times for the fellowship and for a deeper understanding of this community. On one occasion John Randall took a few minutes to describe the beginning of the Word of God community.[1]

Unexpected Renewal   On St. Patrick's Day in 1967 Father John Randall, then a seminary chaplain, attended a Cursillo Leaders' Workshop. This renewal movement, which had come to the United States ten years earlier, emphasized the witness of keen leaders in Christian community.[2] Present at the workshop were Steve Clark and Ralph Martin, on the staff of St. John's Student Parish at Michigan State University and leaders in the national Cursillo Movement.

In February 1967 Clark and Martin had encountered the charismatic renewal on their visit to Duquesne University in Pittsburgh. While confirming much in their experience, it also raised questions for which they needed answers. In March they arrived at the Cursillo Leaders' Workshop in New England eager to talk with John Randall. Here was a mature leader with whom they could talk about the events at Duquesne.

Randall, however, was fearful and disappointed:

We listened to them late into the night and were, to put it mildly, horrified. They told us of the marvelous outpouring of the charismatic gifts, and we quoted St. John of the Cross who warned against spiritual excesses. We begged them, too, not to bring what they had experienced into the Cursillo Movement which was prospering, but had enough difficulties of its own. All I could think of were "Holy Rollers" and all the other pejorative terms that are associated with over-emotional religious practices. I was disillusioned and confused because prior to that Ralph and Steve had given me such hope.[3]

In the weeks that followed John Randall, "interested but distant," read everything he could about the charismatic movement because he could foresee only problems not needed in the Cursillo. In August he read at one sitting *The Cross and the Switchblade* by David Wilkerson, a book influential in the Catholic groups at Duquesne, Ann Arbor and Notre Dame. Involved in his own inner-city work, he was fascinated by this story of the Holy Spirit's power in the slums of New York City, power he had not seen in Providence.

The next year he drove to Brooklyn with several friends to see firsthand the work of Teen Challenge. Their love, joy and power were overwhelming. That night at a rally Donald Wilkerson, David's brother, spoke about prayer. Deeply moved, John Randall and his friends took a most unusual step for Catholics: they accepted the invitation to come forward. As Wilkerson asked what he wanted prayer for, Randall replied, "I work with college students and seminarians. I can use all the help I can get." Wilkerson laid hands on him and asked the Spirit to come in power, to fulfill that request and renew his whole ministry. While nothing unusual happened at that moment, Randall believed in the prayer.

He arrived home at four o'clock in the morning and several hours later conducted an early service. In a new way he experienced the presence of God as he led the worship and preached the sermon. He wondered if this might be the so-called baptism in the Spirit experience.[4]

During the following months John Randall discovered new power and joy in his own life and in others to whom he ministered. He realized that for effective witness and service

Easter must be followed by Pentecost. He had known this in theory, but now it became a central reality in his life.

The Word of God Community   In January 1969 a Sunday afternoon prayer meeting started in an apartment near Providence. By May about fifteen people were attending. With a strong desire to form some kind of community, John Randall and the others were led to the Federal Hill section of Providence. The priest of the Holy Ghost Church invited them to work among his people to create a spirit of prayer in the parish. Two apartments were provided rent free.

A Thursday evening prayer meeting began in the basement of the church. Members of the community spent the morning in prayer; in the afternoon they went out two by two visiting people in their homes and telling the good news of Jesus Christ. The Holy Spirit was manifesting the full range of spiritual gifts reported in the New Testament.

By 1971 five hundred people were attending the prayer meetings. The workload in the Word of God community and the seminary had grown so much that John Randall could no longer continue both commitments. He and Raymond Kelly, the seminary librarian, became convinced that God was leading them to enter parish work. They saw that the ultimate test of the charismatic movement would be its ability to renew the church at the local level in an ordinary city parish. They asked Bishop McVinney for an opportunity to try this approach not just with a weekly prayer meeting but with a whole parish built around the concept of a community empowered by the Holy Spirit, exercising spiritual gifts for building up the body of Christ and serving a variety of human needs.

Randall and Kelly were convinced that God wanted them to move the prayer group from the Holy Ghost Church across town to St. Patrick's to revitalize the decaying inner-city community on Smith Hill. Here they were assigned, and during the next two years they prayed and worked toward making the Word of God community an integral part of the parish.

The initial focus was not on the prayer group but service to the parish.

In 1972 the Word of God community faced the question of reopening the parish school which had been closed two years earlier. As the leaders pondered this idea, they realized that the prayer group had the resources to reopen the school on a new basis—Jesus could really be Lord and children from their early years could be introduced to the working of the Holy Spirit. They were convinced it should be a family-centered school. Therefore they decided to admit only children whose parents were willing to go through an eight-week "Life in the Spirit" seminar so they would understand what their children were learning.

That summer an amazing community building operation took place. People from all over Providence laid new floors, painted walls, prepared the grounds and put in driveways during their free time. During 1972-73 more than two hundred children from all parts of the city and the suburbs attended the school, some traveling an hour each way. Word of God community members came to teach, work in the office and supervise the playground. Some served full-time, others part-time; some received no salary while others were given a stipend. John Randall witnessed a beautiful mingling of people from outside and inside the parish.

Meanwhile a further development took place. In June 1972 the Reverend Graham Pulkingham from the Episcopal Church of the Redeemer in Houston, Texas, came to Rhode Island. He met privately with the leaders from the Word of God community and related God's work through his church in the inner city.[5] He described households that were reliving the Acts of the Apostles as they welcomed individuals with a variety of needs. It involved total commitment, a laying down of life, goods and privacy for the body of Christ.

In November Pulkingham returned to speak to all charismatic groups in Rhode Island at a day of renewal. He stressed the Christian's commitment to God in shouldering responsibility to meet the deepest needs of his brother. Once again members of the Church of the Redeemer had an opportunity to share the lessons they were learning about the vital Christian community. They found it is not enough to get an individual converted and off drugs or alcohol; he requires the love and security of a Christian home that welcomes him as a member of the family as long as he needs to live there.

During the next year several families sold their homes in the affluent Providence suburbs. Among them were two lawyers, two businessmen and a Brown University professor. They purchased "three-decker" houses in Smith Hill, an area dying from social problems, tough youths and disenchantment with religion. They formed households (extended families) which welcomed others not just as guests but as members of the family.

By 1975 there were seven such households with two to five additional members. Four other households had single religious and lay members. *The Providence Journal* reported that the arrival of these families elated residents of the district. "Well-off, impeccably stable families are leaving pleasant and safer suburban fields to live among them, with the vision of Smith Hill becoming a light on the mountain!"[6]

Renewal of a Parish   By early 1973 John Randall saw his vision becoming reality as the Word of God community and parish members joined in the same fellowship and goals. On May 4 a joint committee prepared a St. Patrick's reunion which brought together for a festive evening about twelve hundred parishioners, former parishioners who had moved away and community members from outside who were working in the parish.

The test of union came when each parish was asked to prepare long-range objectives and goals they hoped to achieve during the next five years. At St. Patrick's a goal-setting committee was appointed. Randall recalls,

Now it was vitally important that the parish and the community

share the same vision. The goals decided upon and to which we would pledge our resources in time, in money and in work, would have to be supportable by all. With this in mind some of us fasted for two days prior to the first parish meeting.[7]

At that meeting several leading parishioners affirmed that the first goal should be a true unity of the community and the church. Eventually the community name, *Word of God,* was dropped as the original charismatic prayer group became fully integrated into the life of the parish.

Concern for renewal extended to the social and economic needs of Smith Hill's residents, including many non-Catholics. Among the rows of packed-in frame tenements are signs of its polyglot population—a Polish club, Turkish bathhouse, Armenian church and synagogue. When Carroll Tower opened with apartments for two hundred fifty senior citizens, St. Patrick's held a welcoming party. Since then one sister has devoted her time to visiting the residents. The church supports two full-time social service workers for the area aided by several part-timers. On Thanksgiving Day about four hundred poor residents and lonely strays enjoy a dinner in the school auditorium served by parishioners using their own tableware.

In recent years St. Patrick's and the Chalkstone Presbyterian Church have cooperated in the Capitol Hill Interaction Council (CHIC) to work for the renewal of Smith Hill. Under its auspices a cooperative, Our Daily Bread, makes food available to hundreds of people at the lowest possible prices. The Shepherd's Staff is a center out of which two public social workers and many volunteers work. The Butterfly Shop sells handcrafts made by people in the area.

Individual initiative often comes to the fore. A successful salesman, active in St. Patrick's, resigned his position to start The Earthen Vessel, selling used furniture and clothing. These shops transact more than business; they have become social centers where people linger to talk, with opportunities for Christian witness.

At St. Patrick's the Holy Spirit is expected to manifest the full range of spiritual gifts experienced in the early church. These charisms strengthen the body of Christ for worship and service, equipping its members for evangelism and social concerns. They participate in more than twenty ministries ranging from intercessory prayer, teaching and hospitality to child care, building maintenance and social action. Within five years active membership grew from five hundred to one thousand. About fifty families from the prayer group moved into the parish.[8]

The Word of God community had a profound influence on my thinking about charismatic renewal. Here was a growing body whose members exercised many spiritual gifts I had relegated to the first-century church. A renewed parish was beginning to influence an entire city. Still, I was perplexed. For while it involved the exercise of extraordinary spiritual gifts, the renewal here and earlier at Yale bore little resemblance to my mental image of Pentecostalism.

What was the historical background of this modern charismatic renewal? And how was it related to the Pentecostal movement which arose at the beginning of this century? These questions spurred a quest into the past which uncovered some answers and began to put the pieces together.

4
Charismatic Renewal

The charismatic renewal can be as confusing as Aesop's elephant. Widely differing reports often seem as contradictory as those of the three blind men who described the elephant in terms of its hide, tail and tusk. Much depends on the point of contact.

Unlike many movements in church history spearheaded by one influential leader, this renewal has sprung up spontaneously in a variety of shapes and forms. The river can be traced to no one human source. It is fed by three main streams. While they do not flow in isolated channels, but merge with each other at times, each has distinctive characteristics.

The first is classical Pentecostalism which surged forward at the opening of the century. Fragmented and separatist in its early decades, Pentecostalism since World War 2 has witnessed phenomenal growth in the United States and abroad. A Neo-Pentecostal stream in the late 1950s began to make its way quietly within the major Protestant denominations. In 1961 it came to public attention across the country as the media featured its more unusual spiritual gifts. Neo-Pentecostalism also emerged in the Roman Catholic church in 1967 and has grown rapidly with increasing encouragement from church leaders.

The two later streams, unlike the early Pentecostal movement, have continued to flow within the channels of the churches in which they first arose. Taken together the three have become increasingly influential in what may generally be called the charismatic renewal.

Classical Pentecostalism   This movement, which arose so suddenly on the American scene in the first decade of our century, had many sources. It was fed by a theology and experience dating from the Wesleyan revival of the eighteenth century. The nineteenth-century holiness movement, a branch of Methodism, swelled the stream of twentieth-century Pentecostalism.

Methodist-holiness groups emphasized a "second blessing" of entire sanctification which follows conversion. In America, Charles Finney helped prepare the way for modern Pentecostalism with his theology of the experience he called the "baptism of the Holy Ghost," and his revival methods leading to a crisis experience. The holiness tradition provided the soil, climate and even terminology for Pentecostalism's distinctive view of the baptism with the Holy Spirit.

In October 1900 holiness evangelist Charles Parham started Bethel Bible College in Topeka, Kansas, with about forty students. He was convinced that "while many had obtained real experiences in sanctification . . . there still remained a great outpouring of power for Christians."[1] By December Parham had led his students through the major teachings of the holiness movement, including divine healing. As they began to study the Acts of the Apostles, he left the school for three days on a speaking engagement. He asked the students to search for biblical evidence of receiving the baptism with the Holy Spirit.

Upon his return they unanimously reported their discovery: speaking in other tongues. This conclusion seemed to be confirmed at a December 31 watchnight service as Parham laid hands on Agnes Ozman for the baptism with the Spirit.

Immediately she began speaking in tongues.[2] During January classes were suspended as the whole student body engaged in prayer. Soon a majority of them had had the same experience. Its significance did not lie in the speaking in tongues, a gift already exercised by many. "The importance of these events in Topeka is that for the first time the concept of being baptized (or filled) with the Holy Spirit was linked to an outward sign—speaking in tongues."[3]

During the next four years Charles Parham preached a series of revivals as he spread the Pentecostal message throughout Kansas and Missouri. In 1905 he moved to Houston, Texas and opened another Bible school. One of his students was William J. Seymour, a black preacher who had accepted the holiness doctrine of sanctification as a "second blessing." Now he received Parham's teaching of a "third experience," the baptism with the Holy Spirit evidenced by speaking in tongues and bringing power for witness.

Meanwhile, the Welsh Revival of 1904 also helped prepare the way for events in Los Angeles two years later. Led by Evan Roberts, it witnessed thirty thousand conversions and twenty thousand new church members.[4] Frank Bartleman, a young holiness minister in Los Angeles, was deeply stirred when he heard of this revival in April 1905. During the following months he increasingly desired such a revival in his own city and wrote a tract entitled *The Last Call*. Bartleman was also impressed by the occurrence of speaking in tongues in recent British revivals, including the one in Wales.

In April 1906 Seymour came to Los Angeles to serve as pastor to a small black congregation. When they discovered that he believed in the baptism with the Spirit and speaking in tongues, they asked him to resign. Undeterred, he continued to hold meetings in a rented facility on Bonnie Brae Street and then moved to a former livery stable at 312 Azusa Street. The building had served also as a Methodist Church and a lumber yard. "It had to start in poor surroundings to keep out the selfish human element,"[5] wrote Frank Bartleman who had prayed long for revival in his city. With Seymour's preaching a sustained revival began.

While Seymour was the leader, he encouraged the congregation to participate in worship, prayer and witness. Rich and poor, black and white, educated and unschooled met together. Many began to exercise various gifts of the Spirit and returned home to share these events with others. During the three years of the Azusa Street revival thousands of visitors from all over the country traveled to Los Angeles to see for themselves what was happening. Many of them were convinced of the genuineness of the teaching and practices; others scoffed at the meetings and rejected the doctrine of baptism with the Spirit evidenced by speaking in tongues. Nevertheless, the movement spread throughout North America and also overseas to Scandinavia, Germany, Switzerland and Great Britain. Later it became established in Latin America, Africa and Asia.[6]

While people had spoken in tongues prior to 1906, the Azusa Street revival gave impetus to modern Pentecostalism which views it as the initial physical evidence of baptism with the Spirit. These meetings presented a teaching and experience which attracted many who thirsted for spiritual life and power in the barren theological liberalism and spiritual stagnation which plagued American Protestantism after the Civil War.

The larger denominational churches dismissed this revival as another cultic wave. Many of the holiness churches also dissociated themselves completely from the Pentecostal movement, while leading evangelicals such as R. A. Torrey declared that it was "emphatically not of God."[7] They did not accept spiritual gifts such as healing, prophecy and speaking in tongues which they believed had ended with the first century. Some early Pentecostals were persecuted and excommunicated from their churches, while in turn they often harshly judged Christians who rejected their teaching.

Pentecostalism further isolated itself by hostility toward

higher education and formally educated ministers. While eventually new hearths were built, the movement was divided by disputes over doctrine, church government, finances and cooperation with other denominations. By 1940 a dozen Pentecostal denominations had formed, quite apart from the many small groups which sprang up and died during earlier controversies.[8] During the first half of the century Pentecostalism's influence on mainline American church life was negligible.

In recent decades, however, the movement has matured with the participation of its denominations in the National Association of Evangelicals and in the triennial Pentecostal World Conference.[9] They comprise the largest non-Roman Catholic communion in many countries of Europe and Latin America, and the largest free-church group in Scandinavia.

In 1951 the Full Gospel Business Men's Fellowship International was founded by Demos Shakarian. This lay organization for evangelism and spreading the message of baptism with the Spirit exerted profound influence during the 1960s on the growth of Neo-Pentecostalism among both Protestants and Catholics.[10]

The vitality and influence of Pentecostalism was brought to the attention of the American churches in 1958 by Henry Van Dusen, president of Union Theological Seminary in New York. In a well-publicized article in *Life* magazine he described a "Third Force in Christendom" in which Pentecostalism plays a prominent role. Impressed with its vigor he wrote: "The tendency to dismiss its Christian message as inadequate is being replaced by a chastened readiness to investigate the secrets of its mighty sweep, especially to learn if it may not have important, neglected elements in a full and true Christian witness."[11] During the following decade a readiness to learn grew in the old fireplaces—both historic Protestant and Roman Catholic churches.

Neo-Pentecostalism During the late 1950s a Neo-Pentecostalism began to flow in mainline Protestant churches. Two men were especially influential in this movement. The first was David Du Plessis, a Pentecostal minister in South Africa. He edited a denominational newspaper and became executive secretary of the Pentecostal Fellowship in South Africa. By 1951 he was living in the United States near New York City. That year he felt God was calling him to witness to the leaders of the World Council of Churches. He objected, "Lord, I have preached so much against them, what do I say now? They will not listen to me. Their churches have put our people out of their fellowship."[12] Nevertheless he visited their headquarters where to his amazement he received a warm welcome.

In 1952 Du Plessis was invited to speak at the International Missionary Council in Germany. Since then he has traveled widely throughout the world speaking in a variety of churches as well as to the World Council of Churches and Vatican II. He has given a wide spectrum of Christians a new understanding of the Pentecostal movement.

The second leader was Dennis Bennett, rector of St. Mark's Episcopal Church in Van Nuys, California, from 1953 to 1960. Through his ministry the parish grew to two thousand. Because of the congregation's size, more than seventy "key family areas" were formed for Bible study and prayer. Advanced study classes probed the Scriptures to learn more about the Christian faith. Many with a deepening hunger for God began to pray that the Holy Spirit would manifest himself in greater measure.

In the autumn of 1959 Bennett began to meet with a group who were exercising a wide range of spiritual gifts. Through these meetings he entered a more dynamic relationship with Jesus Christ. During the following months about seventy people in St. Mark's also began to manifest unusual gifts including prayer in tongues. Although they agreed to keep their experience quiet in order that it might not become devisive, eventually rumors began to circulate.

On April 3, 1960 Dennis Bennett stood in his pulpit and related this new work of the Holy Spirit in his life which included praying in tongues. Many in the congregation reacted strongly. That afternoon Bennett was asked to resign from St. Mark's. He consented, feeling that his departure would be better for the congregation as a whole. The bishop sent to the parish a new rector and a pastoral letter banning any more speaking in tongues under church auspices.

Two days after his sermon Bennett sent a letter to his parishioners explaining his conviction:

I'm sorry for the furor, and for the pain that has been caused. I ask every person in St. Mark's, whether he be for me or against me, not to leave the Parish or cancel his pledge. This is a spiritual issue, and will not be settled in this way. . . . It is important that the Spirit be allowed to work freely in the Episcopal Church, and it is to this that I bear witness, and will continue to bear witness. I remind you that we are not alone in this.[13]

Bennett was invited to serve at St. Luke's, a small mission church in Seattle. There he continued to teach and encourage the exercise of spiritual gifts. Soon he was asked to speak in other parts of the country.[14] His preaching and writing encouraged the charismatic renewal in mainline Protestant denominations where many small fellowship groups had quietly come into being.

During the early 1960s a small group of Lutheran pastors and laity enthusiastically took part in this renewal. One of them was Larry Christenson, a recent graduate of Luther Theological Seminary in St. Paul. Early in his ministry he sensed an undefinable lack in his Christian living. The first answer to his uneasiness came through learning about the ministry of healing in the Episcopal Church. After attending several missions, divine healing took firm root in his own convictions and later in his ministry.

At a pastoral care clinic in December 1960 Christenson learned that several people involved in the ministry of healing were also exercising the spiritual gifts listed in 1 Corinthians

12, including speaking in tongues. Eight months later he was invited to a charismatic meeting in nearby San Pedro, California. Afterward, as he was prayed for, nothing appeared to happen. At home, later that night, he started praying in an "unknown tongue." He reported that this new kind of prayer became a valuable part of his devotions. "These initial events were a kind of doorway into a new dimension of spiritual awareness. I have known the reality of Christ in a new way."[15]

In 1963 charismatic renewal took place in the Bel Air Presbyterian Church near Los Angeles. This new congregation had grown rapidly through a program based on commitment to Jesus Christ, the discipline of studying and obeying the Word of God and training lay leadership for group study and prayer. The Holy Spirit taught the basic element of love in an unexpected way as the people responded by moving out to their friends in a ministry of evangelism and healing.

Along the way they discovered the teaching of 1 Corinthians 12 about the exercise of varied spiritual gifts to build up the body of Christ. They began to witness new fruit of love and joy with gifts ranging from service and teaching to healings, prophecy and tongues. The pastor Louis Evans, Jr. explained, "We came to discover that the gifts of the Holy Spirit are not like a box of strawberries. We do not pick and choose the ones we want. Rather we submit ourselves to God, then He provides the gifts of the Holy Spirit which we need."[16]

Inevitably news of the charismatic renewal in major Protestant denominations hit the headlines. This publicity was detrimental in several respects. It made the participants self-conscious, and as a result defensive. Christians newly involved in these events, without time to reflect on them or come to maturity, were forced to defend their experience in the public arena. Some became aggressive and self-righteous, while others withdrew into small groups. But the defensiveness was not all on one side. Many church leaders and congregations harassed the "charismatic" Christians. Some ministers were forced to resign their pulpits, while in many congregations individual members were pressured to leave. Christians involved in this renewal in the early 1960s often found little teaching by their own churches on the nature and exercise of spiritual gifts. Frequently, they turned to the classical Pentecostals, especially local Full Gospel Business Men's Fellowship groups, for encouragement and instruction.

This Neo-Pentecostal stream, however, did not become separatist; it continued to flow within the Protestant churches.[17] As increasing numbers of people became involved, several major denominations appointed committees to study the charismatic renewal. Reports reflecting a positive attitude were published by the two largest Presbyterian churches.[18] Within Lutheran churches growth sparked controversy.[19] The 1972 report of the Missouri Synod took a negative stance, while the 1974 paper of the Lutheran Church in America adopted a positive position.[20] In August 1972 the first Annual International Lutheran Conference on the Holy Spirit convened in Minneapolis with five thousand registered. By 1976 twelve thousand participated in this event.[21] Smaller interdenominational conferences have begun to meet annually in major cities across the United States.

More significant than these gatherings are the hundreds of interdenominational fellowship meetings in homes throughout the country. They convene weekly for worship and praise, Bible study, mutual encouragement and exercise of gifts as the Holy Spirit manifests them. These groups supplement the regular services of churches in which the members are usually active. Even though some of these churches still oppose the charismatic renewal, it continues to flourish within most Protestant denominations.

Catholic Pentecostalism   The third charismatic stream began to flow through the Roman Catholic church in the late 1960s. While its rapid growth began with the "Duquesne Weekend" in 1967, leadership had already been molded by the Cursillo movement which started in Spain after World War 2.[22] This group of clergy and lay intellectuals, concerned over the church's impotence in a de-Christianized world, desired a renewal in which Christians would live intensely their commitment to Jesus Christ through the power of the Holy Spirit.

The early Christian community in Acts with its unity and love in a common life provided the model. They decided to form a body of mature Christian men who would influence their environment and renew the church as they reached out and drew others to Christ.

The movement spread rapidly and came to the United States in 1957. At Notre Dame Steve Clark saw in the Cursillo the evangelistic focus, community emphasis and technique necessary for fundamental church renewal. In 1963 he, Ralph Martin and others who would later become leaders in the charismatic movement started the Cursillos in South Bend, Indiana. As they proceeded, a Christian community came into being. In 1965 Clark and Martin felt that God was leading them to leave their graduate studies in order to be more available for Christian work. They joined the staffs of St. John's Student Parish at Michigan State University and the National Secretariat of the Cursillo, also located in East Lansing.

In the autumn of 1966 several laymen on the faculty of Duquesne University of the Holy Spirit in Pittsburgh desired greater power to proclaim the gospel. While their lives were centered in Jesus Christ, they lacked dynamism in their witness. So they gave themselves to prayer that the Holy Spirit would renew them with the powerful life of the risen Lord. They began to study the New Testament, particularly the parts dealing with the life of the early church, and expected the Spirit to come upon them in the same way.

A friend introduced them to David Wilkerson's *The Cross and the Switchblade*, which opened new windows into biblical teaching. Ralph Keifer, a lay theologian at Duquesne, also read John Sherrill's *They Speak with Other Tongues* which he described to the others. Thereupon they decided that they should contact some Christians having these experiences.

Four members of this Catholic group visited a nondenominational fellowship in early January 1967. After singing four or five hymns, they witnessed a lengthy, spontaneous prayer session followed by sharing from Scripture. The visitors were impressed by the group's warm welcome, joy in worship and love for each other: here was a movement of God.

In mid-February about thirty students and faculty from Duquesne spent a weekend devoted to prayer and meditation on the first four chapters of Acts. Most of them knew little if anything of the gifts of the Spirit, although a majority had read *The Cross and the Switchblade* in preparation for the weekend. This "Duquesne Weekend," one of the most remarkable events in the charismatic renewal, marked the beginning of its rapid growth within the Catholic church.

Saturday evening had been set aside for relaxation and a birthday party. Yet one girl felt drawn to the chapel. Soon by ones and twos the others made their way there. As they prayed the Holy Spirit was poured out upon them.

> *There was no urging, there was no direction as to what had to be done. The individuals simply encountered the person of the Holy Spirit as others had several weeks before. Some praised God in new languages, others quietly wept for joy, others prayed and sang. They prayed from ten in the evening until five in the morning. Not everyone was touched immediately, but throughout the evening God dealt with each person there in a wonderful way.*[23]

During the following weeks God worked in the lives of many others through this group. Some turned from sinful habits and others from intellectual doubt. Throughout the remainder of the spring semester at Duquesne the external gifts and the internal fruit of the Holy Spirit continued to flourish in this little community. They spread the joy of Christ's love to many Catholics in the university area.

About this time Ralph Keifer visited South Bend on business. He spent a weekend with Kevin Ranaghan, a doctoral candidate at Notre Dame, and his wife Dorothy. For two days they talked about Pentecostalism and raised every intellectual, aesthetic and psychological objection they could.

On Saturday evening, March 4, about thirty friends and students met at the Ranaghans' home for fellowship. Ralph Keifer reported on the Duquesne weekend and shared his own experience. The next night nine met again to read Scripture, pray and discuss the events at Duquesne. They asked to be prayed for that they might be filled with the Holy Spirit and that through the gifts and fruit of the Spirit their lives might be more fully Christian. There was no prophecy or speaking in tongues, but for many there was a newness in prayer that marked the beginning of a deeper life of faith.

Realizing that spiritual gifts are designed to build up the body of Christ, they formed a small community. Students and faculty shared each other's concerns and rejoiced together in victories. The focus of their witness was not spiritual gifts but Jesus Christ and the power of his saving love to transform personal relationships.

The general public remained unaware of these events until early April when about forty-five visitors from Michigan State University joined forty from Notre Dame for a weekend retreat held on the campus. Present were several from nearby Pentecostal churches. News of these events stirred criticism and controversy as curious visitors jammed the next Friday evening prayer meeting.

During the following weeks the excitement died down; the rapid growth of early spring gave way to summer. While the spiritual gifts continued, these charisms were seen in the perspective of the Spirit's fruit of love, joy and peace. The new academic year witnessed a slow growth in lessons of personal discipleship and community.[24]

From the beginning of the renewal its leaders stressed the need to integrate the experience of the baptism with the Spirit into a community where the Christian receives support and draws others into this life of joy and service. That year the Word of God community in Ann Arbor also started. It has become an influential center for the charismatic renewal involving classical and Protestant as well as Catholic Pentecostals.

In September 1967 the first annual National Catholic Pentecostal Conference (named in retrospect) was born on the Notre Dame campus with about fifty to one hundred students, faculty and priests. By 1971 it had grown to five thousand and in 1976 the conference over the Memorial Day weekend had an attendance of thirty thousand. By 1977 the number of Catholics involved in the renewal grew to seven hundred thousand.[25]

In July 1971 the *New Covenant*, a monthly magazine with Ralph Martin as editor, began publication in Ann Arbor. The *Catholic Charismatic*, a theological journal, was also started in 1976.

The Committee on Doctrine of the National Conference of Catholic Bishops reported on the renewal in November 1969. Noting that understanding of the movement is colored by emotionalism, the committee recognized its strong biblical basis: while recognizing the abuses of certain charismatic gifts, the report stated that "the cure is not a denial of their existence but their proper use."[26] The committee concluded that the movement should not be inhibited but allowed to develop. The bishops were encouraged to exercise their pastoral responsibility to oversee and guide it.

In 1974 six of the seven cardinals in the United States responded in a positive pastoral way. That year Cardinal Suenens of Belgium, an early supporter, convened a small international group of theologians and lay leaders to prepare a statement on theological and pastoral concerns of the renewal and its role in the life of the church.[27] Originally called the Catholic Pentecostal Movement, it is now termed the Catholic charismatic renewal to differentiate it from classical Pentecostalism, and to recognize that it is not a movement in the full sense with national leadership to whom all are responsible.

All three streams of the charismatic renewal continue to broaden and deepen. Like earlier revivals in the church, it has brought disturbance as well as benefit. No wonder that many Christians both inside and outside the renewal are confused about its theology and practice. In the next chapter we shall summarize classical Pentecostal theology as a point of reference. Then we shall study those New Testament passages crucial for understanding the purpose and function of the gifts of the Holy Spirit. The last section of the book tackles several controversial issues in the current charismatic renewal.

Meanwhile, we should remember that whenever a stream flows swiftly it throws debris onto its banks. Let us not become so preoccupied with the debris that we fail to see the power of the stream itself and rejoice that the riverbed is no longer dry.

5
Pentecostal
Theology

Pentecostalism was born in the arena of experience. Students at Bethel Bible College in Kansas and visitors to Azusa Street in Los Angeles exercised a variety of spiritual gifts for which their churches had not prepared them. They naturally wondered how to integrate this experience into their understanding of the Christian life. How could they explain in biblical terms the events which were taking place?

Turning to the New Testament they found their answer in the Acts of the Apostles. The experiences of the disciples at Pentecost and in the early church seemed similar to theirs. At Pentecost the disciples were baptized with the Spirit,[1] spoke in tongues and preached with power. Now the same thing was happening to them. Thus baptism with the Holy Spirit accompanied by speaking in tongues became the pivotal doctrine of Pentecostalism which took its name from the day these events first occurred. It also became the main theological bone of contention with other churches.

While the Pentecostal denominations have certain doctrinal differences, they are united in their distinctive teaching about the experience of baptism with the Spirit as evidence of a supernatural, postconversion work in the life of the believer. Most of them teach that this baptism comes as the believer fulfills certain conditions, although there is not full agreement on these requirements. Pentecostals also esteem and practice all the spiritual gifts, especially those listed by Paul in 1 Corinthians 12.

Pentecostal doctrine did not develop overnight. Like other theologies in the history of the church, its outline emerged through sustained interaction between experience and Scripture. An understanding of the emergence and historical development of the Pentecostal doctrine of baptism in the Spirit should provide a basis for evaluating not only classical Pentecostal theology but also other streams in the charismatic renewal.

A Second Experience   Eighteenth-century Methodism, mediated through the nineteenth-century American holiness movement, provided the theological framework for twentieth-century Pentecostalism. John Wesley taught a doctrine of sanctification, following conversion, as a "second work of grace." He emphasized conscious religious experience. "A gradual work of grace constantly precedes the instantaneous work of both justification and sanctification.... As after a gradual conviction of guilt and power of sin you were justified in a moment, so after a gradually increasing conviction of inbred sin you will be sanctified in a moment."[2]

When Methodism came to America, the doctrine of entire sanctification as a second experience was transplanted with it. Francis Asbury, appointed to supervise the churches in this country, was also firmly committed to Wesley's teaching. It flourished during the early nineteenth century when perfectionist ideals spurred reform movements such as abolition of slavery, women's rights and prohibition. An influential preacher in these years preceding the great revival of 1858 was Charles Finney. This Presbyterian-turned-Congregationalist taught that entire sanctification is possible in this life.[3]

After the Civil War, churches within the ranks of Methodism declined in vitality and membership. Voices called for a return to the emphasis on sanctification. In 1870 the modern holiness crusade began to recover Wesley's teaching and reached its peak in the 1880s. As opposition to this doctrine grew in the Methodist church, a score of new holiness denominations formed in the decade from 1895 to 1905.[4]

In 1858 William Boardman, a Presbyterian minister, published *The Higher Christian Life* to interpret sanctification to those outside the Methodist tradition. It sold two hundred thousand copies and gained influence in England as well as America. The author wrote, "There is a *second experience* distinct from the first—sometimes years after the first—a *second conversion* as it is called."[5] This book laid out the broad principles which Pentecostalism later used to undergird its theology.

The holiness movement gained strength in England. In the 1880s Boardman and William Booth, founder of the Salvation Army, were active in its preaching. A series of summer conferences began at Keswick for the promotion of the "higher life." The emphasis broadened from sanctification to other dimensions of Christian experience.

Many prominent evangelical leaders such as R. A. Torrey, A. J. Gordon and Andrew Murray witnessed to a second experience subsequent to conversion which they called by different names such as the enduement, infilling or baptism with the Spirit.[6] Torrey taught that "the baptism with the Holy Spirit is a work of the Holy Spirit distinct from and additional to his regenerating work."[7] Its primary purpose is to equip the Christian for service.

A. B. Simpson, however, taught a broader purpose of Spirit-baptism including purifying, refining, quickening and energizing. "It is power to receive the life of Christ; power to be, rather than to say and to do. Our service and testimony will be the outcome of our life and experience."[8]

While many of these leaders rejected the Pentecostal teaching and practice when it developed in the early 1900s, their writings strongly influenced its theology of the baptism with the Spirit.[9] This doctrine of a second experience influenced evangelicals in a variety of denominations and produced a widespread literature. Charles Parham and others in the holiness movement, who had already been sanctified, considered the baptism with the Spirit to be a third experience. In time, however, the second and third stages coalesced into a doctrine of a single baptism with the Spirit, although some Pentecostal groups still teach the original three stages of Christian experience.[10]

Receiving Him Fully   In Pentecostalism the baptism with the Holy Spirit is the full reception of the Spirit which empowers the believer for witness and the exercise of spiritual gifts. Pentecostalists hold that whereas in regeneration each believer *receives* the Holy Spirit, this second experience involves receiving him *fully*. While the Holy Spirit baptizes the believer into Christ at his conversion, Christ later baptizes him into the Spirit. Ernest Williams finds this distinction in 1 Corinthians 12:13: "In the new birth the Holy Spirit is the Agent, the atoning blood the means, the new birth the result; in the Baptism with the Spirit, Christ is the Agent ('He shall baptize you with the Holy Ghost and with fire'), the Spirit is the means, the enduement with power the result."[11]

This doctrine is largely based on the events in Acts where the baptism with the Spirit occurs. On the day of Pentecost the disciples (believed to be already regenerate based on Jn. 20:22) were baptized with the Spirit: "All of them were filled with the Holy Spirit and began to speak in other tongues as the Spirit enabled them" (Acts 2:4). Thereupon they began to preach with great power and exercise spiritual gifts.

As a second experience following conversion, this doctrine of baptism with the Spirit seems to be illustrated by the converts in Samaria. Luke relates that "the Holy Spirit had not yet come upon any of them; they had simply been baptized into the name of the Lord Jesus. Then Peter and John placed their hands on them, and they received the Holy Spirit" (Acts 8:16-17).

Pentecostals find another example in Acts 9:1-19. On his way to Damascus Saul was first converted through his encounter with the risen Lord. Three days later Ananias visited him and said, "Brother Saul, the Lord—Jesus, who appeared to you on the road as you were coming here—has sent me so that you may see again and be filled with the Holy Spirit" (9:17). This subsequent experience was his baptism with the Spirit.

The experience of Cornelius in Acts 10 seems to be an exception; here both conversion and Spirit-baptism occurred at the same time. Pentecostalists stress, however, that these are two, distinct experiences, not to be equated or confused, even though they appear to happen at once. They also point out that this was an "ideal" case which can take place today, although the faith of most Christians is too weak, or their instruction inadequate, for baptism with the Spirit to follow conversion immediately.

The disciples at Ephesus appear to provide further evidence for this teaching. There Paul found some disciples and asked them, "Did you receive the Holy Spirit when you believed?" (19:2). They replied that they had not heard that the Spirit was given and had only received John's baptism. So Paul baptized them in the name of Jesus. "When Paul placed his hands on them, the Holy Spirit came on them, and they spoke in tongues and prophesied" (19:6). Apparently it was only after the Ephesians became disciples that they received the full gift of the Spirit with the promised results.

Pentecostals also appeal to the example of Jesus. Years after he was conceived by the Holy Spirit he was baptized with the Spirit at Jordan. "If there were two operations of the Spirit in the life of Jesus," asks Ernest Williams, "one to bring forth and another to endue Him for service, may it not be equally true that there is a two-fold work of the Spirit in the lives of those who believe on Jesus?"[12]

Pentecostals recognize that the letters of Paul and other apostles do not teach this doctrine explicitly, but they believe that such teaching was unnecessary since these letters were written to established churches in which the majority of the members had already received this experience. Like the first disciples, they were baptized with the Spirit after their conversion.

Requirements for Receiving   If baptism with the Spirit is subsequent to conversion, what are the requirements for its reception? Pentecostals believe that while ideally it can come at or near the time of conversion—as in the case of Cornelius—usually it does not. What then is the responsibility of the believer in receiving this baptism?

Pentecostalism teaches that the Holy Spirit is not expected to fill Christians automatically or imperceptibly; rather they must actively seek this experience for which they are required to meet certain conditions. "There are definite, stated conditions to be met; conditions that had to be met by the disciples; conditions that must be met by all who receive the Holy Ghost today."[13]

The nature and number of these requirements vary with the particular Pentecostal teacher. Many agree, however, on three basic requirements they believe the disciples met prior to Pentecost: obedience, spiritual unity and prayer. The Lord commanded them to wait in Jerusalem until they received power for witness when the Holy Spirit came upon them. After his ascension they obeyed by returning to the city. There the disciples enjoyed unity and continued in prayer (Acts 1:12, 14).

Another model of three conditions appears in Peter's charge to his hearers: "*Repent* and be *baptized.* . . . And you will *receive* the gift of the Holy Spirit" (Acts 2:38). Pentecostals interpret these verbs as three, chronologically distinct, sequential events in the life of the Christian. Repentance involves forsaking all sin; baptism signifies obedience, the removal of all remaining sin to provide a clean heart; reception involves faith, the ultimate means by which the Spirit comes fully. Most conditions listed by various writers fall into the three categories of conversion, obedience and faith. After conversion the believer must progress in sanctification to qualify for baptism in the Spirit. "If we live a yielded, pure and holy life, in close fellowship with Him, the experimental side of this mighty baptism must come."[14]

For those who teach a necessary experience following conversion, the question of requirements arises from a practical problem: how does the Christian get from the first to the second step of conversion? The early *Pentecostals* found the basis of the conditions for a second experience in the writings of the *holiness* and *evangelical* writers previously noted.[15]

But all three groups also had to face another question: what is the evidence for this experience in the life of the believer? How would its fulfillment be known? The holiness groups following Wesley emphasized entire sanctification or freedom from inward sin. Many of the evangelicals with Torrey stressed enduement with power for witness and service. Pentecostals, however, with Parham emphasized an initial speaking in tongues, followed by the exercise of spiritual gifts.

The Great Divide   While early Pentecostalism shared with holiness and evangelical groups the doctrine of a crucial experience subsequent to conversion, it was unique in its insistence that speaking in tongues is *the* initial physical evidence of this experience. This doctrine became the central point of controversy, a "great divide" between Pentecostals and other Christians.

Here also Pentecostal teaching did not develop in a vacuum. Speaking in tongues occurred in nineteenth-century British revivals. It took place among the followers of Edward Irving and in the Welsh revival.[16] It was also reported to have occurred in connection with some of Dwight L. Moody's meetings.

At Pentecost, in the home of Cornelius and at Ephesus (Acts 2, 10, 19), the coming of the Holy Spirit was accompanied by speaking in tongues. While in Samaria (Acts 8), though not explicitly stated, it may be inferred since something obviously happened to attract Simon Magus's attention. This pattern seems to demonstrate that speaking in tongues is the initial physical evidence of the baptism with the Spirit. So Ralph Riggs concludes, "Therefore, all who receive the Baptism in the Spirit today also speak with tongues."[17] This doctrine eventually prevailed in the new Pentecostal movement.

Nevertheless, in 1907 at Nyack, New York there occurred an event of more than historical interest. That year a remarkable Pentecostal revival swept over students and ministers assembled there for the general convention of the Christian and Missionary Alliance. It seemed that this church was well on its way to accepting Pentecostalism when it was discovered that the new movement taught that baptism with the Spirit is always accompanied by speaking in other tongues.

Faced with this doctrinal question, President Simpson made a thorough investigation which led him to reject the position that *all* must speak in tongues as evidence of their baptism. He felt that tongues was only one evidence of the indwelling of the Holy Spirit; it would be allowed in Christian and Missionary Alliance services but not encouraged. A number of prominent men in the Alliance withdrew to join the Pentecostals. Simpson's mediating dictum of "seek not—forbid not" was unique at a time when other groups took a hardline position for or against.[18]

Within the growing Pentecostal movement, speaking in tongues as the necessary, initial physical evidence of baptism with the Spirit was distinguished from the gift of tongues which was not expected for all. This doctrine was not seriously questioned until 1918 when F. F. Bosworth, an influential minister in the Assemblies of God, challenged it. He disparaged the distinction between "evidential tongues" (Acts

2) and the "gift of tongues" (1 Cor. 12—14), contending that *any* manifestation of spiritual gifts is sufficient evidence of the Spirit's baptism.

After a vigorous debate the General Council unanimously adopted a resolution forbidding any minister "to teach contrary to our distinctive testimony that the baptism of the Holy Spirit is regularly accompanied by the initial physical sign of speaking in other tongues as the Spirit of God gives the utterance."[19] Bosworth amicably withdrew and joined the Christian and Missionary Alliance with which he had a long, fruitful ministry including healing services.

Planted in the prepared soil of teaching about a necessary second experience and nurtured in the climate of revival meetings, the seed of Pentecostal theology reaped three doctrines involving the baptism with the Holy Spirit. It is *subsequent to conversion*, experienced through the *fulfillment of requirements*, and initially evidenced by *speaking in tongues*. The new plant weathered the storm of criticism by leaders of revivals already in progress, separated itself from the other Protestant churches and became a new denominational movement. Despite many disputes and divisions about other doctrines, Pentecostalism has preserved these three distinctive elements in its theology.

This theology raises a number of crucial questions. What is the significance of Jesus' anointing with the Spirit at Jordan and its meaning for us? To what extent can the experiences of the disciples in Acts be considered a model for all Christians? What is the meaning of the events at Pentecost in the light of Luke's purpose and historical frame of reference?

Pentecostal theology also stresses the exercise of spiritual gifts, especially those in 1 Corinthians 12. Here also questions arise. Is the baptism with the Spirit an initial or second experience according to Paul? What is the nature and purpose of spiritual gifts in New Testament times and their relevance today?

These questions, raised not only by classical Pentecostalism but also by the current charismatic renewal, can be answered only in the light of Luke's teaching in his Gospel and the Acts, and Paul's teaching in 1 Corinthians, writings essential to Pentecostal theology.

Part Two:

The Spirit in Luke/Acts

6
Christ and the Spirit

Luke's writing covers seventy crucial years, bridging the Old Covenant and the New, Israel and the church, the synagogue and the Christian community. The two eras witness both continuity and discontinuity in God's redemptive activity. In the Old Testament the Spirit came upon individuals and groups at special times for specific tasks.[1] Yet Ezekiel foresaw a day when God would give his people a new heart and put his Spirit within them (Ezek. 36: 26-27). Joel foretold a new era in which God would pour out his Spirit on all, and their sons and daughters would prophesy (Joel 2:28-29).

The same "Spirit of the Lord" who spoke through the prophets now appears in a new role. For Luke the presence and action of the Spirit occupy a central place in the drama of redemptive history. He is prominent at each stage of the coming of the New Age including the revelation of the nature of Jesus' messiahship and mission.

This chapter and the next focus on Luke's teaching about the nature and purpose of the Spirit's activity in the Gospel. More than Matthew and Mark, he highlights the historical and theological importance of this work. Luke has most of their references to the Holy Spirit and another dozen of his own. A grasp of his teaching in the Gospel is foundational for understanding his perspective on the Spirit's mission in Acts.

First Streaks of Dawn   Luke unfolds his message in a carefully designed sequence.[2] Prominent in each episode is the part played by the Holy Spirit. The first act of this drama, with its three visions and three prophecies, features the renewed, expanding activity of the Spirit.

The opening scene breathes the air of the Old Testament as the curtain rises on a Jewish priest performing his duties at the temple in Jerusalem. Zechariah the priest and his wife Elizabeth are upright in God's sight, but they have had no children and are now too old. Though the nation chafes under the yoke of imperial Rome and the voice of God through the prophets has been silent for nearly four hundred years, yet the faithful continue to worship according to the centuries-old ritual of Moses' law.

This day marks the crowning experience of Zechariah's life. To offer this incense is an honor granted only once. But as he stands alone in the Holy Place, Zechariah is startled and terrified when an angel suddenly appears. Gabriel says, "Do not be afraid, Zechariah; your prayer has been heard. Your wife Elizabeth will bear you a son, and you are to give him the name John" (Lk. 1:13). Not only the parents but many others will rejoice over the birth of this child. He will be one of the Lord's great men, preaching in the spirit and power of the great prophet Elijah to prepare for the coming of the Messiah. Gabriel declares that John will be "filled with the Holy Spirit even from birth" (1:15). The fact that the Spirit will so empower him highlights the New Age which is now dawning.

The second scene also features a vision with an angelic announcement of the Spirit's activity. Six months later, after Elizabeth has become pregnant, Gabriel visits a virgin in Nazareth who is engaged to Joseph. He declares,

> *Do not be afraid, Mary, you have found favor with God. You will be with child and give birth to a son, and you are to give him the*

*name Jesus. He will be great and will be called the Son of the
Most High. The Lord God will give him the throne of his father
David, and he will reign over the house of Jacob forever; his
kingdom will never end. (1:30-33)*

When Mary wonders how this can happen, the angel answers,
"The Holy Spirit will come upon you, and the power of the
Most High will overshadow you" (1:35).

In the third scene the Spirit himself acts. Informed by Gabriel that Elizabeth is expecting a child, Mary hurries to visit her.
As soon as Elizabeth hears Mary's greeting, she is filled with
the Holy Spirit and exclaims, "Blessed are you among women,
and blessed is the child you will bear! But why am I so favored,
that the mother of my Lord should come to me? . . . Blessed is
she who has believed that what the Lord has said to her will be
accomplished!" (1:42-43, 45). This prophecy prompts Mary's
great hymn of praise, the Magnificat (1:46-55), which is also a
prophetic word, declaring that the Lord will deliver Israel and
fulfill his promise to Abraham (Gen. 17:8).

Several months later a fourth episode takes place in a more
public setting of family and friends. According to the angel's
promise, Elizabeth bears a son amid much rejoicing. They suggest that he be named after his father. But Zechariah, struck
dumb by Gabriel in the temple for his unbelief, asks for a
tablet and writes, "His name is John." Immediately he begins
to speak and praise God. Filled with the Holy Spirit Zechariah
prophesies, first praising God (1:68-75) and then describing
John's mission (1:76-79):

And you, my child, will be called a prophet
of the Most High;
for you will go on before the Lord to
prepare the way for him,
to give his people the knowledge of salvation
through the forgiveness of their sins. (1:76-77)

Although officially a priest, Zechariah receives knowledge of
God's purpose through the Holy Spirit and speaks as a prophet.

In the fifth scene news of Jesus' birth is brought not to religious specialists but to shepherds. An angel of the Lord appears to them and declares, "Do not be afraid. I bring you good news of great joy that will be for all the people. Today in the town of David a Savior has been born to you; he is Christ the Lord" (2:10-11). Immediately the shepherds hurry to see the baby for themselves, then return to spread the word, praising God for what they have seen and heard.

Jerusalem is the stage of the final scene. After Jesus' birth Joseph and Mary come to the temple to present him to the Lord with the customary sacrifice. Luke introduces a new character described simply as "a man in Jerusalem called Simeon" (2:25). Unlike Zechariah, he has no official position in the religious establishment.

But Simeon does have one thing in common with Zechariah and Elizabeth; he is righteous and devout, looking for the salvation of Israel. "The Holy Spirit was upon him. It had been revealed to him by the Holy Spirit that he would not die before he had seen the Lord's Christ" (2:25-26). On this day, "Moved by the Spirit" (2:27), he comes into the temple courts. When Joseph and Mary enter with Jesus, Simeon takes the baby in his arms and praises God:

Sovereign Lord, as you promised,
  now dismiss your servant in peace.
For my eyes have seen your salvation,
  which you have prepared in the sight of all people,
a light for revelation to the Gentiles
  and for glory to your people Israel. (2:29-32)

After blessing the parents Simeon gives a prophecy to Mary (2:34-35). The Messiah will also be a cause of division, "a sign that will be spoken against." His kind of deliverance will not be welcomed by all. Here Luke introduces the concept of the Messiah suffering with the pain involved in bringing salvation.

At this moment the prophetess Anna arrives. Though not explicitly attributed to the Spirit, Anna's thanksgiving arises from a prophetic knowledge of Jesus' messiahship.

So the first act ends as it began, at the temple in Jerusalem with the Spirit again active in Israel. Luke emphasizes the prophetic vocation found in the Old Testament as he pictures the dawning of the messianic era in terms of the expanding activity of the Spirit. The first two scenes involve a single person and the third a private conversation. The fourth finds family and neighbors present for Zechariah's prophecy concerning the ministry of John. The fifth features an announcement to the shepherds of the Messiah's arrival, while the last scene takes place in the temple courts with Simeon's public prophecy. The variety of people and circumstances involved anticipates the messianic era foretold by Joel. Luke's focus on the prophetic dimension of the Spirit's action from the beginning of his Gospel is clear as individuals, filled with the Holy Spirit, discern the work of God and declare his message.

The New Age Appears　For most new eras in history no one event marks a definitive beginning. The old gradually fades in a series of events which effect a transition to the new. The first act of Luke's Gospel culminates in the birth of Jesus the Christ; the second inaugurates his mission (2:41—4:30). Three major scenes feature the Spirit's activity: Jesus' baptism, his temptation and the sermon at Nazareth.

The first takes place at the Jordan River. When the word of God comes to John, he emerges from the desert to preach a baptism of repentance for the forgiveness of sins. Crowds throng the Jordan to hear and respond. As they are wondering if John might be the long-expected Messiah, he declares, "I baptize you with water. But one more powerful than I will come, the thongs of whose sandals I am not worthy to untie. He will baptize you with the Holy Spirit and fire" (3:16). John's mission is to prepare the way for the Messiah.

Soon Jesus appears on the scene. "When all the people were being baptized, Jesus was baptized too" (3:21). Thirty years of private life in Nazareth have now ended. At the threshhold of his own ministry Jesus humbly identifies himself with his people in their repentance for the sins from which he came to deliver them.

Immediately a second event occurs. As Jesus was praying, "the Holy Spirit descended on him in bodily form like a dove. And a voice came from heaven: 'You are my Son, whom I love; with you I am well-pleased' " (3:22). This brief declaration echoes two significant Old Testament texts. In Psalm 2:7 God addresses the King: "You are my son." Israel nurtured a continuing hope that some day God would bring into the world a messianic Son worthy to rule on David's throne. The second phrase alludes to Isaiah 42:1: "Behold my servant . . . in whom my soul delights." This prophecy pictures the Servant of the Lord who through suffering will bring healing and justice.

This proclamation implies Jesus' double role of messianic Son and suffering Servant. He willingly suffers for his people so that he can take the throne of David and rule the nations. These words from heaven may also be understood as an encouragement to Jesus, the Father's commendation to strengthen him in the struggle with hostile forces he must soon face.

The descent of the Spirit fulfills another element of Old Testament prophecy. Isaiah declared that the Servant would be specially anointed—"I have put my Spirit upon him" (42:1)—and described what this would mean for the Messiah whom God would raise up from David's descendants:

And the Spirit of the LORD shall rest upon him,
   the spirit of wisdom and understanding,
   the spirit of counsel and might,
   the spirit of knowledge and the fear of the LORD. (11:2)

Here at Jordan the pieces of Old Testament prophecy finally fit together. Jesus assumes the dual mission of suffering Servant and messianic Son, empowered by the Spirit of the Lord promised for the New Age.

This experience at Jordan has a special meaning for Jesus

personally as his sense of sonship is reaffirmed and he is anointed with the Spirit. Yet Luke's primary purpose in relating these events is historical—the unfolding of God's redemptive purpose.[3] John's baptism and the Spirit's descent bridge the Old and New Covenants. But the Spirit's coming upon Jesus is unlike his previous activity with the prophets in that here it is visible (the dove) and audible (the voice).[4] The New Age has now arrived in the person of Jesus. He becomes the unique Bearer of the Spirit who introduces a new era in the history of salvation.

The second scene plunges Jesus into conflict with man's ancient enemy, Satan, whom he came to defeat. "Jesus, full of the Holy Spirit, returned from the Jordan and was led by the Spirit in the desert, where for forty days he was tempted by the devil. He ate nothing during those days, and at the end of them he was hungry" (4:1-2). Luke reports two aspects of Jesus' relationship to the Holy Spirit. Fullness of the Spirit is a continuing characteristic of his life. Nevertheless the Spirit acts specifically to lead him in the desert as a preparation for his ministry.

Luke's arrangement of the temptations (different from Matthew's) is such that the climax comes at the temple in Jerusalem, a place prominent in Luke's narrative of salvation history.

The stage is now set for Jesus to begin his ministry. "Jesus returned to Galilee in the power of the Spirit, and news about him spread through the whole countryside. He taught in their synagogues, and everyone praised him" (4:14-15). At the outset of Jesus' ministry Luke emphasizes the source of his power.

The third scene takes place in Jesus' home village of Nazareth. Like every devout Jew, he goes into the synagogue on the Sabbath day. There he stands up and reads from Isaiah 61:1-2.

The Spirit of the Lord is on me;
therefore he has anointed me to preach

> good news to the poor.
> He has sent me to proclaim freedom for the prisoners
>   and recovery of sight for the blind,
> to release the oppressed,
>   to proclaim the year of the Lord's favor. (Lk. 4:18-19)

Jesus realizes that at his baptism he was anointed by the Spirit of the Lord so that he is the one in whom this prophecy is fulfilled. Also, his ministry will have the dimensions of preaching and healing. Jesus is sent to give sight to the blind as well as to declare good news to the poor. Finally, his understanding of God's purpose makes clear to him which parts of Old Testament prophecy are descriptive of his ministry and which are not. Jesus' message is one of God's favor and not of vengeance; he stops short of quoting the last half of Isaiah 61:2.

As the eyes of everyone in the synagogue are fastened on him, Jesus declares, "Today this scripture is fulfilled in your hearing" (4:21). The long-awaited time has arrived. Jesus understands that the Spirit descended upon him at Jordan to anoint him as the Messiah (Hebrew "anointed one").

As the people wonder about his words, Jesus challenges them to accept him, not as Joseph's son but as a prophet. Because of their unbelief they reject him and his message, even try to kill him, but he escapes and continues his ministry in Capernaum.

Luke's narrative features the presence and activity of the Spirit in the inauguration of Jesus' ministry. His initiative is central in these three events—baptism, temptation and sermon. The Spirit both directs his path and empowers his activities. Luke continues to present the prophetic dimension of the Spirit's function as he anoints and fills Jesus for his mission

Preaching and Healing In his record of the events following the sermon at Nazareth, Luke makes it clear that Jesus' ministry consistently centers in preaching and healing.[5] Both words and acts lie at the heart of his mission.

While teaching in the synagogue, Jesus commands a demon to come out of a man and the demon leaves (4:33-37). Jesus heals Simon's mother-in-law of a high fever, and she immediately gets up and begins to serve them. Then "the people brought to Jesus all who had various kinds of sickness, and laying his hands on each one, he healed them" (4:40). After calling Peter, James and John to be his disciples, Jesus heals a leper and, as the news spreads, whole crowds come "to hear him and to be healed of their sicknesses" (5:15).

Jesus' preaching and healing through the Spirit receive opposite responses seen in the following two events. While the crowds gladly receive his ministry, some of the spectators begin to attack it. One day religious leaders from every village of Galilee and from Judea and from Jerusalem were present. "And the power of the Lord was present for him to heal the sick" (5:17). Suddenly some men carry in a paralytic whom Jesus heals both spiritually and physically. "Friend, your sins are forgiven. . . . Get up, take your mat and go home" (5:20, 24). He stands and walks out carrying his mat and praising God. Everyone is amazed and filled with awe.

Luke has shown that Jesus' ministry of preaching and healing, intended to reach every dimension of human need, is exercised in the power of the Spirit. Having made this clear, he does not need to keep repeating it. But on one other occasion Jesus specifically attributes his healing power to the Spirit of God.

When one day he drives out a demon, some of the onlookers say, "By Beelzebub, the prince of demons, he is driving out demons" (11:15). Jesus answers with a logical argument: "If Satan is divided against himself, how can his kingdom stand? . . . But if I drive out demons by the finger of God, then the kingdom of God has come to you" (11:18, 20). Matthew's version uses the phrase "by the Spirit of God" (Mt. 12:28). Either way the point is clear: Jesus does not claim to exorcise demons in his own power.

This passage throws light on Jesus' statement in Luke

12:10: "Everyone who speaks a word against the Son of Man will be forgiven, but anyone who blasphemes against the Holy Spirit will not be forgiven." Personal criticism of Jesus is forgivable. But since he casts out demons by the Spirit of God, rejection of this ministry is an entirely different matter. To attribute to Satan the evident power of God in overcoming illness and evil is to commit the unpardonable sin.

Luke makes one other reference to the Spirit in Jesus' conflict with Satan. The seventy disciples, sent out to heal and to preach the kingdom of God, return with joy and report that even the demons submitted to them in his name. Jesus replies, "I saw Satan fall like lightning from heaven. I have given you authority to trample on snakes and scorpions, and to overcome all the power of the enemy" (10:18-19). Luke reports that Jesus "rejoiced in the Holy Spirit" (10:21 RSV). He sees these exorcisms not only as healing of the sick but also as victory over Satan.

According to Luke's record Jesus' miraculous healings are more than his ministerial credentials, the validation of office expected of prophets in Israel. They demonstrate the purpose and scope of his mission. Just as sin has ravaged every dimension of human existence, salvation extends to the total person. The Greek word *sōzō*, often translated "save", also means "heal."[6] It can connote salvation from disease as well as from eternal death.

Furthermore, these healings—especially the exorcisms—are a sign of the New Age. This binding of evil powers, expected at the end of the present age, has already begun. The final battle with Satan has begun and is being won.

The Spirit and Jesus   In recent years concern has grown over the neglect of the Holy Spirit in many areas of theology, especially in the ministry of Jesus.[7] This neglect is due in part to the nature of the Spirit's work as the agent of God—he represents another and not himself. He reveals the divine message to the prophets in the Old Covenant, while in the New

Covenant he is sent by the risen Christ to indwell and empower believers. Jesus tells the disciples that the Spirit speaks neither on his own authority nor about himself (Jn. 16:13-14). By the very nature of his mission the Spirit points to the Father and the Son.

A second reason, however, lies in the historical development of theology. In the early centuries, heresies concerning the person of Christ forced the church to face difficult questions. One of these was posed by the Docetists who were perplexed by a logical dilemma: if Jesus suffered he was not God; if he was God he did not suffer. Since they firmly believed that Jesus was divine, they concluded that he could not have suffered as a human being. Ignatius found it necessary to affirm a Jesus Christ "who was truly born, who ate and drank, who was truly persecuted under Pontius Pilate, was truly crucified and truly died."[8]

In our century appreciation of this reality has suffered for a different reason: Jesus' deity has required so much defense in the face of its strong denial that his true humanity has often been neglected. Therefore, it is important to recognize Luke's teaching about Jesus' genuine growth to manhood and his ministry through the Spirit.[9] "The child grew and became strong; he was filled with wisdom, and the grace of God was upon him. . . . And Jesus grew in wisdom and stature, and in favor with God and men" (2:40, 52). Since Jesus was a perfect man, he made progress like other men using his powers of soul, mind, will and affections.[10]

Jesus' growth in favor with God and others involved increasing self-understanding since knowledge of self comes mainly through relationships. "Through the relationships that developed between Jesus and others the Spirit taught him. . . . Jesus' knowledge of God and his knowledge of himself grew apace."[11]

Luke describes Jesus as anointed, filled, led and empowered by the Spirit.[12] Jesus himself attributes both his power (*dunamis*) to heal and his authority (*exousia*) to preach as manifestations of the Spirit. "The demons obeyed, the blind saw, the lepers were cleansed; the poor and the sinner experienced forgiveness and acceptance; or in a word, power to bring wholeness of mind, of body and of relationships."[13] In Jesus Christ we see the unified Act and Word of God; life and message are one as he teaches by example and precept. And the results affected not just the minds but the total lives of those who heard and responded.

The relationship between Jesus and the Spirit also had implications for the latter's ministry. In the Old Covenant, the Spirit of the Lord spoke in a variety of ways through the prophets. Now he initiates the New Age in the person of Jesus. "Picking up from the Old Testament, Jesus is conceived, guided, filled with the Spirit. He centers in Jesus who will bring salvation."[14] God's presence through the Spirit comes to focus in the character and ministry of his Son. From now on all teaching and experience attributed to the Spirit must be in harmony with that of Jesus.

Yet soon the work of the Spirit in the One will include the many. According to John the Baptist, the Bearer of the Spirit will also baptize with the Spirit, who is to be poured out on the disciples.

7
The Promise
of the
Spirit

To speculation that he was the Messiah, John the Baptist answered, "I baptize you with water. But one more powerful than I will come.... He will baptize you with the Holy Spirit and fire" (3:16). What was the meaning of this promise for Jesus' disciples? What would be the relationship of the Spirit to these men whose experience bridged the old and new eras?

Holy Spirit and Fire   While all four evangelists record the promise that Jesus would baptize with the Holy Spirit, only Matthew and Luke add "and fire." Though the meaning of this phrase is not perfectly clear,[1] in the Old Testament fire pictures both cleansing and destruction. Malachi, looking forward to John's mission, speaks of God's fire which purifies the faithful and burns up the wicked (Mal. 3:1-3; 4:1). John's statement apparently indicates that the *same* persons ("you") are to be baptized with both the Spirit and fire. Therefore it is probable that for the disciples the fire refers to the purifying power of the Messiah's baptism.

In the New Testament, Luke uses the words *baptize* and *baptism* in two ways: literally to signify the water rite and figuratively to describe spiritual experiences. In his Gospel the verb and noun occur thirteen times, ten of which refer to John's water baptism for the forgiveness of sins. (By submitting to this baptism Jesus identified himself with his people living under the Old Covenant.)

The other occurrences denote two quite different experiences: the suffering of the cross and the coming of the Spirit. Before Jesus could fulfill John's promise of baptizing others with the Spirit and fire, he must experience his own baptism of the cross. Jesus said, "I have come to bring fire on the earth, and how I wish it were already kindled! But I have a baptism to undergo, and how distressed I am until it is completed!" (12:49-50). In both cases baptism is an apt metaphor, since Jesus' passion is a flood into which he would *plunge*, and the Holy Spirit would be *poured* out.

Having been anointed with the Holy Spirit to inaugurate the New Age, the servant and representative of his people had to endure for them the "fire" of judgment. Jesus' ministry of preaching and healing must culminate in the cross to atone for his people's sins and make possible their forgiveness. Only then—after his death, resurrection and ascension—could he baptize others with the Spirit and fire.

Prayer and Witness   Prior to his crucifixion, however, Jesus taught his disciples and gave them, among other things, a promise of the Spirit's activity in connection with their prayer and witness. The Gospels show that Jesus himself was a man of prayer. After a strenuous day or before a crucial decision he often engaged in a time of prolonged prayer. But this communion with the Father was not reserved for special occasions; it formed the fabric of his life.

One day a disciple saw Jesus praying and asked, "Lord, teach us to pray, just as John taught his disciples" (11:1). In the following verses Luke clusters four teachings about prayer, two of which involve the Holy Spirit.

The first is a sample prayer, combining elements of worship and petition, which has come to be known as the "Lord's

Prayer." It starts with the familiar words: "Father, hallowed be your name, your kingdom come" (11:2). Another version of Luke's wording appears probably as early as the second century. Instead of "your kingdom come" it reads: "May the Holy Spirit come upon us and cleanse us."[2] This alternative harmonizes with Jesus' teachings about the Spirit in Luke 11. It also suggests that in later liturgical usage the gift of the Spirit was considered a vital characteristic of the kingdom.

Next comes a parable teaching the importance of persistence in prayer (11:5-8), followed by a threefold command reinforcing this principle: "Keep on asking . . . keep on seeking . . . keep on knocking. . . . For every one who asks *and* keeps on asking receives, and he who seeks *and* keeps on seeking finds, and to him who knocks *and* keeps on knocking the door shall be opened" (11:9-10 Amplified).

After this sample prayer, parable and command, Jesus concludes his teaching with these words:

Which of you fathers, if your son asks for a fish, will give him a snake instead? Or if he asks for an egg, will give him a scorpion? If you then, though you are evil, know how to give good gifts to your children, how much more will your Father in heaven give the Holy Spirit to those who ask him!" (11:11-13)

This passage clearly teaches three basic truths about the Holy Spirit. First, it is God's purpose to bestow the Spirit on the disciples. Second, this bestowal is a gift, not something to be earned or demanded. Third, the reception of the Spirit is to be expected and sought.

The application of this verse poses difficulty if it is interpreted to mean the initial reception of the Spirit in regeneration. But if we stay within the context of Luke's teaching concerning the Spirit's prophetic, vocational activity—that is, his empowering for witness and service—there is no problem. There is good reason to seek the Spirit's power for these activities.[3]

Luke also records a promise of the Spirit's help for witness when suffering persecution. Jesus instructs his disciples,

"When you are brought before synagogues, rulers and authorities, do not worry about how you will defend yourselves or what you will say, for the Holy Spirit will teach you at that time what you should say" (12:11-12).

Shortly before his death Jesus gives a similar teaching (21: 12-15). Again he tells the disciples they will be arrested and put in prison for his sake. As a result they will be witnesses. "But make up your mind not to worry beforehand how you will defend yourselves. For I will give you words and wisdom that none of your adversaries will be able to resist or contradict" (21:14-15).

The disciples are not to worry in advance about the content or form of their defense; these will be given at the time. In the first promise, the wisdom comes from the Holy Spirit, while in the second Jesus says that *he* will give it. Their action on behalf of the disciples is one and the same: the exalted Lord will work through the Spirit. This theme of joint activity leads to Jesus' promise that he will send the Holy Spirit to his disciples.

Power for Witness   The last chapter of Luke's Gospel records the first of three statements about the Holy Spirit's coming at Pentecost. In them, Jesus explains what this event will mean for the disciples.

After his resurrection, Jesus appeared in a room where the disciples were gathered and opened their minds to understand the Scriptures.

This is what is written: The Christ will suffer and rise from the dead on the third day, and repentance and forgiveness of sins will be preached in his name to all nations, beginning at Jerusalem. You are witnesses of these things. I am going to send you what my Father has promised; but stay in the city until you have been clothed with power from on high. (24:46-49)

Seven elements make up Jesus' last instruction recorded in the Gospel. First, the heart of the gospel is the death and resurrection of Christ; it calls for repentance and offers forgiveness of sins. Second, the disciples will preach this salvation to all nations; God's redemptive purpose is worldwide. Third, they will start at Jerusalem. Fourth, the disciples are witnesses to these events; the basis of apostolic preaching is personal testimony. Fifth, the coming event is something the Father has promised. Sixth, the disciples are to wait for it in Jerusalem. Finally, at Pentecost they will be clothed with power for witness.

With this Jesus blessed them and parted from them. The suffering Servant, through death and resurrection, is now exalted to the place of power as the triumphant Son of David.

Moving from the Gospel to the Acts of the Apostles, we read, "In my former book, Theophilus, I wrote about all that Jesus began to do and to teach until the day he was taken up to heaven, after giving instructions through the Holy Spirit to the apostles he had chosen" (Acts 1:1-2). This summary of Luke's Gospel makes clear the intended continuity of Luke and Acts. First, the Gospel tells what Jesus *began* to do and teach; by implication Acts will report the continuation of his work. Second, just as Jesus taught and healed for several years in the power of the Holy Spirit, so he continued his postresurrection ministry through the Spirit.

In the first few verses of Acts, Luke again recounts Jesus' activities between his resurrection and ascension, this time emphasizing his proofs that he was alive and his teaching about the kingdom of God. On one occasion he gave them a second command and promise similar to the one recorded at the end of the Gospel. "Do not leave Jerusalem, but wait for the gift my Father promised, which you have heard me speak about. For John baptized with water, but in a few days you will be baptized with the Holy Spirit" (1:4-5).

This overlap with Luke 24:47-49 forms a double link in the chain of events stretching from John at the Jordan to Paul in prison at Rome. The statement at the end of the Gospel looks forward to the mission which develops in the Acts; these words at the beginning of Acts look back to the events at Jordan. The baptism with the Spirit foretold by John is the promised gift of the Father about which Jesus has spoken. These two passages unite the Gospel and the Acts in their continuous record of Jesus' redemptive ministry through the Spirit, first as the suffering Servant and then as the ascended King.

Still, the disciples did not grasp the meaning of their ministry. As often before, their old way of thinking missed the main point. So they asked him, "Lord, are you at this time going to restore the kingdom to Israel?" (1:6). The disciples were still thinking of the kingdom as a geo-political conquest within the present age. They had yet to learn that its present manifestation is the reign of God in human hearts no matter where they live. Jesus used this misunderstanding to give further instruction.

It is not for you to know the times or dates the Father has set by his own authority. But you will receive power when the Holy Spirit comes on you; and you will be my witnesses in Jerusalem, and in all Judea and Samaria, and to the ends of the earth. (1:7-8)

A third time Jesus mentions Jerusalem as the place where they will be baptized with the Holy Spirit and begin an international witness with power.

In these three statements (Lk. 24:47-49; Acts 1:4-5; 1:8) Jesus describes the nature and purpose of his promised baptizing with the Spirit. As the Holy Spirit comes upon the disciples, they will be clothed with power from on high to become Christ's witnesses to the ends of the earth. Well before Pentecost, the baptism with the Holy Spirit is given theological interpretation—empowering for mission.[4]

Jesus then ascended out of their sight into a cloud. The ascension has two sides. In the Gospel it is the final event in Jesus' earthly life; exaltation to God's right hand vindicates his servant. In the Acts it is the opening event in the risen Christ's activity to build his church. His glorification precedes the pouring out of the Spirit.

Luke deliberately repeats his narrative of both Jesus' commission of the disciples and his ascension in order to connect the work of Jesus and the Spirit. To view the Gospel as the story of Jesus and the Acts as the story of the Spirit is to misunderstand Luke's teaching. At the beginning of the Gospel Jesus becomes the Bearer of the Spirit (Lk. 4:18); in the Acts he is the Giver of the Spirit (Acts 2:33). James Dunn notes that at each stage Jesus enters into a new relationship with the Spirit:

> *First, when his human life was the creation of the Spirit (Luke 1:35); second, when he was anointed with the Spirit and thus became the Anointed One, the unique Man of the Spirit (Luke 3:22; 4:18); third, when he received the promise of the Spirit at his exaltation and poured the Spirit forth on his disciples, thus becoming Lord of the Spirit.*[5]

The ministry of the Spirit in Acts cannot be dissociated from that of the risen Christ. Through the Holy Spirit Jesus continues in his church the ministry he conducted publicly during the preresurrection mission. (John's perspective is markedly different from that of the Synoptic writers. See Appendix A for a discussion of the "impartation" of the Spirit in John's Gospel.)

The closing scene of Luke's Gospel is similar to the first: the disciples "returned to Jerusalem with great joy. And they stayed continually at the temple, praising God" (24:52-53). The story began in the temple where Zechariah, a righteous priest of the Old Covenant, served before God with a petition for the redemption of Israel. It closes with Jesus, the resurrected High Priest of the New Covenant, blessing the new Israel. In obedience to their Lord, his followers return to the temple with prayers of praise to wait for the promise of the Father.

8
Pentecost

The day of Pentecost marks the beginning of a third stage in the Holy Spirit's role in the coming of the New Age. His renewed prophetic activity had preceded the birth of the Messiah. At Jordan he anointed Jesus for his messianic ministry. Now, at this Pentecost, the Spirit comes on the disciples to empower their witness. The next two chapters focus on the Holy Spirit's activity in the mission of the church as Luke records it in the Acts of the Apostles.

Descent of the Spirit   Pentecost was celebrated fifty days after Passover. Marking the end of the spring harvest, the ceremony on Pentecost offered the first two loaves of new grain. It was one of the three great pilgrimage festivals which required Israel's attendance at the temple (Deut. 16:16), so Jerusalem was thronged with pilgrims from other parts of the Roman Empire. Amidst the festive activities of the Pentecost following Jesus' ascension, a sudden and dramatic event took place.

When the day of Pentecost came, they were all together in one place. Suddenly a sound like the blowing of a violent wind came from heaven and filled the whole house where they were sitting. They saw what seemed to be tongues of fire that separated and came to rest on each of them. All of them were filled with the Holy Spirit and began

to speak in other tongues as the Spirit enabled them. (Acts 2:1-4)
Several elements in this account are significant. First is the
timing. The disciples had obeyed their Lord as day after day
they had waited in Jerusalem for the fulfillment of his promise. Yet the descent of the Spirit is linked not to their spiritual
readiness but to the sovereign action of God in history. Pentecost would be the day of greatest impact as the pilgrims, now
swelling Jerusalem's population, soon returned home with
the new message. They would be the first fruits of a worldwide
spiritual harvest.

A second element in this event is its *origin*. It was not produced by human endeavor; the gift came suddenly from
heaven. The downward movement from God to man continued to demonstrate the divine initiative. Luke pictures the
disciples gathered together, available but not active. They
were sitting, not kneeling or standing (the usual Jewish pos-
tures of prayer).

Third, Luke uses two *symbols* to describe the Spirit: wind
and fire. The Greek word here translated "wind" occurs only
one other time in the New Testament. At Athens Paul declared that God "gives all men life and breath" (Acts 17:25).
The use of "wind" echoes Jesus' words to Nicodemus about
the wind (spirit) blowing wherever it pleases (John 3:8). The
Old Testament links wind and fire in Psalm 104:4, quoted
in Hebrews 1:7: "He makes his angels winds, his servants
flames of fire." Thus John the Baptist: "He will baptize you
with the Holy Spirit and fire" (Lk. 3:16). Just as wind represents the Spirit, so fire connotes God's purification of his
people.

A fourth element has to do with the *recipients*. The tongues
like fire rested on "each" of them and "all" were filled with the
Holy Spirit. Probably the whole body of one hundred and
twenty involved in the preceding chapter (1:15) were present,
not just the Twelve. The main point is that here, as elsewhere
in Acts, the Spirit did not come on part of a group. All the disciples were baptized with the Spirit by the ascended Christ on

this feast of Pentecost.

Too Much Wine? A fifth element is the immediate *result* of the Spirit's coming. Those present heard a specific sound— not just the inarticulate rushing of the wind, but a speaking in other tongues. Luke lists more than a dozen different countries and districts represented by these pilgrims. "Utterly amazed, they asked: 'Are not all these men who are speaking Galileans? Then how is it that each of us hears them in his own native language? . . . We hear them declaring the wonders of God in our own tongues! . . . What does this mean?' " (2:7-8, 11-12). While some were perplexed, others made fun of the disciples with a ready answer: "They have had too much wine" (2:13).

Today we face the same question of what this strange phenomenon meant, and now as then a variety of explanations is offered. Some scholars note that the returning Jews would have known the two languages spoken in Palestine— Aramaic and Greek—and then assert that the disciples were simply speaking in an unusually clear manner.[1] But does this explanation do justice to the data? Sometimes the significance of an event is revealed by the reaction of its observers. Luke says they were bewildered, utterly amazed, perplexed. Is this the kind of reaction to be expected if the disciples were doing nothing more than speaking a purer Aramaic or Greek without their Galilean dialect?

Another view rejects a miraculous element because it did not seem to serve any practical purpose at the time.[2] But is this a valid criterion for accepting or rejecting a possible miracle? Surely our acceptance of biblical events cannot depend on whether at the moment their purpose is obvious.

Some assert that the miracle consisted not of the *speaking* of the disciples but in that the visitors from other countries heard and understood. It is assumed that speaking in tongues here is the same as at Corinth where they are not known, foreign languages. Therefore, at Pentecost the disciples "spoke a heavenly language to God—not of angels, but a language above the influence of sin.... Hence the understanding of this language was also a work of the Holy Spirit."[3] But this is not what Luke records. He clearly identifies the Spirit's activity with the speaking and reports that the visitors heard it in their own languages (2:4, 6). (Furthermore there is reason to question whether the phenomenon at Pentecost was indeed the same as later occurrences in the Acts or at Corinth. To make the miracle one of hearing requires more theological inference than the passage warrants.)

The most straightforward interpretation is that the disciples were speaking in languages other than their own, namely, those of the countries and districts represented.[4] Luke reports that they spoke in "other" (or "different") tongues.[5] Only at Pentecost does Luke report a variety of linguistic groups hearing a message in miraculously given tongues. The pilgrims didn't require this phenomenon, since they understood Aramaic or Greek. But in the circumstances it served both a practical and a symbolic purpose.

Practically, this speaking in other tongues attracted the attention of visitors from other countries. It succeeded in bringing together a crowd perplexed and curious to know more about what was happening.

But this speaking in foreign languages was not a side show; it was a sign or symbol of the Lord's purpose to proclaim the good news not just in Jerusalem and Judea, but "to the ends of the earth" (1:8). In the providence of God the nations of the world were represented in these God-fearing Jews gathered in Jerusalem. Soon the message would spread with missionaries to the distant countries from which they came. The miracle of tongues at Pentecost captures at one place and time a preview of the church's mission over the miles and throughout the years. "Nothing more aptly expressed the will of God for the world mission of the Church than proclaiming the great deeds of God in the world's languages."[6]

Peter's Sermon   When Peter stood up with the other eleven disciples to address the crowd, he first set the record straight on the charge of drunkenness. While it was a possibility, since wine flowed freely at festivals, Peter pointed out that the disciples were not drunk. It was only nine o'clock in the morning. Rather, this was the fulfillment of Joel's prophecy (Joel 2: 28-29).

In the last days, God says,
* I will pour out my Spirit on all people.*
Your sons and daughters will prophesy,
* your young men will see visions,*
* and your old men will dream dreams.*
Even on my servants, both men and women,
* I will pour out my Spirit in those days,*
* and they will prophesy. (Acts 2:17-18)*

What did Joel proclaim about the future coming of the Spirit and how did Peter apply this prophecy? First, the coming of the Spirit is eschatological, that is, for the last days. Peter equates this outpouring of the Holy Spirit with the experience of filling which he and the other disciples have just had. It is evidence that the New Age foretold by the prophets has arrived.

Second, the nature of this gift is prophetic. The words "and they will prophesy" at the end of 2:18 do not occur in Joel. Their addition here in Peter's otherwise direct quotation shows his concern to emphasize the prophetic nature of this speaking in tongues. In this instance it takes the form of praise in "declaring the wonders of God" (2:11).

Third, this giving of the Spirit is universal. He is poured out on all people and not just on a few select prophets or disciples. It is for men and women, young and old, slaves and free; all will prophesy, without distinction of sex, age or social position.

Peter ends the quotation with Joel's universal offer: "Everyone who calls on the name of the Lord will be saved" (2:21). He then bears witness to the Messiah himself:

Jesus of Nazareth was a man accredited by God to you by miracles, wonders and signs, which God did among you through him, as you yourselves know. . . . You, with the help of wicked men, put him to death by nailing him to the cross. But God raised him from the dead. (2:22-24)

From the outset the heart of apostolic preaching empowered by the Holy Spirit was witness to the life, death and resurrection of Jesus the Christ.

Going on, Peter cites two Old Testament passages (Ps. 16: 8-11; 110:1) whose fulfillment in Jesus prove him to be the Messiah. Peter again witnesses to Jesus' resurrection and then links him with the Spirit: "Exalted to the right hand of God, he has received from the Father the promised Holy Spirit, and has poured out what you now see and hear. . . . Therefore, let all Israel be assured of this: God has made this Jesus whom you crucified both Lord and Christ" (2:33, 36).

These words cut the hearers to the heart, and they ask the apostles, "What shall we do?" Peter responds with a call to repentance.[7]

Repent and be baptized, every one of you, in the name of Jesus Christ so that your sins may be forgiven. And you will receive the gift of the Holy Spirit. The promise is for you and your children and for all who are far off—for all whom the Lord our God will call. (2:38-39)

Peter's command echoes the message of John the Baptist, but now baptism is in the name of Jesus Christ. Like Joel's prophecy Peter's preaching ends with a promise of salvation, universal in time (to "your children") and in distance (to "all who are far off").

Luke records three central and related elements involved in becoming a Christian: repentance, water-baptism and reception of the Spirit. Peter's three verbs are repent, baptize and receive. Two are commands and one is a promise. Repentance is the sinner's active response to the gospel;[8] water-baptism is performed by the Christian community; the gift of the Holy Spirit is received from God.[9]

It should be noted that Luke presents no standard formula for conversion. In the following chapters he varies the sequence and sometimes omits one of the three elements in his narrative. This practice is understandable in light of the author's purpose: to record the prophetic activity of the Spirit as he inaugurates the New Age and empowers the disciples for witness and service. Luke does not unfold the inner spiritual life of the disciples but the growth of the early church.

Christian Community Peter concluded his sermon with words of warning and invitation. "Those who accepted his message were baptized, and about three thousand were added to their number that day" (2:41). Luke then describes the early Christian community. While he doesn't answer all our questions, he sketches a remarkably clear picture in about one hundred words.

The entrance requirement was clear; people didn't just drift into this fellowship. Individual repentance and faith was accompanied by baptism, a visible initiation into the community.

The Christians "devoted themselves to the apostles' teaching and to the fellowship, to the breaking of bread and to prayer" (2:42). The members recognized the authority of the apostles. They had much to learn from these men who had lived and worked with Jesus for three years, and who would be further taught by the Spirit as he had promised (Jn. 14:26). The believers were also devoted to each other in a close fellowship (*koinonia*). Their worship found expression in the Lord's Supper and the prayers (Acts 3:1).

The community had a deep social concern. "All the believers were together and had everything in common. Selling their possessions and goods, they gave to anyone as he had need" (2:44-45). This pooling of property demonstrated their concern for physical need, following the example of their Lord who not only preached but also healed and provided bread for a hungry crowd and wine for a wedding feast.

The believers continued as devout Jews in their familiar forms of worship. "Every day they continued to meet together in the temple courts" (2:46). They also enjoyed each other's company in a larger context than their "religious" activities. "They broke bread in their homes and ate together with glad and sincere hearts, praising God and enjoying the favor of all the people. And the Lord added to their number daily those who were being saved" (2:46-47). This was the character of the community which grew up after the outpouring of the Holy Spirit.

The Meaning of Pentecost What is the significance of the day of Pentecost? It is already apparent that Pentecost is a complex event. It was foretold by Joel, promised by John the Baptist, explained by Jesus before his ascension, described as it happened by Luke and afterward interpreted by Peter. Here we concentrate on the meaning of Pentecost for Jesus, for the disciples and for the people who responded to their message.[10]

For Jesus this day has a twofold significance. He had been anointed and filled with the Spirit for his own public ministry. Now, exalted at the right hand of God, he pours out the Holy Spirit on his disciples to empower their mission. On Pentecost Jesus baptizes them with the Spirit as John the Baptist foretold. The Bearer of the Spirit becomes the Giver of the Spirit.

For Jesus Pentecost also marks the vindication of his ministry in this first public witness which gathers three thousand into his church. Peter now proclaims Jesus of Nazareth as the Messiah. Though rejected and crucified by his people, he has been raised from the dead and exalted as both Lord and Christ.

What is the meaning of Pentecost for the disciples? Luke's answer draws on several sources: quotations from Jesus, Joel and Peter as well as his own description of the disciples' experience.

On three occasions before his ascension (Lk. 24:49; Acts

1:5, 8) Jesus explained the promised experience. He said to the disciples: "I am going to send you what my Father has promised.... You will be baptized with the Holy Spirit.... You will receive power when the Holy Spirit comes on you." Jesus also stated the purpose: "You will be my witnesses ... to the ends of the earth." The purpose of Spirit-baptism was proclamation.

Peter explained this event to the astonished crowd in somewhat different words. He first declared it to be the fulfillment of Joel's prophecy. "I will pour out my Spirit on all people. Your sons and daughters will prophesy" (Acts 2:17). Later in his sermon, Peter connected this action with the exalted Christ who "has poured out what you now see and hear" (2:33). Again the prophetic dimension of the Spirit's activity is emphasized.

In addition to recording Jesus' promise and Peter's interpretation, Luke describes the disciples' experience with a phrase of his own. He reports that the disciples were "filled with the Holy Spirit" (2:4); as a result they began to speak in other tongues and declare the wonders of God in the diverse languages of the pilgrims. With one exception (Eph. 5:18) "filled with the Holy Spirit" is used only by Luke, and it is his most common description of the Holy Spirit's activity.[11] It occurs early in Luke's Gospel with Elizabeth and Zechariah, and later in Acts with Peter and Paul, recording specific results of the Spirit's action. Both individuals and groups are filled with the Spirit. Furthermore, this experience is not once and for all; it can be repeated, as was the case with Peter.[12] Throughout Luke-Acts filling with the Spirit always results in prophetic speaking, in its broadest sense, whether worship or witness or judgment.[13]

For Luke, as historian and theologian, no one term adequately describes the coming of the Spirit at Pentecost. As Christ *poured out* the Spirit the disciples were *baptized, filled, clothed* with power. As a result they immediately spoke in other tongues, declared the wonders of God and boldly witnessed to

Jesus Christ. These disciples had been demoralized and scattered by their Lord's trial and crucifixion. Even after the resurrection they were huddled behind closed doors in fear. Now, less than two months later, they stood fearlessly in Jerusalem proclaiming Jesus of Nazareth as Messiah and Lord. What made the difference? According to Luke it was this coming of the Spirit.

Luke draws a remarkable parallel between the descent of the Spirit at Jordan and at Pentecost: in both cases the purpose of the anointing is ministry.[14] Both Jesus and the disciples are praying as the Spirit descends. Physical manifestations of sight and sound are in each situation. Both ministries begin with a thematic sermon which appeals to the Old Testament, highlights Jesus' ministry and speaks of his rejection. This parallelism emphasizes the prophetic activity of the Spirit to inaugurate public ministry.

For the three thousand who responded to Peter's sermon, Pentecost involved a distinctly different experience from that of the disciples in terms of personal need, required response and result. Unlike the disciples they were not already followers of Jesus commissioned for service, waiting for the Spirit to empower their witness. Rather these residents and visitors in Jerusalem were hearing the gospel of Christ for the first time. A response of repentance was required from them before they could participate in the New Age. As a result they received the gift of the Holy Spirit to begin their Christian life.

A Spiritual Model   Pentecostals take the experience of the first disciples as a model for all later Christians. They interpret the disciples' baptism with the Spirit on Pentecost as a necessary second experience subsequent to conversion. Those who reject this two-stage concept of salvation reply that, on the contrary, Pentecost marks the disciples' regeneration and incorporation into the body of Christ.

While this controversy is dealt with in chapter fifteen, two points should be noted here. First, the uniqueness of the disciples' experience rules it out as a model for all later Christians. Born and raised under the Old Covenant, their understanding and faith grew gradually during their years with Jesus in his public ministry. Only after the resurrection did they grasp the meaning of his mission as he opened their minds so they could understand the Scriptures (Lk. 24:25-27). And only at Pentecost did the pieces of the puzzle regarding the New Age and the message of salvation fit together.

There is a second reason why the disciples' baptism with the Spirit at Pentecost does not provide the model for a second inner experience following conversion: this is not Luke's interpretation of the event. He does not relate it to *salvation*, whether a first or second stage, but to *service*.

In Luke-Acts the primary significance of the Spirit's activity is historical and prophetic. Luke's narrative is shaped according to the unique pattern of redemptive history unfolding in Jesus Christ and his church. The Spirit's coming on the disciples at Pentecost anoints them for their role in this drama. Initial *and repeated* filling with the Spirit empowers a prophetic ministry. This is the hallmark of Luke's teaching about the Holy Spirit. He does not intend to present a model of inner experience designed for all Christians.

Nevertheless, the disciples' experience at Pentecost does present a model for the church's mission in the world. Filling with the Holy Spirit for effective witness and service is normative for all Christians.[15] And the early Christian community provides an example of continuing in the apostles' teaching, fellowship, worship, social concern and evangelism, demonstrating the love and joy the Lord desires in his people.

9

*The Church
in Action*

"You will be my witnesses in Jerusalem, and in all Judea and Samaria, and to the ends of the earth" (Acts 1:8). That these words of the risen Lord found fulfillment in Jerusalem is recorded in Acts 1—8. But as the church flourishes a tide of opposition begins to swell. Soon it will sweep many believers out to Judea and Samaria. The gospel will move into the Gentile world at Caesarea, then north and west until a Christian community is established in Rome.

Luke's record of this ever-widening expansion continues to feature the activity of the Holy Spirit, who directs and empowers the church. At each crucial stage his guidance is evident as he works in a variety of ways through individuals and groups.

Jerusalem   One day Peter and John entered the temple to pray. They talked with a lame man whom Peter healed in the name of Jesus Christ. His jumping and praising immediately attracted a crowd which soon became an audience for Peter's preaching. Though many believed, the priests had the two disciples arrested and put in jail overnight.

The next day they were called before the religious leaders

for questioning. "Then Peter, filled with the Holy Spirit" (4:8), preached Jesus Christ to them also. Deeply disturbed, the council could only threaten and release them because the people were praising God for this miraculous healing.

Peter and John returned to the Christian community and reported on their encounter with the chief priests and elders. Instead of reacting in fear, these men and women prayed for boldness to preach in the face of these threats. "After they prayed, the place where they were meeting was shaken. And they were all filled with the Holy Spirit and spoke the word of God boldly" (4:31).

Sometime later another disciple, Stephen, encountered opposition to his preaching. "But they could not stand up against his wisdom or the Spirit by which he spoke" (6:10). Called before the Sanhedrin, he infuriated them with his indictment of their unbelief. "Filled with [or full of] the Holy Spirit" (7:55), Stephen looked into heaven, saw Jesus standing at the right hand of God and reported this vision to them. Enraged, they dragged him out of the city and stoned him to death.

As at Pentecost, so now in the face of opposition, filling with the Holy Spirit empowered the disciples to give effective witness. We have seen that this action of the Spirit was repeatable; Luke records three such experiences for Peter. It involved both individuals and groups, and the result was prophetic in the sense of powerful proclamation.

Luke also uses the term "full of the Spirit" to describe a continuous state. In the Christian community sectional prejudice soon precipitated a quarrel. The Grecian Jews accused the Aramaic-speaking members of shortchanging their widows in the daily food distribution. To settle this problem the apostles said, "Brothers, choose seven men from among you who are known to be full of the Spirit and wisdom" (6:3) to assume responsibility for this distribution. Among these was Stephen, "a man full of faith and of the Holy Spirit" (6:5). The Holy Spirit provided wisdom and faith for ongoing responsibilities within the church.

While "full of the Spirit" usually indicates a condition, it can also describe an event (7:55). Whether in witness to the world or service to the community, the believers depended on the Spirit for guidance and power.

Samaria   On the day of Stephen's death a great persecution began which scattered many believers throughout Judea and Samaria. Among those in this area who preached the Word, Philip became an evangelistic pioneer. In one city of Samaria he performed miraculous healings and preached Christ with power. The crowds received his ministry with joy. Many believed his preaching and were baptized.

When the apostles in Jerusalem heard that Samaritans had accepted the Word of God they sent Peter and John to investigate. Their arrival set the stage for an event involving the Holy Spirit which has proved perplexing and controversial.

When they arrived, they prayed for them that they might receive the Holy Spirit, because the Holy Spirit had not yet come upon any of them; they had simply been baptized into the name of the Lord Jesus. Then Peter and John placed their hands on them, and they received the Holy Spirit. (8:15-17)

This is the only record in the New Testament of persons who believed and were baptized in the name of Jesus Christ, yet had not received the Holy Spirit. In the light of Luke's narrative to date this situation presents an apparent contradiction. Since the Samaritans had believed and been baptized in the name of the Lord Jesus (8:12, 16), they must have become Christians. Hadn't they satisfied the conditions Peter preached at Pentecost? But since they did not receive the Spirit before Peter and John arrived, how could they already have been Christians? What is the explanation?

One interpretation holds that the Spirit's absence from and coming to the Samaritans is the critical factor in this narrative. "It is not sufficiently realized that in New Testament times the possession of the Spirit was *the* hallmark of the Christian."[1] Luke reports that "Simon himself believed and was baptized"

(8:13) just like the rest, yet Peter's harsh words that Simon's heart was not right with God, that he was "full of bitterness and captive to sin" (8:23), hardly indicate true conversion. Apparently, it was possible that the others also professed faith, were baptized and yet did not become truly Christian until later when they received the Holy Spirit. Their first response therefore was defective.

A basic weakness of this interpretation lies in its assumption that receiving the Spirit here refers to regeneration, his initial coming to indwell the believer. It is true that without the Spirit a person is not really a Christian, as Paul teaches in Romans 8:9. But why assume that Luke is writing from this perspective?

Both context and usage reveal that Luke is teaching a different lesson. His narrative does not intend to describe the Spirit's reception in terms of the Christian's regeneration and sanctification (Paul's categories for the individual's spiritual life). Luke explains what he means by receiving the Spirit in quite different terms: "the Holy Spirit had not yet come upon any of them" (8:16). This is the phrase Jesus used when he promised the disciples they would receive power for witness (1:8)—a result of the Spirit's being poured out at Pentecost.

Luke does not report what happened when the Samaritans received the Holy Spirit, but based on Simon's reaction there seems to have been something specific which he wanted to purchase and produce. Probably it was speaking in tongues and prophecy as at Pentecost.[2] The main point is that, as elsewhere when the Spirit comes upon someone, Luke reports not an internal change but an external happening.

It thus appears that the Samaritans were truly converted earlier when they believed and were baptized. This later receiving of the Spirit was a charismatic manifestation, not the completion of their conversion-initiation into the church.[3] It provided evidence to Peter and John that the Samaritans were on a par with the Christians in Jerusalem,[4] empowered for cooperation in the missionary task.

The fact that the Spirit came upon them through this laying on of hands may also have been a lesson to the Samaritans.[5] The age-long animosity between them and the Jews still existed. This visit by Peter and John from Jerusalem may have been designed to heal this historical wound so that two independent churches would not develop on opposite sides of the "Samaritan Curtain."[6] Christian experience outside Judea is thereby linked to the Jerusalem church.

This event in Samaria, like Pentecost earlier, cannot be taken as a model either for conversion and incorporation into the church or for a necessary second experience of the Spirit for the Christian. These are not Luke's concerns. Perplexity and debate over seemingly contradictory statements arises from asking the wrong questions. When Luke's purpose guides interpretation, his meaning is clear. Here again he teaches the prophetic or vocational role of the Spirit in the historical development of the church.[7] Samaria represents a significant religious boundary initially crossed by the growing church, just as Caesarea and Ephesus later represent racial boundaries crossed.

The Gentile World   Back in Jerusalem Saul, who had witnessed Stephen's death, was breathing out murderous threats against the disciples. Soon he was on his way to Damascus with warrants for the arrest of any Christian men and women he might find. En route a light flashed from heaven and a voice said, "I am Jesus whom you are persecuting" (9:5).

Blinded, Saul arose as instructed and was led into the city. Three days later the Lord sent a disciple named Ananias to Saul with these words: "Brother Saul, the Lord—Jesus, who appeared to you on the road as you were coming here—has sent me so that you may see again and be filled with the Holy Spirit" (9:17). Saul immediately regained his vision, arose and was baptized.

In this narrative some see another example of two distinct experiences for Saul: conversion on the road to Damascus in his encounter with the risen Lord and baptism in the Spirit later through the visit of Ananias.[8] Others conclude that since his reception of the Spirit and his baptism did not occur until after Ananias' visit, Saul's conversion was not complete until then; his experience of blindness and inactivity for three days was a single, traumatic unit during which he had to reassemble the pieces of his shattered life around a new center.[9]

Here again the controversy arises from an attempt to get answers to questions Luke does not consider. Consistent with his purpose which has become so clear, he concentrates on the mission of the church. The risen Lord told Ananias that he had chosen this zealous Pharisee, his persecutor, to "carry my name before the Gentiles and their kings and before the people of Israel" (9:15). The context for Saul's being filled with the Spirit, as well as Luke's consistent usage of this phrase, is commission and not conversion.

Luke does not report exactly when Saul was filled with the Spirit and any immediate result. He is not concerned to teach a specific sequence of repentance, baptism, reception of the Spirit and the need for a particular manifestation as evidence of his filling. (See Paul's own account in Acts 22:3-16.) The main point is that the Lord has called his servant and equipped him for an unprecedented mission to the Gentiles.

The time had arrived for the gospel to bridge the gulf between Jews and Gentiles. God had prepared a bridgehead on the other side in the life of a Roman army officer. Cornelius was a centurion in the Italian Regiment. Luke relates the steps which led this devout man to send for Peter who was also being prepared for his assignment. Again the Spirit directed the mission as he instructed Peter to go to Cornelius' home in Caesarea (10:19-20).

There Peter presented to a large gathering the good news about Jesus Christ. His witness has much the same content as at Pentecost: the ministry, death and resurrection of Jesus of Nazareth, whom God anointed with the Holy Spirit and power. When he declared, "Everyone who believes in him receives forgiveness of sins through his name" (10:43), a dramatic event occurred.

While Peter was still speaking these words, the Holy Spirit came on all who heard the message. The circumcised believers who had come with Peter were astonished that the gift of the Holy Spirit had been poured out even on the Gentiles. For they heard them speaking in tongues and praising God.

Then Peter said, "Can anyone keep these people from being baptized with water? They have received the Holy Spirit just as we have." So he ordered that they be baptized in the name of Jesus Christ. Then they asked Peter to stay with them for a few days. (10:44-48)

Peter immediately equated this "receiving" of the Spirit with his own experience at Pentecost.[10] Luke here uses the same terminology of the Spirit's being "poured out" and "coming on" as he reported for the disciples (2:33; 1:8). And he records the same results: speaking in tongues and praising God (2:4, 11).[11] Unlike the disciples at Pentecost, the Gentiles were also converted and baptized, but the purpose of the Spirit's coming remains the same. Luke's emphasis on the prophetic dimension of the Spirit's activity continues.[12]

The speaking in tongues here also served a practical purpose, but one different from that at Pentecost. It was a testimony to Peter and his friends that God accepted the Gentiles on the same basis as he did the Jews: through repentance and faith in Jesus Christ. Accordingly he took the unprecedented step of baptizing the new converts immediately, bringing them directly into the Christian community without the usual preparatory period of instruction in Jewish law.

That the Spirit's prophetic activity in the New Age was not limited to the apostolic leaders in Jerusalem Luke shows unambiguously by another event.[13] The persecution following Stephen's death pushed some Christians north to Antioch. Here Barnabas, "full of the Holy Spirit and faith" (11:24), and Saul spent a year strengthening the church. During this period a prophet named Agabus "through the Spirit predicted that a severe famine would spread over the entire Roman world" (11:28). The disciples immediately responded by sending their gifts to the brothers in Judea by Barnabas and Saul.

Paul's Mission   Until now Peter, based in Jerusalem, had led the church's expanding mission. With Saul's arrival in Antioch the center of missionary leadership shifted. While Jerusalem remained the seat of apostolic authority, Antioch became the primary base of operations for the mission into Europe.

In this growing church at Antioch there were several prophets and teachers besides Barnabas and Saul. "While they were worshiping the Lord and fasting, the Holy Spirit said, 'Set apart for me Barnabas and Saul for the work to which I have called them' " (13:2). After fasting and praying they laid their hands on the two and sent them off. "Sent on their way by the Holy Spirit" (13:4), Barnabas and Saul sailed to the island of Cyprus to begin the first of three extensive missionary journeys.

The last recorded reception of the Spirit in Acts occurs several years later at Ephesus where Paul was preaching. He asked some disciples, "Did you receive the Holy Spirit when you believed?" (19:2).[14] They replied that they had not even heard that the Holy Spirit had been given; it was John's baptism they had received. Paul responded that John told the people to believe in Jesus who was coming after him. "On hearing this, they were baptized into the name of the Lord Jesus. When Paul placed his hands on them, the Holy Spirit came upon them, and they spoke in tongues and prophesied. There were about twelve men in all" (19:5-7).

In the Pentecostal theology of Spirit-baptism, this third account of speaking in tongues following the coming of the Holy Spirit is key. This interpretation holds that the twelve Ephesians were already Christians before Paul met them. His question implied that one can be a Christian without receiving fully the Holy Spirit. When the disciples responded to Paul's teaching, he laid his hands on them to impart the baptism with the Spirit. But was this the case?

This narrative raises perplexing questions: were these Ephesian disciples of John already Christians? Or did they become true believers only after Paul's preaching?

This situation must be understood in the context of the preceding passage about Apollos who had recently preached in Ephesus (18:24-28). Although he had a thorough knowledge of the Scriptures and taught accurately about Jesus, he knew only the baptism of John. So Priscilla and Aquila gave him more adequate instruction. Similarly the twelve disciples whom Paul met needed more teaching.

What, then, is the meaning of Paul's initial question: "Did you receive the Holy Spirit when you believed?" (19:2)? Paul certainly knew that all true Christians have the Spirit dwelling in them (Rom. 8:9). His question seems to indicate that he considered them to be Christians[15] (although this assumption is questioned by some interpreters[16]). He may well mean a reception in terms of being filled with the Spirit, with some resulting manifestation characteristic of Luke's record. For Paul found no tension between the reality of the indwelling Spirit and additional experiences of his filling (Eph. 5:18).

Fortunately, understanding the main teaching of this passage does not depend on knowing what was in Paul's mind or in the Ephesians' hearts. Luke simply reports that "the Holy Spirit came upon them, and they spoke in tongues and prophesied" (19:6). Again his lesson lies in the vocational or prophetic function of the Holy Spirit's filling; that is, when the Holy Spirit comes upon a believer, he does so in order to equip for "declaring the wonders of God" (Acts 2:11).

This event marks another decisive moment in missionary history. Ephesus was soon to be a new center of the Gentile mission. Luke's historical purpose draws a parallel between the ministries of Peter and Paul. At Samaria the new Christians were linked to the church in Jerusalem as the Holy Spirit came upon them through Peter and John. At Ephesus he comes upon the twelve through Paul. "By this exceptional procedure, then, they were associated in the apostolic and missionary task of the Christian Church."[17]

Although this is the last dramatic outpouring of the Holy Spirit recorded by Luke, he continues to mention the Spirit's activity until the end of the book. The Holy Spirit, also called the Spirit of Jesus, directs Paul where he shall preach and where he shall not (16:6-7). Paul speaks of being bound by the Spirit who continually tells him of persecution to come (20:22-23). He reminds the Ephesian elders that the Holy Spirit has made them guardians of the flock (20:28).

At Tyre, disciples tell Paul through the Spirit not to go to Jerusalem (21:4); and later in Caesarea Agabus declares through the Spirit that Paul will be bound in Jerusalem and handed over to the Gentiles (21:11). Paul's final sermon speaks of the Holy Spirit's prophesying through Isaiah (28:25). From beginning to end Luke's narrative highlights the Holy Spirit's activities to direct and empower the mission of the church.

Luke the Theologian   While the excellence of Luke's history has long been recognized, appreciation of his theology has not kept pace. The Acts of the Apostles is often studied as an illustration of the Holy Spirit's activity in the early church, but rarely for a doctrine of the Spirit. One reason for this attitude is the misleading statement that theology should be based primarily on the *didactic* passages rather than those which are *descriptive*.[18] Thus a doctrine of the Holy Spirit should come from Paul rather than Luke.

This distinction is intended to emphasize that the experiences of people recorded in the Bible are not necessarily meant to be ours today. While this is true, a sharp distinction between didactic and descriptive passages has several weaknesses. At a practical level it doesn't solve the problem of understanding God's purpose for us. Much explicit teaching in so-called didactic passages is no more meant for Christians today than many of the experiences found in descriptive passages.[19] The problem of interpreting the current relevance of a given Scripture is more complex than this distinction implies.

At a deeper level this distinction fails to recognize that Bible history itself is revelatory. To a large extent God has chosen to reveal his character and purpose by his actions, the way he deals with men in judgment and mercy.[20] Most of the biblical revelation comes in the form of description—narratives of individuals, families and nations. These accounts are not simply a record of "brute facts." They are carefully selected sequences designed to teach.

Furthermore, this distinction tends to limit doctrinal data to explicit instruction and to those narratives which are immediately explained. Hence, it fails to recognize the variety of literary forms biblical writers have been inspired to use in their teaching. An unqualified distinction between didactic and descriptive is artificial. Didactic simply means "used for teaching, intended for instruction."[21] Many, if not all, of the descriptive passages have this same purpose. Often the narrative itself makes the point clear without any explanatory comment. For example, some of Paul's most effective teaching is given by personal testimony—a description of his experiences —although not all are meant to be ours.

Thus the basic question is not whether historical passages have doctrinal value, but how to interpret what they teach. Gordon Fee notes how little has been written on the interpretation and application of the historical sections of Scripture. He stresses the importance of discovering what the author intends to teach: "Historical precedent, to have normative value, must be related to *intent*. That is, if it can be shown that the purpose of a given narrative is to *establish* precedent, then such precedent should be regarded as normative."[22]

Luke, like other historians, has his own *perspective* on events and a particular *purpose* for reporting them which guide his selection of the facts, the way he relates them and the meaning they communicate. The narratives in Acts are no more "purely descriptive" than are the testimonies of Paul. Both are designed to teach. Each event Luke records serves his theological purpose. "Because he was a theologian he had to be a historian. His view of theology led him to write history."[23] The narratives in Acts are a valuable source for Luke's doctrine of the Holy Spirit because they reflect his theological concern.

The Holy Spirit in Acts We have endeavored to understand what Luke intends to teach about the activity of the Holy Spirit in the early church. The terms he uses have been interpreted within his own context and usage. Study of Luke-Acts reveals Luke's distinctive doctrine of the Holy Spirit. He records his prophetic action in inaugurating the New Age and empowering the mission of the church. This teaching differs from, but complements, that of John and Paul. While Luke notes that the gift of the Spirit is an essential element in conversion (2:38), he does not describe the inner spiritual development of the disciples. In line with his historical purpose, he emphasizes the Holy Spirit's role in directing and empowering their worship, witness and service in carrying out the commission of their Lord.

In Acts the presence of the Spirit is evidenced in a visible, dynamic and often dramatic way. It is "charismatic" in the sense of directly manifesting his power. The result is prophetic in the broad sense of praise and worship, witness and preaching. Luke's dynamic terminology demonstrates that when the Spirit was present something happened. People knew that God was active in their midst.[24]

The Spirit "fell on" (3), "came upon" (2), was "poured out" (2). Correspondingly the believer "received" (2) or was "filled with" (5) the Spirit. This action produced observable results: speaking in tongues (3), healing (3), preaching (2), witness with power (1). (Figures in parentheses indicate number of occurrences in Acts.) These manifestations stirred praise, strengthened the community and empowered it for service. The initiative was with the sovereign Lord. The subject of the verbs is God (Father or Son) who "poured out" or "anointed," or the Spirit who "came upon" or "fell on." The disciple "received" or "was filled."

Luke also describes the Spirit's activity in another way. Four times he speaks of individuals as "full of" the Holy Spirit, usually with no specific action or result, but accompanied by a certain quality or characteristic. Seven men "full of the Spirit and of wisdom" were selected to supervise the food distribution (6:3). Among them was Stephen, a man "full of faith and of the Holy Spirit" and also "full of God's grace and power" (6:5, 8). Barnabas was also "full of the Holy Spirit and faith" (11:24). Sometimes this characteristic was accompanied by action, as with Stephen's signs and wonders, or his looking into heaven at his stoning to see Jesus standing at the right hand of God (6:8; 7:55). Nevertheless, the phrase emphasizes a state of *being* full of the Spirit, as well as manifesting his power.

The example of these vital early Christians sparks the search for a normative model, a standard pattern of spiritual growth. But it is fruitless because Luke does not intend to provide one. He does not picture the inner life of great Christians, but the growth of the church in its mission.

No single event in the Acts provides the model for the sequence of the individual's repentance and faith, water-baptism and the reception of the Spirit. Nor does Luke provide a standard pattern for subsequent manifestations of the Spirit. If there is a pattern, it is one of diversity in the sovereign action of the Spirit who blows when and where he wills.

In the Acts, Luke pictures an effective community directed and empowered by the Holy Spirit. Its commitment to the Lord, concern for its members and openness to the Spirit provide an example for every generation. But for teaching about the Spirit's work in the inner life of the individual believer and the proper exercise of spiritual gifts we turn to the writings of Paul.

Part Three:

The Spirit in Paul's Letters

10
Life
through the Spirit

The letters of the Apostle Paul are not theological treatises. Though permeated with theology, they are letters to churches and individuals in specific situations.

The apostle's teaching is well anchored in history; it arises from life and speaks to life. Just as events must be interpreted, so doctrines must be historically understood. The teaching of Paul (and Luke) constantly unites principle and practice, the truth of God and personal application.

This section (Part III) does not consider all of Paul's teaching about the Holy Spirit. Rather it concentrates on his teaching regarding the exercise of spiritual gifts by members of the body of Christ. This chapter views the Spirit's work in the spiritual growth of the Christian as an individual and as a member of the body. The following three chapters discuss the teaching of 1 Corinthians 12—14 which undergirds the charismatic renewal.

The Spirit and Salvation in Christ   Paul calls the New Age the "dispensation of the Spirit" (2 Cor. 3:8 RSV). He teaches that salvation comes *from* God, *in* Christ, *through* the Spirit.[1] First, it is God who takes the initiative. "God was reconciling the world to himself in Christ, not counting men's sins against them" (2 Cor. 5:19). Second, salvation is provided *in Christ*—Paul's favorite term for being a Christian. "Therefore, if anyone is in Christ, he is a new creation; the old has gone, the new has come! All this is from God" (2 Cor. 5:17-18).

Third, this new life is produced *through* (or *by*) *the Spirit.* Paul tells Titus that God "saved us through the washing of rebirth and renewal by the Holy Spirit" (Tit. 3:5). To the Romans he declares: "God has poured out his love into our hearts by the Holy Spirit, whom he has given us" (Rom. 5:5). The believer's regeneration or rebirth and the growth of this new life takes place through the activity of the Holy Spirit.

Paul uses a variety of words to describe the work of God in the life of the individual (for example, election, conversion, justification, regeneration, sanctification, sealing, redemption). Salvation is a gem with many facets. Systematic theology generally summarizes these words in "the two-fold concept of justification and sanctification."[2] God puts the righteousness of Christ to the account of the sinner and declares him righteous (Rom. 4:24-25). God also sanctifies him and calls him to be holy (1 Cor. 1:2). Yet this systematic summary tends to obscure a work of the Spirit signified by the other names. Not even Paul's terminology, much less Luke's, can be pressed into this "twofold" schema without loss of meaning.[3]

For Paul the central element in salvation is *charis* ("grace"), God's act of unmerited favor. Far more than an attitude, it is his loving action in Christ. And more than a past event to be believed, God's grace, for Paul, is a present, continuing experience sustained by the Holy Spirit, who is always at work in the life of the believer. Paul's typical greeting, "Grace and peace to you," is no mere formality; it expresses his earnest desire that his converts may constantly experience the gracious power of the Spirit in their lives. "The whole of life is for Paul an expression of grace: always of grace, and grace is all. . . . Grace gives the believer's life both its source, its power and its direction."[4]

This conviction lies behind Paul's many statements about the gracious action of the Spirit in the Christian's life and service. "Those who are led by the Spirit of God are the sons of God. ... The Spirit himself testifies with our spirit that we are God's children. ... The Spirit helps us in our weakness" (Rom. 8:14, 16, 26). Of wisdom he says: "God has revealed it to us by his Spirit"; of spiritual gifts: "Now to each man the manifestation of the Spirit is given for the common good" (1 Cor. 2:10; 12:7). And Paul speaks of "worship by the Spirit of God" (Phil. 3:3).

These actions are not automatic, however, for the Spirit is a person with whom the Christian has a responsible relationship. Paul commands: "So I say, live by the Spirit" (Gal. 5:16) and "Do not grieve the Holy Spirit of God" (Eph. 4:30). Although the Holy Spirit is a person, Paul uses the metaphor of fire: "Be aglow with the Spirit" (Rom. 12:11 RSV) and "Do not put out the Spirit's fire" (1 Thess. 5:19).

Just as in Acts the Spirit is poured out by the exalted Christ, so in the letters of Paul the Holy Spirit is the Spirit of Christ. "If anyone does not have the Spirit of Christ, he does not belong to Christ" (Rom. 8:9; compare Gal. 4:6; Phil. 1:19). Only through the Holy Spirit can one say "Jesus is Lord" (1 Cor. 12:3). The Spirit transforms believers into the likeness of Christ (2 Cor. 3:18). For Paul the test of all experience of the Spirit is conformity to the character of Jesus Christ.

Filled with the Spirit   Paul's single use of the phrase "filled with the Spirit" is likewise a command. He instructs, "Be filled with the Spirit. Speak to one another with psalms, hymns and spiritual songs. Sing and make music in your heart to the Lord, always giving thanks to God the Father for everything, in the name of our Lord Jesus Christ" (Eph. 5:18-20). In Acts an individual or group was usually filled with the Spirit on a particular occasion to meet a specific need, whether for bold preaching or prophecy or healing. And, again usually, there was a visible or audible result; something happened.

To what extent is Paul's use similar?

The immediate context gives an answer. (Paul's writings abound with truth about what it means to be filled with the Spirit, using a variety of other terms, in the full range of his fruit and gifts. So although this is the only occurrence of the phrase in Paul's letters, it is neither necessary nor valid to derive its full meaning from this one passage, as if it were his only teaching on the subject.) The form of the verb "be filled" is significant in several respects. It is a *command;* this action for Christians is not optional but imperative for all. Furthermore, it is in the *present tense* and better translated as "keep on being filled." Paul has in mind not a once-for-all event but a repeated experience. The verb is also *passive*. While the believer is responsible to be open to him, it is the Holy Spirit himself who fills and manifests his power.

Finally, the verb is in the *plural*, addressed not only to individuals but also to the Christian fellowship. So it is not surprising that the immediate consequences are corporate: "speak to one another.... Sing and make music ... always giving thanks to God" (5:19-20).[5]

The meaning of the first phrase is illuminated by the parallel passage in Colossians 3:16: "Let the word of Christ dwell in you richly as you teach and counsel one another with all wisdom." One result of being filled with the Spirit is building up the body of Christ through gifts such as encouragement, teaching and wisdom provided for that purpose (Rom. 12: 7-8; 1 Cor. 12:8).

A second result is singing and making music wholeheartedly to the Lord. The Holy Spirit glorifies the Lord Jesus by inspiring the praise of his people. The verb *psallō* ("making melody") may be taken as singing psalms, its meaning in 1 Corinthians 14:15 and James 5:13. Commenting on Ephesians 5:19-20, F. F. Bruce writes: "If we are to distinguish between the three kinds of musical composition, 'psalms' may refer to the Old Testament Psalter; ... 'hymns' may denote Christian canticles such as have been recognized in several places in the New Testament (including verse 14 above); 'spiritual songs' may be unpremeditated words singing 'in the Spirit,' voicing praise and holy aspirations."[6]

A third element is giving thanks always to God for everything in the name of Christ. To do this in difficult circumstances in the face of much for which we are not naturally thankful requires the power of the Spirit.

Taken together in their God-ward and man-ward dimensions, these three results strengthen the fellowship. As Christians enjoy right relationships with their Lord and each other, they are enabled to "submit to one another out of reverence for Christ" in the ways Paul then describes (Eph. 5:21ff). In this passage the meaning of "filled with the Spirit" parallels Luke's. Both Paul's use of the verb and its context connote not so much a settled state as a repeated activity—an activity which is prophetic in the broad sense of teaching, counseling, praising and giving thanks.

Fruit and Gifts   Paul also teaches a fullness of the Spirit evidenced by Christlike character. An essential activity of the Spirit in the life of the believer is cultivating what Paul calls the fruit of the Spirit. In the last analysis the value of all we do depends on who we are; apart from right attitudes and motives even the best actions mean nothing.

"The fruit of the Spirit is love, joy, peace, patience, kindness, goodness, faithfulness, gentleness and self-control" (Gal. 5:22-23). Love is the most important. Without love all spiritual gifts and sacrificial service mean nothing (1 Cor. 13:1-3). The entire law is summed up in the command to love God with all your heart and your neighbor as yourself.

Spiritual gifts which build the body of Christ for worship, service and witness supplement this fruit. Sometimes the distinction (between fruit and gifts) is blurred or, if the distinction is kept clear, one is elevated at the expense of the other. The difference between fruit and gifts lies in their nature and purpose.

The first distinction involves being and doing, character and action. The fruit of the Spirit describes the kind of person a Christian should *be,* his attitudes and motivation: loving, joyful, patient, gentle, self-controlled. The gifts of the Spirit describe what the believer *does* as a member of the body of Christ, for example, teaching, encouraging, speaking a word of wisdom or prophesying.

Second, a gift by nature is received rather than demanded. Paul *requires* Christians to bear the fruit of the Spirit: love one another, be joyful, be at peace, be patient. But nowhere does he command believers to exercise spiritual gifts. Rather they are to be desired and received as the Spirit gives them.

Third, fruit is Christlike character which the Spirit desires to produce in *all* Christians. No one may say, "Don't expect me to love; this isn't my gift." Everyone is to bear all of the fruit. Spiritual gifts are just the opposite. In diversity, members of the body exercise different gifts as the Spirit chooses to manifest them.

Finally, the fruit of the Spirit is for all times and places, while spiritual gifts are for specific times and needs. The Spirit, like the wind, blows where he wills; we can neither predict nor program his activity.

Paul neither blurs the distinction nor severs the connection between fruit and gifts. The fruit of the Spirit does not appear in his lists of spiritual gifts, but he expects the latter to be exercised in love and with self-control. Some Christians emphasize spiritual gifts with insufficient concern for spiritual fruit. Others claim that the real evidence of the Spirit's filling lies in Christian character rather than spiritual gifts. But Paul does not offer a choice. Both are necessary for the church's health and effectiveness.

The Body of Christ Perhaps Paul's best model for this healthy unity and diversity is the body. Paul teaches that a person in Christ is a member of the body of Christ. The members are united with each other in Christ who is the head; at the same time, they are diverse in their activities. The body is strong and balanced only when its members are fulfilling their functions. For this purpose they receive and exercise spiritual gifts.

Just as *charis* ("grace") is central in Paul's teaching about salvation, so *charisma* ("gift") is important for his doctrine of the church. *Charisma* is a "gift (freely and graciously given), a favor bestowed."[7] This word is distinctively Pauline; of seventeen occurrences in the New Testament only one appears in another author, and that passage is very much like Paul's writing (1 Pet. 4:10). *Charisma* appears only twice in the Greek translation of the Old Testament.

In general this gift is the gracious act of God in Christ: "The gift of God is eternal life through Christ Jesus our Lord" (Rom. 6:23). Most frequently, however, *charisma* is a particular manifestation within the Christian community. The prominence of spiritual gifts (charisms) in Paul's teaching shows the close connection between his theology and his experience.

Another distinctively Pauline word is *pneumatikos* ("spiritual") which occurs twenty-six times in the New Testament. Only twice is it used by another author (1 Pet. 2:5). This term is important in Paul's teaching because it clearly conveys the sense of belonging to the Spirit. In Romans 1:11 he combines it with *charis*: "I long to see you so that I may impart to you some *spiritual gift*" (emphasis added).

Paul's letters contain three major lists of gifts for building the body of Christ.[8] These are frequently combined as if they were not significantly different. But while the model of one body with many members is the same, the context and wording of each list are sufficiently different to warrant separate study. Otherwise, important distinctions are blurred.

In Romans 12 the giver is God and the *charismata* ("gifts") are offered to God as acts of service which please him. In Ephesians 4 the giver is Christ, the head of the body; each *dōrea* ("gift") is a person to help prepare all the members for their ministry and maturity. In 1 Corinthians 12 the giver is the Holy Spirit, and the *charismata* are manifestations of the

Spirit for the common good. (Only Rom. 12 and Eph. 4 will be discussed in this chapter.)

Service to God   Romans 12 opens with a call to sacrificial living, renewal of the mind and discovery of God's will. Then Paul describes this life in the service of God and others. He urges the Christians, "Do not think of yourself more highly than you ought, but rather think of yourself with sober judgment, in accordance with the measure of faith God has given you" (v. 3). In Christ the members form one body in which they belong to one another.

> *Having gifts* [charismata] *that differ according to the grace* [charis] *given to us, let us use them: if prophecy, in proportion to our faith; if service, in our serving; he who teaches, in his teaching; he who exhorts, in his exhortation; he who contributes, in liberality; he who gives aid, with zeal; he who does acts of mercy, with cheerfulness. (12:6-8, RSV)*

Paul describes these charisms as a practical expression of God's grace. Several are acts of service generally considered ordinary or natural. But Paul doesn't distinguish between what we call "supernatural" and "natural," as if only the former can be attributed to divine activity.[9] All are "new-creation" gifts of God.

The listing seems to be a random sample of varied functions performed by members of the body. While in Paul's lists the first item often has special importance for the immediate context, the sequence itself cannot be taken as an order of rank. (See Appendix B.) Last place, far from being least, is sometimes a position of prominence. Here it is occupied by showing mercy, one of the great attributes of God (Ex. 34: 6-7).

Prophecy is especially important in Paul's teaching on spiritual gifts. As an immediate communication of God's word to his people, it is valuable for building the body. Prophecy is to be exercised "in proportion to ... faith" (12:6). In other words, the individual should say only what God gives at the time, however much or little. Here prophecy, like the charisms which follow, is exercised by a member of the body; it is not a ministerial office limited to a select few.[10]

Service, or ministry, is used generally for a variety of Christian ministrations, although at times it refers specifically to relief for the poor. Teaching explains and applies the truth of revelation already given, while encouraging appeals to the heart and will. Some of these gifts overlap, however, and are not to be unnaturally systematized into separate categories. With the last three, Paul indicates the right attitude for their exercise; contributing wholeheartedly, exercising leadership diligently and helping others in distress cheerfully.

Paul immediately follows this list with a command: "Love must be sincere. . . . Be devoted to one another in brotherly love. Honor one another above yourselves" (12:9-10). Charisms are to be exercised in love. The gifts and fruit of the Spirit always belong together. Use of spiritual gifts without love can be an ego trip, while professed love which disparages these gifts fails to strengthen the body of Christ.

Gifts of Christ   A second list of gifts appears in Ephesians. Paul begins chapter 4 urging the Christians to live worthy of their calling. They are to bear with one another in love and keep the unity of the Spirit in the bond of peace. Paul emphasizes the unity of the body in a trinitarian statement involving one Spirit, one Lord, one God and Father of all (Eph. 4:2-6).

In this passage Christ is the giver: "But grace [*charis*] was given to each of us according to the measure of Christ's gift [*dōrea*]" (Eph. 4:7 RSV). Although Paul doesn't call this gift a *charisma*, it is related to *charis*. He pictures the exalted Christ fulfilling the words of Psalm 68:18 which describes a victorious king in his triumphal procession. He now occupies the supreme place from which he sends his gifts.

It was he who gave some to be apostles, some to be prophets, some to be evangelists, and some to be pastors and teachers, to prepare God's people for works of service, so that the body of Christ may be built up until we all reach unity in the faith and in the knowledge of the Son of God and become mature, attaining the full measure of perfection found in Christ. (Eph. 4:11-13)

Here the gifts are certain *individuals* with special ministries, not charisms (as in Rom. 12:6-8 and 1 Cor. 12:8-10) manifested throughout the body.

An apostle is essentially a representative or messenger. The New Testament notes two groups of apostles. The Twelve and Paul were apostles of Christ in a special sense. Earlier in Ephesians Paul says the church is "built on the foundation of the apostles and prophets, with Christ Jesus himself as the chief cornerstone" (Eph. 2:20; compare 3:5 also). A larger group were apostles of the churches (2 Cor. 8:23).[11] Although not all of the latter were eyewitnesses of the resurrection, their apostolic ministry was recognized.

A prophet speaks directly through the Spirit. The first prophets, with the apostles, served a unique function in the church. Yet Paul as well as Luke indicates that in the New Age prophecy is potentially a gift to all Christians (Acts 2:17-18; 1 Cor. 14:5, 31). It performs a vital role in building the body of Christ.

An evangelist is literally one who presents the gospel. He has a special gift of bringing people to Christ. Pastors and teachers guide in the way of truth those who have been converted. Whether or not these comprise one or two ministries, they surely are related in the way they strengthen the church.

The order in which Paul lists these gifted individuals seems to follow a developmental pattern: apostles and prophets establish the church; evangelists bring in new members; pastors and teachers guide and instruct. Again the value of a gift cannot be determined simply from its place on the list. Teachers are hardly considered least important because they are last on the list.

These gifted individuals are designated by Christ to equip

the members for *their* ministry of building up the body. Some translations erroneously imply a threefold function of these special ministries on behalf of the congregation: *"for* the perfecting of the saints, *for* the work of the ministry, *for* the edifying of the body of Christ" (Eph. 4:12 KJV). This implies that it is the responsibility of a few gifted individuals (1) to equip the saints, (2) do the work of the ministry and (3) build the body.

A correct translation shows that Paul teaches a much different concept. These gifted individuals are given by Christ: "for [*pros*] the equipment of the saints unto [*eis*] the work of the ministry, unto [*eis*] the building up of the body of Christ." It is the members who minister and build up the body. This model provides opportunity and freedom for the exercise of spiritual gifts by all the members, rather than limiting them to a few offices in the church.

Finally, as in Romans 12:9-10, Paul stresses the importance of love. "Speaking the truth in love . . . [the whole body] grows and builds itself up in love, as each part does its work (4:15-16). Truth without love can be brutal; love without truth is sentimental. Genuine love conveys the truth in a constructive manner.

Just as a car needs a steering wheel to direct it, the church requires gifted individuals for special ministries (Eph. 4:11). But a car also needs a motor for power; likewise, the church must have the dynamic of the Holy Spirit manifesting diverse spiritual gifts through all the members (Rom. 12:6-8; 1 Cor. 12:8-10). A car with a motor and no steering wheel is dangerous, as church history has shown on many occasions when uncontrolled spiritual gifts caused havoc. No wonder that the steering wheel has gained such prominence. "To be sure, it is essentially less dangerous for a car to have a steering wheel without a motor. One can steer in utmost peace without causing any kind of havoc—but at the same time the car does not move! Motor and steering wheel belong together."[12]

The ministries have a steering function within the church,

a responsibility to encourage and guide the spiritual gifts of the members without squelching them. Paul is particularly concerned about the corporate exercise of the charisms. On this subject he wrote at length to the church at Corinth.

11
Gifts
of the Spirit

Corinth commanded a strategic position in the ancient world. Standing on the isthmus between Athens and Sparta, the city had ports on two seas and was on the major land route between East and West. A center of commerce, Corinth was the chief city of Greece in political authority, wealth and luxury. Also the center for worship of Aphrodite, the goddess of love, the city became known for its sexual immorality.

After leaving Athens Paul came to Corinth and stayed eighteen months to preach, teach and establish the church. He then continued his travels to Ephesus where he lived for two years. During this period the intellectual pride and moral laxity of Corinth began to trouble the church.

Cultural currents flowed through the Christian community, influencing its value system and lifestyle. Eventually a variety of serious problems emerged. Given the commerce between Corinth and Ephesus, Paul probably heard frequent news of conditions in the church. Disturbed over these developments, he endeavored to deal with the issues by mail.

A Church with Problems   Paul's first letter to the Corinthians is practical, dealing with problems ranging from party spirit and false wisdom to sexual immorality and disorder in public worship. While Paul emphasizes correct practice, his instructions are grounded in theological principles.

He begins positively with thanks to God for his grace given to them in Christ. "In every way you were enriched in him with all speech and all knowledge . . . so that you are not lacking in any spiritual gift" (1:5, 7 RSV). At the outset Paul relates enrichment in Christ to the exercise of spiritual gifts. The two go hand in hand. He is also confident that God will keep the Corinthian believers strong until the day of our Lord Jesus Christ. But at present the church is weakened by major problems with which it must deal.

The first is quarreling and divisions which have been reported to him. "One of you says, 'I follow Paul'; another, 'I follow Apollos'; another, 'I follow Cephas'; still another, 'I follow Christ' " (1:12). It is not certain what the different emphases were, but apparently each group claimed primacy for some special teaching of the apostle they chose to follow. A fourth group may have acknowledged no human leadership, claiming that their position came from Christ himself!

Paul condemns these divisions as worldly and affirms that the apostles, including himself, are only servants through whom God has done his work (3:5-9). The seriousness of schism is revealed in his verdict: "If anyone destroys God's temple, God will destroy him; for God's temple is sacred, and you are that temple" (3:17).

This divisiveness is closely linked to a theme to which Paul gives much attention throughout this letter—Christian speech and knowledge. The Corinthians have been enriched in "every kind of speech," with gifts of the Spirit including prophecy, teaching, speaking in tongues and interpretation; and in "every kind of knowledge," including gifts of wisdom and knowledge. "The troubles in Corinth were due not to a deficiency of gifts but to lack of proportionate balance in estimating and using them."[1]

Accordingly Paul devotes most of the first four chapters

to problems involving true and false wisdom. Apparently the Corinthians' understanding of wisdom was wrong in two respects. First, they overestimated the value of the content and persuasive form of human wisdom, which captivated the Greek mind. Paul reminds them that God made foolish the wisdom of the world; not many of them were wise according to worldly standards (1:20, 26). He declares, "I did not come with eloquence or superior wisdom. . . . My message and my preaching were not with wise and persuasive words, but with a demonstration of the Spirit's power" (2:1, 4). He did not depend on human wisdom for either the content or the presentation of God's truth.

Second, the Corinthians were apparently misusing spiritual gifts of wisdom and knowledge. Not only were they judging Paul, but their knowledge, exercised without love, produced a "knowing" attitude (4:3, 8:1f.). Paul reminds them that Christ is their wisdom and they are not to "go beyond what is written" (1:30; 4:6).

In chapters 5 and 6 Paul deals with moral lapses in the areas of sexual immorality and initiating lawsuits against each other. In 7 to 10 he answers questions raised by the Corinthians, including problems about marriage and meat offered to idols. He then reprimands them again for division and for disorder when they convene for the common meal and celebration of the Lord's Supper (chapter 11). Chapters 12 to 14 concern the nature, purpose and practice of spiritual gifts, while chapter 15 clears up a misunderstanding about the resurrection.

Spiritual Gifts   The twelfth chapter of 1 Corinthians may be considered to have four main divisions: the nature of spiritual gifts, a list of nine charisms, the body and its members, and a list of ministries and gifts. Paul's opening statement declares his purpose: "Now about spiritual gifts, brothers, I do not want you to be ignorant" (12:1). The Greek word *pneumatikoi* literally means "spirituals" and can be translated either "spiritual gifts" or "those who possess spiritual gifts."[2] At the outset Paul makes it clear that they are activities initiated by the Holy Spirit, and not simply natural talents or abilities.

Paul begins his discussion of the nature of spiritual gifts by pointing out that they focus on Christ. He reminds the Corinthians of their former pagan religion in which they were *forcibly influenced* by demonic powers, in contrast to their new life in Christ in which they are now *led* by the Spirit. Far from violating people (as did the evil spirits in the Gospel records), the Holy Spirit frees them to develop their potential. Also, the Spirit never leads anyone to say "Jesus be cursed."[3] Rather it is he who enables one to make the true confession of Christian faith: "Jesus is Lord" (12:3). Spiritual gifts can be properly exercised only as an expression of a personal relationship with the Lord Jesus Christ brought about by the Holy Spirit.

Second, the source of the variety of spiritual gifts is God. "There are different kinds of spiritual gifts, but the same Spirit. There are different kinds of service, but the same Lord. There are different kinds of working, but the same God works all of them in all men" (12:4-6).

Paul uses three different words: *charisma* ("spiritual gift"), *diakonia* ("service") and *energēma* ("working"). Each teaches something about the nature and purpose of spiritual gifts.[4] They originate not in the believer but in divine grace; *charisma* quite literally is a gift. Their purpose is to serve others, not the recipient. Finally, they are functional; they produce results.

Paul states that there are "different kinds" (*diaireseis*) of gifts, service and working. This word can also mean distribution (12:11). Underlying this remarkable diversity is an essential unity because the same Spirit, the same Lord and the same God are distributing the different kinds of gifts. The charisms are from God, through the Spirit, in the service of the Lord Jesus Christ.

Paul introduces and concludes his list of spiritual gifts with statements which shed additional light on their nature, purpose and occurrence. "To each is given the manifestation of the Spirit for the common good. . . . All these are inspired by one and the same Spirit, who apportions to each one individually as he wills" (12:7, 11 RSV).

Phanerōsis ("manifestation") is especially significant as it conveys the idea of disclosure or announcement. In the only other New Testament occurrence, Paul speaks of his "open statement" (2 Cor. 4:2 RSV) of the truth. The spiritual gift is more than a talent or ability; it is an announcement of the presence and action of the Holy Spirit which belongs to the new creation.

Second, the manifestation *is given* (continuous present) not once and for all, but repeatedly. Paul urges believers to "keep on being filled" with the Spirit (Eph. 5:18). Third, the purpose of these gifts is for the *common good,* not to promote individual status.

Fourth, the gifts are for *all;* three times Paul makes it clear that each believer participates (12:6, 7, 11). As Joel promised and Peter preached, the Spirit is poured out on young and old, men and women, slave and free. No one has all the gifts, and none are left out. Paul teaches that spiritual gifts are not limited to office or position in the church (a truth demonstrated by the reality of the body and its members which he soon describes in detail).

And finally, while neglecting no one, the Spirit distributes the gifts as he determines; he gives to one and to another *as he wills.* It is not for the Christian either to demand or to disparage certain gifts according to what he considers important or unacceptable. The sovereign Lord through the Spirit will build his church according to his purpose and in his own way.

Nine Charisms   *To one is given through the Spirit the utterance of wisdom, and to another the utterance of knowledge according to the same Spirit, to another faith by the same Spirit, to another gifts of healing by the one Spirit, to another the working of miracles, to another prophecy, to another the ability to distinguish between spir-*

its, to another various kinds of tongues, to another the interpretation of tongues. (12:8-10 RSV)

Several features of this list are significant. First, it is not exhaustive but rather representative. (Several charisms listed in Rom. 12:6-8, for example, do not appear here.) Since Paul's letter to the Corinthians is problem-oriented, the list here is probably "stacked" with those they most misunderstood or misused.

Second, their value cannot necessarily be determined from the order of appearance. Such a conclusion is not valid for any list unless it is the clear intent of the author to rank the items in order of importance. (An example is 1 Cor. 12:28; see Appendix B.)

Third, Paul doesn't rigorously classify these gifts. They sometimes overlap or occur together. He makes no distinction between what we call supernatural and natural, spectacular and ordinary, logical and emotional. Paul's one concern is that they be understood and properly exercised to supplement one another in building up the body of Christ. Some writers reclassify these gifts into three groups of three according to the functions of knowing, speaking and doing. Such a grouping may prove helpful for study providing that it is made clear that the grouping is not Paul's.[5] We will follow Paul's order, which seems to group the gifts in terms of knowledge, miracles and inspired speech.

Fourth, the significance of these gifts should be understood in light of the fundamental error in the Corinthian church. Underlying the specific problems was pride—the attitude that spiritually they had "arrived." Paul declares: "Already you have all you want! Already you have become rich! You have become kings—and that without us! How I wish that you really had become kings . . ." (4:8). Such a Christian community actively exercising spiritual gifts needed teaching about their true nature and use. Rather than fostering pride, the charisms should generate humility: the Corinthian Christians should remember their constant dependence upon the grace (*charis*) of God in continuing to exercise gifts (*charismata*) of the Spirit.

A brief description of each of the nine charisms listed in 1 Corinthians 12:8-10 follows. The precise nature and function of some gifts in this list is not clear from this passage alone. Experience is crucial for understanding biblical truth, whether it be of conversion, discipleship, prayer or spiritual gifts. It opens windows into passages previously overlooked or misinterpreted. While the interpretation must ultimately be grounded in the text, practice of biblical principles illuminates their meaning. Thus current manifestations of spiritual gifts, including their use and misuse, can aid our understanding of Paul's teaching.

1. *Word of Wisdom.* Paul uses the words *sophia* ("wisdom") and *sophos* ("wise") twenty-eight times in this letter, all but two of which occur in the first three chapters. Worldly wisdom depends on human ideas and eloquence (1:17; 1:20ff.; 2:1, 4). God's wisdom is revealed in Jesus Christ (1:24, 30). Against the philosophy of this world Paul sets the crucified Christ (1:23); against its eloquent words he sets the power of Christ and the Spirit (1:24; 2:4).

The gospel as God's "wisdom," once secret and hidden, has now been revealed by the Spirit to his people. Similarly, a "word of wisdom" is a charismatic message applying God's wisdom in Christ to a specific situation. "The *charisma* of God is the particular word given to a particular instance and is 'mine' only in the act and moment of uttering it."[6] Thus "word of wisdom" is not a quality a person *possesses*, but a message he *speaks* by the Spirit's power.

2. *Word of Knowledge.* Paul's use of *gnōsis* ("knowledge") in this letter is less clear. He says the rulers of this age do not know God's wisdom, while the Christians do know it as they are taught by the Spirit (2:8, 12, 13). In this sense knowledge and wisdom are synonymous: to know is to have wisdom. On the other hand, as a spiritual gift knowledge is similar to prophecy. It is also the accurate perception of Christian

truth.[7] "Word of knowledge" then is a message which speaks the truth desired by the Spirit for a specific situation.

Some of the Corinthians prided themselves on their gift of knowledge. In one of the controversies they apparently claimed special knowledge for their behavior: "Now about meat sacrificed to idols: 'We all possess knowledge,' as you say" (8:1 alternative trans.). But since this gift was exercised without the fruit of the Spirit, Paul responds: "Knowledge puffs up, but love builds up. The man who thinks he knows something does not yet know as he ought to know" (8:1-2). These Christians needed to understand that manifesting a "word of knowledge" is not simply having the truth, but through the Spirit speaking it in love (see Eph. 4:15). The importance of these gifts of wisdom and knowledge, and the serious consequences of their misuse, may well be a reason why Paul lists them first (compare 4:7, 18-20).

3. *Faith.* From Genesis to Revelation the Bible emphasizes the importance of faith. Yet the word has several different meanings. Saving faith is the response to God's offer of salvation through which the sinner is justified and receives the Spirit (Rom. 5:1; Gal. 3:2). Since this faith is the means by which all become Christians, it cannot be the special gift Paul lists here. Nor is it a body of truth, "the faith that God has once for all entrusted to the saints" (Jude 3).

The gift of faith, exercised by some, designates the confidence in a specific situation that God is about to act. It is often the assurance that God is working through me—the one gifted with faith. "Faith is thus both the irresistible knowledge of God's intervention at a certain point and the authority to effect this intervention through the power of the Holy Spirit."[8] The special nature of this faith, like the kind that can "move mountains" (13:2), is emphasized by healings and miracles listed next.

4. *Healings.* Paul uses the double plural "gifts of healings" to indicate that there are different kinds of healings, either by various means or in different dimensions of illness. The

Greek word *sōzō* often translated "to save" also means "to heal." The Gospels record healings that are physical, psychological and spiritual. Jesus' ministry of preaching and healing saved individuals from leprosy, blindness, deafness and paralysis; psychological disorders, sometimes accompanied by demon possession; and spiritual sickness requiring forgiveness and forsaking of sin.

The disciples continued this ministry which is recorded in the Acts. No doubt Paul had these healings in mind. His mention of these gifts three times in this chapter indicates there were cures in the Christian communities for which no natural explanation would suffice.

These gifts are not a power possessed by an individual; the healing is initiated by the Spirit. Every healing is a special gift exercised in dependence upon the divine Giver. There is no formula or technique for programming God's healing power. (See chapter 17, Healing.)

5. *Miracles.* Paul describes this gift as "workings of miracles" (or miraculous powers). It covers a wide range of mighty acts which display God's power, including some involving the gifts of faith or healing. The nature of the miracle is suited to the situation which calls for the exercise of this gift.

While working of miracles is often one sign of an apostle (2 Cor. 12:12), it is not limited to the apostles.[9] Paul recognizes the fact that this gift is exercised more widely in the churches, some of which have no apostle. He mentions it three times in this chapter and also in his letter to the Galatians (3:5). The miracle, like the other gifts, is due to the charismatic activity of the Spirit.

6. *Prophecy.* This is the first of several gifts of inspired speech which conclude the list. For Paul the Spirit and speaking go together, whether in the church's mission of witness and preaching, or in its worship and building up the body. Among the different kinds of inspired speech, prophecy is of prime importance; it is the only one which appears (as a gift or a gifted individual) on all of Paul's lists.

In the Old Testament a prophet is God's spokesman who proclaims the divine message to his people in a specific situation. The prophecy usually evaluates the situation, looks into the future and calls the hearers to action. New Testament prophecy continues to exercise this function. In the New Age, however, prophecy is not limited to a select few. The examples of more widespread prophecy in the Acts are confirmed by Paul's teaching on the exercise of this gift in 1 Corinthians 14. He urges the church eagerly to seek this gift.

Prophecy is a message from God to his people given directly through an individual. It may be exercised by any member of the body as the Spirit determines. "Prophecy as *charisma* is neither skill nor aptitude nor talent; the charisma is the actual speaking forth of words given by the Spirit in a particular situation and ceases when the words cease."[10]

7. *Discerning of Spirits.* The gift of "discernings of (or distinguishing between) spirits" is an essential partner of prophecy. Old and New Testaments know both true and false prophets, as well as evil spirits working against the Holy Spirit. Genuine spiritual gifts exalt Jesus Christ as Lord. The gifts of inspired speech must conform to the revelation already given in Scripture. Since prophecy has great potential for good or evil, the companion gift of discernment is needed. It is not designed to be exercised independently, but as a test of prophecy to guard against its abuse.

While *diakrisis* is usually taken as distinguishing between spirits, it can also mean interpretation of inspired revelations. As a charism it is more than a logical analysis of the message. In the Corinthian context Paul's use of this gift seems to call for evaluation as well as testing, for a determination of significance as well as source.[11] As the congregation is listening to a prophecy, this gift enables them to know whether it is a word of the Spirit and to discern its significance (14:29).

8. *Speaking in Tongues.* Another gift of inspired speech is "different kinds of tongues." Several characteristics of this gift are significant. First, the Greek word *glōssa* means "tongue"

both as an organ of speech and "language." Speaking in tongues is not, as often assumed, an inarticulate babbling and rolling of the tongue. "The tongue plays no other role in glossolalia than it does in normal speech. The Greek word *glōssa* carries the force here exclusively of 'language.' "[12] Second, the nature of this language, of which Paul says there are different kinds, must be determined from other passages where the gift is either manifested or discussed. (See chapter 16, Prophecy and Tongues.)

Third, there is nothing in the word itself to associate speaking in tongues with ecstasy, "a state of being overpowered with emotion . . . a trance."[13] Since some pagan religions have a glossolalia involving frenzy and trance, it is often assumed that the Christian experience is similar. These religions also have ordinary prayer, meditation and sacrifice, but their meaning is hardly determinative for the Christian expression. On the contrary, the Corinthians were not possessed by evil spirits but were led by the Holy Spirit. In fact Paul assumed that they could control their speaking in tongues (14:28).

The Corinthians may have exercised this gift with strong emotion, just as they may have prayed, prophesied or sung emotionally. But this style of expression is not inherent in the gift. Paul considers speaking in tongues a charism of value for building the body when properly exercised.

9. *Interpretation of Tongues*. The Spirit who leads one person to speak in a language not understood by the congregation, enables that person or someone else present to interpret the message. There is nothing to indicate that it is an exact translation, as if the interpreter were required to understand the unknown language. Both speaking in tongues and interpretation as charisms are not dependent on our understanding of how they work.

Apparently at Corinth there was some uninterpreted, and therefore unintelligible, speaking in tongues in the congregation. Paul deals with this problem at length in 1 Corinthians 14. Significantly, while some pagan religions have speaking in tongues, there is no evidence that they are interpreted.

Paul concludes this list of charisms by making three important points (12:11). These varied gifts are the work of one Spirit; and as the work of *one* Spirit they cannot be made the focus of rivalry or comparison. He distributes them according to his own purpose; they are not programmed by the recipients. The Spirit gives them to each member of the body whose functioning Paul now describes.

One Body, Many Members   Paul first notes that the human body is a unit even though it has many parts. So it is with Christ of whose body the Corinthian Christians are members. "For we were all baptized by [in] one Spirit into one body—whether Jews or Greeks, slave or free—and we were all given the one Spirit to drink" (12:13). Paul emphasizes the *unity* of the Spirit before explaining the *diversity* of his gifts.

This is Paul's only use of the phrase "baptize in the Spirit." While several versions translate the preposition *en*, "by," its use in the New Testament with the verb "baptize" designates the element of the baptism and not the one who performs it. The Corinthians had been baptized *with* or *in* (not *by*) the Spirit.[14] Paul also describes this event as being "given the one Spirit to drink." In both phrases the tense of the verb indicates a single experience in the past common to all, not just to some of the Christians.

Paul's use of the term "baptize in the Spirit" is markedly different from that of Luke. Here it describes the Corinthians' incorporation into the body of Christ. In Acts, baptism in the Spirit is a clothing with power for witness and mission. This difference in meaning is understandable when each author's usage and the dissimilar contexts are considered. In each case, the nature and results of the Spirit's activity suit the author's teaching.

With the unity of the body affirmed, Paul makes four observations about its members. First, there is variety: "Now the body is not made up of one part but of many" (12:14). The foot is needed as well as the hand, the ear as well as the eye, if the body is to exercise its several functions.

Second, the design is of God, who has "arranged the parts in the body, every one of them, just as he wanted them to be" (12:18). Any complaints about the kind and number of members must be taken up with the Creator!

Third, Paul shows how the members are interdependent, not only in their functions but also in their feelings. "The eye cannot say to the hand, 'I don't need you!' And the head cannot say to the feet, 'I don't need you!'. . . . If one part suffers, every part suffers with it; if one part is honored, every part rejoices with it" (12:21, 26). All members are bound together for better or worse. And "those parts of the body that seem to be weaker are indispensable" (12:22). They must be valued and not disparaged.

The social structure as a body was a common analogy in the Greek and Roman world. But Paul considers it a reality. "Now you *are* the body of Christ, and each one of you *is* a part of it" (12:27). The church as a body provides the context for appreciating each spiritual gift.

Frequently today certain charisms are categorically designated more (or less) important than others. Such an evaluation overlooks the truth that just as no member of the body is always more important than another, neither is a spiritual gift. If someone asked which member of your body is most important, you might reply: "For what purpose? First tell me the specific need and I'll answer your question." The value of a member at a given time depends upon its relevance to a particular situation. Only one part of the body is of greatest importance at all times—the head.

Suppose you are walking near a lake and suddenly *hear* a cry for help. As you turn toward the water you *see* that a child has fallen off a dock, whereupon you *run* to the spot and *pull* the youngster out. It is obviously absurd to argue about which member of the body was most important to the rescue—ears, eyes, feet or hands—since each met a specific need. If any of them had not functioned at the right time the child would not have been saved.

By the same token, the importance of a spiritual gift cannot be determined apart from the need of the body. If it is perplexity, wisdom is required; if illness, then healing; if a message from the Lord, then prophecy. When this concept is grasped, says Paul, no member has reason to feel inferior and complain because he manifests a "lesser" gift, nor can another be proud because hers is a "greater" gift.

Paul concludes this chapter with a fourth list of eight gifts. "And God hath set some in the church, first apostles, secondarily prophets, thirdly teachers, after that miracles, then gifts of healings, helps, governments, diversities of tongues" (12:28 KJV).[15] The first three are gifted individuals which are also mentioned in Ephesians 4:11.[16] The last five are spiritual gifts (*charismata*), three listed earlier in this chapter and two similar to several in Romans 12:6-8.

Paul reaffirms this distinction in his rhetorical questions. "*Are* all apostles? *Are* all prophets? *Are* all teachers? *Do* all work miracles? *Do* all have gifts of healing? *Do* all speak in tongues? *Do* all interpret?" (12:29).

Following this second list of spiritual gifts, Paul changes the subject. Having stressed diversity, he shows how these diverse elements cohere harmoniously. His attention centers in the crucial issue of motivation. In what way does the Lord desire these charisms to be manifested?

12
The Excellent Way

The profound truth and literary beauty of Paul's discourse on love stir the imagination and probe the heart. This love (*agape*) is rooted in the nature of God, demonstrated in Jesus Christ and imparted through the Holy Spirit.

Our Lord sums up the entire law in the command to love God with all your heart and your neighbor as yourself. Following suit, Paul shows that without love the greatest demonstration of spiritual gifts and self-sacrifice amounts to nothing. This chapter forges a vital link between his teaching about the nature and purpose of charisms and instruction for their exercise.

The Vital Link The marked change of content and style in this passage has raised questions about its place in the letter. Some believe that, set as it is between chapters 12 and 14, it breaks the stream of Paul's teaching about the principles and practice of spiritual gifts. They argue that this "hymn to love," which can stand by itself, was written at another time and later inserted here.

A further difficulty is the seeming lack of smooth transition from chapter 12: "But eagerly desire the greater gifts. And now I will show you the most excellent way" (12:31). "It may be that the awkwardness of the sentence is due to the fact that the connection between chapter 12 and chapter 13 is somewhat artificial."[1]

Alternatively, however, the awkwardness of this sentence may be due to mistranslation. Verse 31 consists of two statements, one looking back to Paul's teaching about spiritual gifts and the other introducing the way they are to be exercised. Most modern versions, with minor variations, translate the first as a command: "But eagerly desire the greater gifts." Apparently Paul is urging the Corinthians to seek the more important spiritual gifts.

But this interpretation is inconsistent with Paul's teaching so far. At Corinth some were not satisfied with the gifts they were exercising while others were proud of theirs. This snobbish, human tendency to create ladders on which each person feels inferior to those above and superior to those below was weakening the church, not strengthening it. Paul deals with this problem by describing at length the interdependence of bodily functions. "Those parts of the body that seem to be weak are indispensable, and the parts that we think are less honorable we treat with special honor" (12:22-23). Having just taken the Corinthians off their ladder and into the body (where there are no "greater" or "lesser" members), why, then, would Paul command them to desire the *more important* gifts?

Furthermore, if this were Paul's command, why wouldn't he explicitly say which are the greater and lesser gifts, or give the criteria by which they could be recognized? The apostle is hardly known for ambiguity in his instructions for practicing the principles he teaches. But Paul does not rank the charisms distributed throughout the body. Degree of importance cannot be determined from the place on the list, as if in 12:28 Paul were saying that miracles and healings are always more important than helpful deeds and administration. (See Appendix B.) It is true that he does rank the first three gifted individuals, but is he urging all the Corinthians to become apostles, prophets and teachers?

The solution to this problem may lie in an overlooked alternative translation, which also makes a smooth transition to the second clause of 12:31. The Greek form of the verb *zēloute* ("desire") can be translated either in the imperative as a command or in the indicative as a description of what is already happening. The context determines which is the better translation. Verse 31a can equally well read: "You are earnestly desiring the greater gifts." This reading has the merit of describing what the Corinthians were doing (and getting into trouble as a result) and avoids the difficulty of making Paul contradict what he has just taught. It has the added grace of leading naturally to Paul's description of the right way of exercising spiritual gifts (1 Cor. 13).

The second half of the verse says, "And now I will show you the most excellent way." Most modern versions translate it "a still more excellent way," implying a comparison between spiritual gifts and love. On this basis many conclude that Paul now turns attention to the greatest gift, love, which after all is more important than spiritual gifts. But this interpretation encounters three difficulties: translation, the nature of love and the difference between gifts and fruit.

First, the Greek words *kath huperbolē* mean "according to excellence." It is "a way according to extraordinary quality"[2] or "an excellent way." Charles Hodge notes: "Here no comparison is implied. The idea is not that he intends to show them a way that is better than seeking gifts, but a way *par excellence* to obtain these gifts."[3]

Second, talk about love being *better than* spiritual gifts fails to appreciate love's radical absoluteness. Paul doesn't say, "If I have mountain-moving faith without love, my effectiveness is sharply reduced. If I give my body to the flames without love, my sacrifice counts for less." He says that without love, "I am nothing. . . . I gain nothing" (13:2-3). Exercise of charisms without love is valueless. By the same token, so-called love without the gifts which build up the body is hollow.

This fact highlights a third point. Love is not a gift, not even the greatest of gifts. In the New Testament love is never called a charism. Rather, love is the underlying motive for exercising charisms. It provides the way to seek and manifest them since love focuses on others and the needs of the body. Through his gifts the Holy Spirit provides the means to express the love of Christ in specific and practical ways. Paul links the Spirit's fruit and gifts in the connection between chapters 13 and 14: "Follow the way of love and eagerly desire spiritual gifts" (14:1).

The alternative translation of 12:31 now reads: "You are eagerly desiring the greater gifts, but now I will show you the excellent way."[4] Rather than standing as separate sentences (RSV, NIV), these connected clauses contrast the wrong and right ways to exercise spiritual gifts. Instead of an awkward connection, this sentence becomes a logical and necessary link between the two chapters. It is evident not only that Paul wrote this discourse on love, but also that he composed it especially for this occasion. Love is the one way to build up the body of Christ through the harmonious functioning of its members.

Love and the Gifts   Paul begins chapter 13 with a dramatic scene of spectacular gifts without love. He describes representative charisms of speaking, knowing, acting and giving to the utmost.

> *If I speak in the tongues of men and of angels, but have not love, I am only a resounding gong or a clanging cymbal. If I have the gift of prophecy, and can fathom all mysteries and all knowledge, and if I have a faith that can move mountains, but have not love, I am nothing. If I give all I possess to the poor and surrender my body to the flames, but have not love, I gain nothing. (1 Cor. 13:1-3)*

"Tongues of men and of angels" encompass all languages, human or divine. Even in its highest form, this gift without love has no value. The resounding gong and clanging cymbal were ancient single-toned instruments which could not produce a melody and were frequently used in pagan worship.[5] Without love, the gifts of prophecy and knowledge also amount to nothing. Truth is necessary but not sufficient. This principle extends to mountain-moving faith and even martyrdom.

Without love spiritual gifts neither please God nor strengthen Christian character. In the exercise of spiritual gifts the decisive question is this: "Is *love* translated into deed through this *charisma* or not? Does the neighbor encounter the ascended Lord in the gift or just the man exercising the gift? Is Christ incarnate being glorified and lifted up or does the gift serve to glorify man?"[6] Since the gifts are meant to be functions of Christ's body, through which his love is demonstrated on earth, their value lies only in the extent to which his love is conveyed.

Love in Action For Paul love is neither an abstract ideal nor a sentimental feeling. He doesn't define what love *is*, as an end in itself, but how it *acts* and *reacts* in the rough and tumble of life. This is not so much a "hymn to love" as the "way of love" when the members of the body are controlled by the love of Christ (2 Cor. 5:14).

Love is the motivation for good relationships and positive action. In the last analysis love is not something we have, but the way we live.

> *Love is patient, love is kind. It does not envy, it does not boast, it is not proud. It is not rude, it is not self-seeking, it is not easily angered, it keeps no record of wrongs. Love does not delight in evil but rejoices in the truth. It always protects, always trusts, always hopes, always perseveres. (13:4-7)*

The first brief sentence captures love in both quantity and quality. Love's patience never runs out; it is willing to endure; for love there are no hopeless cases. Love is also kind; it is merciful in its demonstrated concern for the other's welfare.

Love's duration and depth know no limits.

Paul then lists eight ways love does *not* act: five verbs describe unloving action *to* others and three depict unloving reaction to wrong done *by* others. Applied to the situation at Corinth, love doesn't *envy* the more prominent spiritual gifts of others, nor does it *boast* about miracles and healings. Love is not *proud* of spiritual wisdom and knowledge. Love is not *rude* or *self-seeking* in the exercise of prophecy and speaking in tongues.

So much for wrong action; what about reaction to the sins of others, especially fellow Christians who make things difficult? Since love is patient it is not *easily angered* by injuries, whether real or imagined. Love *keeps no record of wrongs* but allows the brother to start over with a clean slate. Love does not *delight in evil.*

Paul concludes the section on a positive note with five actions love performs. Love *rejoices in the truth,* wherever it is found. Love *always protects* others, concerned for their welfare; *always trusts,* willing to give others the benefit of the doubt; *always hopes,* confident in God even when the darkness prevails; *always perseveres,* enduring the assaults of suffering, misunderstanding and persecution.

When the implications of this description sink in, initial inspiration can be swallowed by despair. Who is able to perform to this standard? Hope revives with the realization that the first meaning of these words is found in the nature of God. God is love. This *agape* is the way he deals with us. It is most fully demonstrated in the character and actions of his Son, Jesus Christ. He is supremely patient and kind, not easily angered or keeping a record of wrongs, always protecting and persevering, even to death on the cross for our sins.

Love lies at the most basic level of life—relationships with God and others. It anchors the soul far below the waves of surface activity, even spiritual gifts. This love of Christ must first be received, experienced in the depths of our being. Only then can we express it, as a fruit of the Holy Spirit, in the practical ways Paul describes.

The Permanence of Love   Paul now demonstrates the transience of spiritual gifts and the permanence of love.

> *Love never fails. But where there are prophecies, they will cease; where there are tongues, they will be stilled; where there is knowledge, it will pass away. For we know in part and we prophesy in part, but when perfection comes, the imperfect disappears. (13: 8-10)*

A time will come when charisms of prophecy, tongues and knowledge are no longer needed. Paul calls it *to teleion* ("perfection").

Interpretations of this event differ. One view takes it to be the completion of the New Testament, after which revelational gifts are no longer necessary.[7] But this interpretation has two major difficulties. First, Paul describes the perfection as the time when "we shall see face to face" and "know fully, even as I am fully known," that is, perfectly (13:12). This condition did not exist at the end of the first century, and will not occur until the end of the age at the coming of Christ.[8] Second, this view narrows the function of these gifts to the few apostles and prophets through whom inspired Scripture was written. Paul, however, teaches a wider purpose for these charisms— constantly building the body of Christ. These three gifts, as well as the others, are needed as long as the church continues its pilgrimage.

But the charisms, valuable as they are for the church in time, will not be needed in eternity. Prophecy, the revelation of God's purpose indirectly through an intermediary, will give way to a direct understanding of his will. Speaking in other languages will no longer be necessary. Words of knowledge will become superfluous as we shall then know fully. "Knowledge and prophecy are useful as lamps in the darkness, but they will be useless when the eternal Day has dawned."[9]

Paul next teaches the difference between the present imperfection and this future day. Each illustration makes its contribution to our understanding. The first is based on the difference between childhood and maturity in human development. "When I was a child, I talked like a child, I thought like a child, I reasoned like a child. When I became a man, I put childish ways behind me" (13:11). A child naturally talks, thinks and reasons like a child.[10] How else? A child's understanding of life and response to it are appropriate to this stage of development. They serve well at this stage and prepare for the next step on the path to maturity. A child's thinking and speaking is good as far as it goes; but eventually "childish ways" are left behind.

So it is with spiritual gifts. In the providence of God they meet the present needs of the church; they serve a useful purpose now even though eventually they will cease.

The second illustration contrasts seeing an object by imperfect reflection and seeing it directly. It suggests the ancient mirrors of polished metal. "Now we see but a poor reflection; then we shall see face to face" (13:12). Corinthian mirrors were famous, but even the best of them gave an imperfect, somewhat distorted reflection. Nevertheless, this kind of mirror served its purpose, reflecting the original object and not something entirely different. The picture was useful to the viewer; equally important, he knew it was only an imperfect reflection and not the real thing.

So it is with our knowledge of God in this life. It comes through the imperfect medium of human language as well as symbols, pictures and vision. But while partial, this knowledge is adequate for its purpose of leading to a holy life.

Paul concludes with a brief statement: "And now these three remain: faith, hope and love. But the greatest of these is love" (13:13). In what way does Paul use "now"—temporal in the sense of "here and now," or logical meaning "now we have demonstrated"? In favor of the latter is the fact that here faith and hope are united with love as remaining or abiding, and earlier Paul says that love endures forever.[11]

The integral relationship between 1 Corinthians 12 and 13

is now clear. Although Paul's essay on love can stand by itself, perhaps gracing a wedding ceremony, its message is essential to the exercise of spiritual gifts. "It is shaped and created for the very purpose of demonstrating the solution to the tensions in the Corinthian congregation."[12] At Corinth the full range of charisms was present. Yet because the right motivation was lacking, they served to puff up, rather than build up the body of Christ. Love makes the difference between an ego trip and constructive service.

As important as love is to spiritual gifts, the relationship is not a one-way street. Chapter 13 of 1 Corinthians should be read in the light of chapters 12 and 14. It is no accident that Paul's teaching on love comes in this context. The charisms are an essential manifestation of love in the body of Christ. The Corinthians were not to affirm their love for others without being ready to meet their needs through mercy, knowledge or healing as the Spirit desired. Spiritual gifts are not the servants of love but full partners.

Paul is ready now to provide guidelines for exercising gifts of inspired speech. He presents a model for their use when the Christians come together in corporate worship.

13
Order in Worship

As the Christians at Corinth were enriched in Christ, they exercised the full range of spiritual gifts. Yet some of these charisms were misunderstood and misused with serious consequences. Apparently among the most controversial, then as now, were prophecy and speaking in tongues. In 1 Corinthians 14 Paul discusses their purpose and practice, providing guidelines for their proper exercise in worship.

Assessment of speaking in tongues is complicated by the fact that Paul's letter seems to have a proof-text for every point of view! Some happily quote, "Where there are tongues, they will be stilled" (13:8), while others urge "I would like every one of you to speak in tongues" (14:5). Many in the middle cautiously note the instruction, "Do not forbid speaking in tongues" (14:39).

Much of the difficulty in understanding 14:2-25 lies in the style of argument. Paul is not writing a theological treatise, but a letter in which he shares elements of his own experience as well as illustrations from life. Seeming contradictions emerge as he alternates between prophecy and speaking in tongues, comparing one with the other.

The key to understanding Paul's teaching about speaking

in tongues lies in his repeated concern that the church be edified. Spiritual gifts are designed to strengthen the body of Christ. If they are to achieve this goal, charisms of inspired speech obviously must be understood. "Unless you speak intelligible words with your tongue, how will anyone know what you are saying? . . . You may be giving thanks well enough, but the other man is not edified" (14:9, 17). The problem with speaking in tongues at Corinth was a lack of communication. Speaking in tongues without interpretation failed to achieve its purpose of building up the body of Christ because its message was not understood. The basic issue is intelligibility.

Prophecy   Paul begins with an instruction involving both the fruit and gifts of the Spirit: "Follow the way of love and eagerly desire spiritual gifts, especially the gift of prophecy" (14:1).[1] The context of this command and the verses which follow it is the gathering for public worship. In this setting the most relevant charisms involve inspired perception and speech (14:26). Here prophecy has special value for believers as it declares God's message to the community. "But everyone who prophesies speaks to men for their strengthening, encouragement and comfort. . . He who prophesies edifies the church" (14: 3-4).

Prophecy serves a broader purpose than providing new revelation from God to be recorded in Scripture; it also strengthens, encourages and comforts—functions the church will always need. In this way, prophecy effectively "builds the house." Paul's choice of the word *oikodomeō* reinforces his earlier statement to the Corinthians, "You are . . . God's building" (3:9, see p. 126). Through this charism God makes known his purpose, strengthens the will and encourages the spirit of his people.

Prophecy also reaches the unbeliever:

But if an unbeliever or someone who does not understand comes in while everybody is prophesying, he will be convinced by all that he is a sinner and will be judged by all, and the secrets of his heart

will be laid bare. So he will fall down and worship God, exclaiming,
"God is really among you!" (14:24-25)

Paul highly regards his special office of apostle and prophet through which new revelation is given. But lest it be thought that this gift is meant only for a select few, he teaches the Corinthians that prophecy in its broader use is potentially present for every believer. "I would like *every one* of you to speak in tongues, but I would rather have you prophesy.... But if an unbeliever ... comes in while *everybody* is prophesying.... For you can *all* prophesy in turn" (14:5, 24, 31). Paul's view of widespread prophecy in the New Age confirms what was predicted by Joel, preached by Peter and taught by Luke.

Tongues and Interpretation   Concerning speaking in tongues in public worship, Paul criticizes only the uninterpreted exercise of this charism. His first comparison of tongues and prophecy makes this clear:

He who speaks in a tongue edifies himself, but he who prophesies
edifies the church. I would like every one of you to speak in tongues,
but I would rather have you prophesy. He who prophesies is greater
than one who speaks in tongues, unless he interprets, so that the
church may be edified. (14:4-5)

Paul affirms the greater value of prophecy with a qualification that is frequently overlooked: prophecy is greater *unless* the tongues are interpreted. With interpretation, speaking in tongues also edifies since the message is understood. Thus it has a place with prophecy in the model of public worship (14:26ff.).

His one concern is intelligibility:

Unless you speak intelligible words with your tongue, how will
anyone know what you are saying? You will just be speaking into
the air.... If then I do not grasp the meaning of what someone
is saying, I am a foreigner to the speaker, and he is a foreigner
to me.... For this reason the man who speaks in a tongue should
pray that he may interpret what he says. (14:9, 11, 13)

In light of these preliminary qualifications at the outset of 1

Corinthians 14, Paul's succeeding observations should be understood as referring to speaking in tongues in public worship *without interpretation.* Thus:

> *For anyone who speaks in a tongue [without interpretation] does not speak to men but to God. Indeed, no one understands him; he utters mysteries with his spirit. . . . If you are praising God with your spirit, how can one who finds himself among those who do not understand say "Amen" to your thanksgiving, since he does not know what you are saying? You may be giving thanks well enough, but the other man is not edified. I thank God that I speak in tongues more than all of you. But in the church I would rather speak five intelligible words to instruct others than ten thousand words in a tongue [without interpretation]. . . . So if the whole church comes together and everyone speaks in tongues [without interpretation], and some who do not understand or some unbelievers come in, will they not say that you are out of your mind? (14:2, 16-19, 23)*

The charism of tongues exercised without interpretation neither builds the church nor converts unbelievers.

Paul illustrates the need for intelligibility with two familiar examples, musical instruments and foreign languages. If a flute or harp does not distinctly sound its notes, no one knows what tune is being played. And if the trumpet doesn't give a clear call, who will prepare for battle? (14:7-8). Likewise, if someone speaks a language the hearer doesn't understand, they are foreigners to each other (14:10-11). Paul desires for the Corinthians the recognized tune and clarion call of understandable messages.

Paul makes one other comparison of prophecy and tongues in public worship based on a condensed quotation of Isaiah 28:11-12:

> *In the Law it is written:*
> > *"Through men of strange tongues*
> > *and through the lips of foreigners*
> *I will speak to this people,*
> > *but even then they will not listen to me,"*
> *says the Lord.*

Tongues then are a sign, not for believers but for unbelievers;
prophecy, however, is for believers, not for unbelievers. (14:21-22)
This difficult passage has given rise to several different interpretations, depending on the understanding of two key
words: *sign* and *tongues*.[2] Does *sign* mean proof, wonder, warning of punishment or simply indication of God's presence?
And does *tongues* mean the gift of tongues or just a foreign
language? We will treat these questions in order.

First, when Israel was obedient, God sent them prophets
speaking their own language. When they were disobedient he
sent foreigners, in the case of this passage from Isaiah the
invading Assyrians whose language they could not understand. The lesson is that unbelievers will be sent unintelligible
teachers, while believers will be sent those who can be understood. In this sense the sign is the active presence of God dealing with people in different ways.

Second, a tongue or language may be unknown in two
senses—to the speaker or to the hearer. At Pentecost the
tongues spoken by the disciples were unknown to them but
well understood by the hearers from other countries. At Corinth the tongues in public worship were unknown to both
speakers and hearers, including the unbelievers who might be
present. It was not uncommon for the latter to visit Christian
assemblies as well as synagogues. For them it was not a saving
sign, but one of judgment on their disobedience as God's
message came in a language they could not understand.[3]

Paul's expressed concern, then, for public speaking in
tongues is not for the style but for the content. Though commentaries on 1 Corinthians often disparage speaking in
tongues as ecstatic and emotional, like the frenzied practice
of pagan religions, Paul does not state that the gift was being
exercised in this manner. *Glōssa* is sometimes translated "ecstatic speech," but the word itself has no connotation of ecstasy. In fact, Paul assumes that speaking in tongues can be
controlled (14:28).

The Christians at Corinth may have exercised this charism,

as well as others, with great emotion and unexpected results, but for Paul the issue is one of intelligibility; whether loud or soft, the message must be understood. He criticizes only the exercise of tongues without interpretation. The recurring contrast in this passage is between prophecy and *uninterpreted* tongues.

Private Prayer   Paul also teaches that private speaking in tongues can strengthen the individual.

> *For any one who speaks in a tongue does not speak to men but to God. Indeed, [without interpretation] no one understands him; he utters mysteries with his spirit [by the Spirit]. . . . He who speaks in a tongue edifies himself. (14:2, 4)*

This speaking in tongues is a form of prayer. With his spirit (literally, *in spirit*), the individual speaks mysteries, that is, divine truths. Although any hearers wouldn't understand him, this speaking has value. It builds up the individual, not the congregation. Therefore it is not designed for public worship. Without interpretation, "the speaker should keep quiet in the church and speak to himself and to God" (14:28).

How does speaking in tongues differ from ordinary prayer?

> *For this reason the man who speaks in a tongue should pray that he may interpret what he says. For if I pray in a tongue, my spirit prays, but my mind is unfruitful. So what shall I do? I will pray with my spirit, but I will also pray with my mind; I will sing with my spirit, but I shall also sing with my mind. (14:13-15)*

The first statement follows from the main argument so far: unless the message is interpreted, speaking in tongues cannot build the church. The speaker does not understand what he is saying; otherwise he would not have to pray for an interpretation.

Verses 14 and 15 are among the most difficult of the chapter and so give rise to conflicting interpretations. First, what does Paul mean by saying that his spirit prays? Some take it as an expression of feeling. But in this discussion Paul never uses "spirit" for the feelings, which play no part in his teaching about tongues. Rather this praying in a tongue is the exercise of a spiritual gift. The speaker is under the influence of the Holy Spirit and ought not to be marked as a frenzied enthusiast or someone full of new wine.

Paul explains further by noting that in this kind of prayer his mind or understanding is unfruitful. Some interpret this unfruitfulness in terms of the hearers; it does them no good because they cannot understand the message.[4] However, Paul's words focus not on the result but on the process: "[my] *mind is unproductive*, because it is not active."[5] Paul teaches that when one prays with tongues, it is the Spirit, rather than his own intellect, who determines what he says.

A final question concerns the relationship between spirit and mind in verse 15. Based on the definition above, Paul apparently is talking about two kinds of praying and singing: with his spirit in tongues and with his mind in ordinary language. Some insist that these be combined, although they do not explain how one can do both at the same time. Once the difference between the two modes is recognized, it can be seen that each serves its own purpose (see pp. 203ff.).

According to Paul a person may speak in tongues in public worship providing there is interpretation. If not, he is to be silent, speaking to himself and to God (14:28). In his private prayer he may speak either in a tongue by the Spirit or in ordinary language controlled by his mind. This understanding of the passage guides the contemporary exercise of tongues in most charismatic fellowships. In public only a few manifest the gift of speaking in tongues, accompanied by interpretation. Many use this means of prayer silently in meetings and in their private devotions. They find that it does edify them, as Paul indicates.

A Model for Worship   If speaking in tongues caused a problem, what was the solution? One quick answer might have been to eliminate the practice. Some at Corinth may have had this action in mind since Paul thought it necessary to command, "Do not forbid speaking in tongues" (14:39). Paul's solution was to use this charism properly with the gift of interpretation to build the church.

Having corrected the misuse of speaking in tongues and its consequences, Paul provides a model for its proper use with prophecy in orderly worship. "What then shall we say, brothers? When you come together, everyone has a hymn, or a word of instruction, a revelation, a tongue, or an interpretation. All of these must be done for the strengthening of the church" (14:26). When the Corinthians gathered together they all expected to participate in the service with a variety of spiritual gifts. While all would not necessarily take part in any one meeting, the significant point is that any of them might do so. The picture here reflects the meetings sketched in Ephesians 5:18-20 and Colossians 3:16-17. The list has several representative gifts of inspired speech which are designed to strengthen the Christian community in its public services.

Paul next gives specific instructions for the exercise of speaking in tongues and prophecy. "If anyone speaks in a tongue, two—or at the most three—should speak, one at a time, and someone must interpret. If there is no interpreter, the speaker should keep quiet in the church and speak to himself and God" (14:27-28). In a given meeting only a few are to speak in tongues, and those one at a time. There must always be interpretation. Paul assumes that the believers are not carried away in ecstasy, but have the power to control this speaking.

Then come guidelines for prophesying:

Two or three prophets should speak, and the others should weigh carefully what is said. And if a revelation comes to someone who is sitting down, the first speaker should stop. For you can all prophesy in turn so that everyone may be instructed and encouraged. The spirits of the prophets are subject to the control of the prophets. (14:29-32)

Here also only two or three are to speak at one meeting. Paul guards against two possible misuses of prophecy. With the gift of prophecy becoming widespread in the church, there was a danger that some prophecies might not be valid. Paul doesn't assume that the believer exercising this gift is infallible; his message should be carefully weighed. Foreign elements can creep in to cloud or distort God's message. Here is the opportunity and need for the gift of discernment—the ability to distinguish between spirits immediately after a prophecy has been given.

A second difficulty can involve the way prophecies are given. There are to be only a few, one at a time. Furthermore, no one is to dominate the meeting. If a revelation comes to someone else, the one who is speaking should conclude and allow the other to speak. Such an interruption and transition can be made in an orderly way because "the spirits of the prophets are subject to the control of the prophets." Whatever the precise meaning of "spirits of the prophets," Paul's point is clear: the first prophet has the power to bring his message to an orderly conclusion so that the other can speak. "For God is not a God of disorder but of peace" (14:33).

Great opportunities entail great risk. Prophecy is valuable and yet open to the possibility of both error and confusion. Paul guards against the danger but not so as to discourage the exercise of this gift (compare 1 Thess. 5:20).

Significantly Paul does not instruct the church to deal with possible misuse of speaking in tongues and prophecy through authoritative control by its leaders. He says nothing about an organizing group to program the service. Rather these gifts have the built-in balance of the two supplementary gifts of interpretation and discernment. Paul's confidence lies in control by Christ, the head of the body, through the Holy Spirit as he manifests his power and direction through the individual members.

Speaking in tongues and prophecy, as direct communication from God, are designed to strengthen the body. Prophecy is superior to *uninterpreted* tongues. But when the charism of tongues is followed by the gift of interpretation it can have the same value. Both are spoken in the Spirit to convey a divine message. Yet in a given meeting their exercise is limited to two or three persons. Whether loud or soft, enthusiastic or calm, the question is not one of volume and emotion but content. Prophecies must be tested by those with the gift of discernment. Speaking in tongues and prophecy, like other spiritual gifts, are to be exercised in love. Their message should exalt Jesus Christ as Lord and build his body, the church.

It is evident that the misuse of tongues at Corinth was mainly a failure to interpret. And possibly many people speaking at the same time produced disorder. But Paul does not declare that tongues was causing the greatest difficulty because the Christians prized this gift above the other charisms. His severest criticism occurs in the first eleven chapters and is aimed at the party spirit, divisions, sexual immorality, lawsuits and disorder at the Lord's Supper. The charism of tongues appears to be less of a problem to Paul than it is to modern interpreters who call it overvalued and ostentatious.[6]

Paul concludes his teaching by reaffirming his authority. "If anybody thinks he is a prophet or spiritually gifted, let him acknowledge that what I am writing to you is the Lord's command" (14:37). Paul's prophetic office enables him to speak with certainty and truth.

The chapter ends with three commands briefly summarizing the instruction he has given. "Therefore, my brothers, be eager to prophesy, and do not forbid speaking in tongues. But everything should be done in a fitting and orderly way" (14:39-40). The first reflects his teaching elsewhere: "Do not put out the Spirit's fire; do not treat prophecies with contempt" (1 Thess. 5:19-20). The second insures that his teaching about speaking in tongues with interpretation will be practiced. Paul's command should be translated, "Stop forbidding speaking in tongues."[7] Apparently one faction in the church wanted to solve the problem by dispensing with this charism.[8] The third command undergirds the others: when spiritual gifts are exercised in an orderly way they build the body of Christ.

Without the experience of grace (*charis*) there is no being "in Christ." Without the experience of spiritual gifts (*charismata*) the body of Christ cannot grow strong. According to Paul as well as Luke, the Christian community needs the full range of charisms to fulfill its mission in the world. *All* are spiritual gifts. *Each* performs a valuable function, but only when exercised in love. "The inspiration, the concrete manifestations of Spirit in power, in revelation, in word, in service, all are necessary—for without them grace soon becomes status, gift becomes office, ministry becomes bureaucracy, body of Christ becomes institution, and *koinonia* becomes the extension fund."[9]

Part Four:
Contemporary Issues

14
Spiritual Gifts Today

How relevant today is Paul's model of a Christian community? Should we expect the Holy Spirit to manifest the full range of charisms appearing in the letters to Corinth and Rome? Both classical Pentecostalism and the charismatic renewal in mainline Protestant and Roman Catholic churches answer yes. They witness to the occurrence of all these spiritual gifts for strengthening the body of Christ. In doing so they challenge the doctrine that many charisms were designed only for the first-century church.

When unexpected events seem to contradict their theology, Christians face a dilemma. Something has to yield if we are to keep our thinking and living integrated. Either this purported activity by God is spurious or our theology needs to be revised. We must either find good reason for rejecting the witness to unexpected manifestations of the Holy Spirit, or accept them as windows for viewing biblical teaching in a new light.

By its very nature a renewal questions long-held traditions and beliefs. Yet every such challenge is not necessarily valid. Embracing new experiences, however vital, without the test of Scripture can lead into a morass of subjectivism and even heresy. On the other hand, refusal to accept the possibility that

God is acting in unexpected ways, opening the eyes of his people to scriptural truths long overlooked or misunderstood, runs the risk of smothering a fire being kindled by the Holy Spirit.

Church history reminds us that renewals are times of vigorous action and reaction. Biblical teaching reopened and relived often conflicts with established beliefs and programs. Custodians of the fireplace sometimes resist the painful remodeling necessary to accommodate the new fire. The charismatic renewal questions the doctrine that certain "miraculous" spiritual gifts were designed to launch the church in the first century, after which they were meant to cease. In this chapter we shall examine the historical and biblical arguments for this view as we consider the use of spiritual gifts in the church today.

Historical Evidence   The doctrine that certain extraordinary spiritual gifts were intended only for the first century was derived largely from experience. During the second century some began to claim that these charisms died with the last of the apostles. The early Christian apologist Justin Martyr (ca. A.D. 100-165) contradicted this assertion: "It is possible now to see among us women and men who possess gifts of the Spirit of God."[1]

Irenaeus (ca. A.D. 130-200) confirmed this fact as he described many spiritual gifts in the church of his day, including prophecy, discernment and healing. He writes, "Others have foreknowledge of things to come: they see visions, and utter prophetic expressions. Others still, heal the sick by laying their hands upon them, and they are made whole."[2]

At the beginning of the third century, Tertullian (ca. A.D. 160-220) reported witnessing extraordinary gifts of the Spirit, although their manifestation was waning with the increasing formalism of the church. A strong defender of orthodoxy, Tertullian maintained vigorously that spiritual gifts constituted the full Christian experience and challenged his skeptical contemporaries by citing the Apostle Paul.[3]

This brilliant theologian was won to Montanism, a reform movement which protested against the religious establishment and combined a desire for return to apostolic purity with a revival of charismatic gifts. The movement produced courageous missionary pioneers and martyrs. But their zeal and enthusiasm provoked a strong reaction by church leaders as many Montanists fell into fanaticism and heresy. As a result the church became wary of supernatural manifestations of the Spirit. Ironically, the Montanist excesses served to tighten the very ecclesiastical control against which they were protesting.

Nevertheless, some church leaders continued to advocate the full range of spiritual gifts. Presbyter Novatian (d. A.D. 257) wrote concerning the Holy Spirit:

This is He who places prophets in the Church, instructs teachers, directs tongues, gives powers and healings, does wonderful works, offers discrimination of spirits, affords powers of government, suggests counsels, and orders and arranges whatever other gifts there are of charismata; and thus makes the Lord's church everywhere, and in all, perfected and completed.[4]

A century later Bishop Hilary (d. A.D. 367) quoted Paul's list of gifts in 1 Corinthians 12 and commented: "Here we have a statement of the purpose and results of the Gift; and I cannot conceive what doubt can remain, after so clear a definition of His origin, His action, and His powers."[5] The argument that the charisms ended with the apostolic era is simply untrue. Not only did they persist, but their full exercise was taught by some of the church's ablest leaders during the first four centuries.

In the fifth century Augustine (A.D. 354-430), influential theologian and Bishop of Hippo, reported that the gifts of the Spirit could occasionally be seen. But by this time the Western church generally viewed these charisms as given for the founding of the church and then withdrawn because they were no longer necessary. Augustine developed this argument mainly in order to explain their general absence. Ultimately some spiritual gifts did disappear from general use, although not completely. They waned, not in a church which otherwise was growing in spiritual power, but in one which was departing from other New Testament principles and practice as well.

External political and social developments also influenced the church's attitude toward spiritual gifts.[6] After the western part of the Roman Empire fell in the fifth century, the stream of Christian thought and life divided and separated. The Roman or Latin tradition developed a different attitude toward spiritual gifts and speaking in tongues from that of the Greek or Orthodox tradition. In the West, civil government disintegrated as a result of barbarian invasions and the church remained as the only viable organization of civilized life. Forced by necessity to exercise many functions of secular authority, it became very practical and this-worldly. Western Christianity thus developed an authoritative pattern in which the unity of the body was stressed at the expense of the diversity of its members. With the emphasis on authority rather than on individual religious expression, it is not surprising that the congregational exercise of spiritual gifts held little place in the life of the church.

The eastern part of the Roman Empire, however, retained at Constantinople a strong central government which until 1451 provided a stable society in which the church could develop. As a result it was not forced to take over the secular functions assumed by its counterpart in the West. The Eastern Orthodox church remained more other-worldly and mystical with the encouragement of introspection and individuality. It gave greater encouragement in the diversity of the body's members through which the gifts of the Spirit could flourish. "The spiritual gifts of 1 Corinthians 12, with the possible exception of glossolalia, have always been considered normative by nearly all of the Orthodox within the life of the Church."[7]

In the Western church, the doctrine of withdrawn spiritual

gifts was refined in the heat of controversy during the Reformation. The Roman Catholic church validated its authority on the basis of miracles performed in its midst. John Calvin countered this claim by arguing that miraculous gifts were given to the early church to support its preaching of the Word, and for strength while it was still young and weak. After the death of the apostles these gifts were no longer needed; God withdrew them, leaving the primary focus on the preaching of the Word. "The gift of healing, like the rest of the miracles, which the Lord willed to be brought forth for a time, has vanished away in order to make the new preaching of the Gospel marvelous forever."[8]

During the following centuries this view was affirmed and transmitted by influential theologians. John Owen wrote: "It is true that those extraordinary effects of his power, which were necessary for laying the foundation of the church, have ceased."[9] Charles Hodge commented on 1 Corinthians 12:28: "In that age there was a plenitude of spiritual manifestations and endowments demanded for the organization and propagation of the church, which is no longer required. We have no longer prophets, nor workers of miracles, nor gifts of tongues."[10]

Dispensational theology also subordinates miracles to preaching. It holds that the purpose of miraculous gifts was to validate the prophetic message at particular times in history when God worked in a special way.[11] He sent his Son to initiate the New Age and establish the church. The apostles, validated by signs and wonders, preached the new revelation which they committed to writing. With the launching of the spiritual ship and the passing of the apostles, the church's voyage through the centuries, guided by the canon of Scripture, no longer needed the exercise of miraculous gifts.

Nevertheless, post-Reformation Protestantism was not unanimous in this verdict. John Wesley observed a correlation between lost gifts and the general state of the church:

The causes of their decline was not as has been vulgarly supposed because there was no more need for them, because all the world were become Christians . . . the real cause was: the love of many, almost all Christians so called, was waxed cold . . . this was the real cause why the extraordinary gifts of the Holy Spirit were no longer to be found in the Christian Church; because the Christians were turned heathen again and had only a dead form left.[12]

While he did not believe that miraculous activities of the Spirit had ceased, Wesley didn't consider the question to be of great importance.

Whenever there is a wide gap between biblical teaching and the church's experience, two explanations are possible: it may be due to divine intention or to human failure. Some principles and commands in the Bible do not apply to the church today. But others, which should be fully operative, are sometimes overlooked or neglected. An operational gap between God's standards and our performance is usually due to a low level of expectation on our part or to disobedience. We often recognize this fact in such areas of holy living, prayer, evangelism, stewardship and missions. The same principle applies to the exercise of spiritual gifts.

In order to break through the limitations of historical and cultural conditioning, we must start with a scriptural understanding of their nature and purpose. While our experience influences what we see in Scripture, in the last analysis our doctrine must be based on the teaching of the biblical writers.

Biblical Teaching   Paul's teaching of the church as a body uncovers several critical weaknesses in the doctrine of the temporary nature of certain charisms such as prophecy, speaking in tongues and miracles. First, the New Testament nowhere teaches that these spiritual gifts would be withdrawn. Paul devotes three chapters of his first letter to the Corinthians to the nature, purpose and use of spiritual gifts. Here, if anywhere, one would expect him to identify any temporary gifts and prepare the believers for their phasing out. On the contrary, he not only emphasizes the importance of each charism, but also takes pains to instruct this new Christian community in the proper use of prophecy and tongues in public worship.

Second, if certain charisms were meant only for the first century, which are they and what are the biblical criteria for deciding? The usual answer is that the supernatural gifts were temporary. Yet Paul does not make the distinction between "natural" and "supernatural" which has become ingrained in Western thought.[13] Prophecy and service, healing and helping, tongues and administration stand side by side in his lists without these labels. All are manifestations of the Holy Spirit. Giving aid or teaching in a specific situation is no less a charism than prophesying or healing.

Third, the limitation of miraculous gifts to the first-century church is based on too narrow a view of their purpose. It sees the apostles' miracles only as a temporary validation of the prophetic revelation. While miracles, signs and wonders indeed authenticated a prophet's ministry, the New Testament shows that they served a broader purpose in their own right. Jesus' healings, for example, were an integral part of his ministry. His great love and compassion moved him to make people whole in every dimension of life. And he committed this ministry of preaching and healing to his disciples. In 1 Corinthians 12—14 Paul teaches not that the miraculous gifts were designed to validate the revelation given to the apostles, but that their purpose with the other charisms is to build up the body. The Christian community is weakened by the loss of gifts as the body is crippled by the paralysis of its members. Paul rejoiced that the Corinthians lacked no spiritual gift.

Both Old and New Testaments have the model: revelation is validated by miracle and preserved in Scripture. But in the New Age the Spirit, no longer limited to a select few, is poured out on all God's people. His widespread activity now provides a broader and more continuous model: prophecy and miracle daily adding to and building up the body. The closing of the canon of Scripture surely did not end the church's need for the full range of charisms to inspire its worship, conduct its service and empower its mission.

The Church As Body   Paul's description of the church as the body of Christ should direct our theology and practice of the charisms. The diversity of service and ministry, with each member contributing his unique part through the Holy Spirit, is essential to the very life and growth of the church. Each member meets a need, and all work together harmoniously.

A return to this New Testament model of the body of Christ can reverse two other trends in Western Christianity: institutionalization and individualism. After the third century there was a shift from ministry as *charism* to ministry as *office*. The most significant gifts were no longer expected to be exercised by members of the body; they became special functions of the clergy. Spiritual gifts such as preaching, teaching and pastoring came to be exercised almost exclusively by ministers appointed to or called by the congregation. Commenting on Romans 12:6-8 Abraham Kuyper concludes: "From these passages it is evident that among these charismata St. Paul assigns the first place to the gifts pertaining to the ordinary service of the church by its ministers, elders, and deacons."[14] In this respect the Protestant churches of the Reformation did not fully break free from the structure of the medieval church.

This institutional view of the church has recast Paul's teaching into a radically different model. According to it a professional clergy now performs ministerial functions *for* the laity. The role of the congregation is reduced to the exercise of a few more or less natural talents and acts of service. Most modern churches have come a long way (not just in distance and time) from Corinth where everyone had "a hymn, or a word of instruction, a revelation, a tongue or an interpretation . . . for the strengthening of the church" (1 Cor. 14:26).

Spiritual gifts have also become overly individualized. They are commonly called abilities, talents, endowments or capacities—terms which convey the idea of personal possessions or characteristics.[15] Too often spiritual gifts are considered a matter of one's individual relationship with God. Yet Paul explains a charism in different terms: "To each . . . the manifestation of the Spirit is given for the common good" (1 Cor. 12:7). This statement makes three important points.

First, it describes the gift as a "manifestation" of the Spirit, a clear evidence of his presence which can be seen or heard. Second, it is not given to *have* but to *use*.[16] The gift is not a *possession* but an *exercise* by the power of the Spirit. Third, its purpose is the "common good." The charism is meant to strengthen the body. The context is corporate, not private.

Therefore, the believer does not struggle to discover his or her individual gift and then wonder where to use it.[17] Instead, the Christian participates in the body and, sensitive to the needs of others, trusts the sovereign Spirit to manifest whatever gifts will meet the needs of the community. The community benefits from and controls the exercise of gifts.

In Paul's model the charisms are neither an exclusive function of a few officers nor the private possession of individual members. They are actions initiated by the Spirit through *all* the members in the body.

Charisms and Experience   Having shown the perennial usefulness and purpose of spiritual gifts, however, we remember that one of the most common criticisms of the charismatic renewal is in the area of experience. Charges of emotionalism and subjectivism are directed toward the exercise of certain charisms. Since the time of the Montanists, Western theology has been wary of enthusiasm, many times with good reason. Nevertheless, experience lies at the heart of biblical faith.

The greatness of men and women such as Abraham, Moses, Hannah and Mary lay in their personal relationship with God, their experience of faith and obedience. The Psalmist invites, "Taste and see that the Lord is good" (34:8). Peter, James and John enjoyed an inner circle of experiences with their Lord. Paul confessed his one aim in life: "I consider everything a loss compared to the surpassing greatness of knowing Christ Jesus my Lord" (Phil. 3:8).

God's revelation calls for personal response. His truth is meant to be lived (2 Tim. 3:15-17). And obedience to his commands opens windows of new understanding (Jn. 7:17). The Christian's goal is a deepening experience of God in Christ through the Spirit (Eph. 1:17).

This kind of experience moves out to interact with objective reality in relationships with God and others. Christian prayer is not just a "mystical experience" but communion with our Lord. Love is not a sentimental feeling but a way of living with others.

True spiritual experience is the opposite of a self-centered kind which, like a boomerang that fails to hit its target, curves back to end where it started. Such a trip may involve drugs, alcohol or subjective religious experiences (whether charismatic, evangelistic or liturgical). No dimension of Christian life is immune to the pursuit of experience as an end in itself. But temporary enthusiasm sinks into hangover and depression. Paul contrasts these two kinds of experience: "Do not get drunk on wine, which leads to debauchery. Instead, be filled with the Spirit" (Eph. 5:18).

Authentic charismatic experience is response to the initiative of the Holy Spirit in the body of Christ. "Experience as used here does not mean something man does or something man causes to happen. Experience is concrete knowledge of the God who approaches man. . . . This act of God is appropriated by man at the personal level."[18] This is the nature of all valid Christian experience, not just the charisms. The believer both *receives* the gracious action of the Holy Spirit and *shares* it with others. The boomerang hits its target—the welfare of the community.

Not surprisingly, then, Scripture provides several practical tests for spiritual gifts. First, a genuine manifestation of the Spirit exalts the *person* of Jesus Christ. Paul declares, "I tell you that no one who is speaking by the Spirit of God says,

'Jesus be cursed,' and no one can say, 'Jesus is Lord,' except by the Holy Spirit" (1 Cor. 12:3). The Spirit of Christ exalts the Lord—the Giver of the Spirit.

Second, authentic charisms build the *body* of Christ. They are given "for the common good" and are to be exercised in an "orderly way" (1 Cor. 12:7; 14:40). As meaningful as they may be in the individual's spiritual growth, their primary purpose is to edify the church.

A third test is the fruit of the Spirit, the *character* of Jesus Christ. Genuine spiritual gifts foster "love, joy, peace, patience, kindness, goodness, faithfulness, gentleness and self-control" (Gal. 5:22-23). All religious experience, charismatic or otherwise, is worth nothing if it is not a manifestation of the love of God in Christ.[19]

A further misconception should be cleared up. Experience is often mistakenly equated with emotion or crisis or individualism. But Christian experience, whether conversion or charism, should not be identified with a certain kind of feeling. It may be highly emotional or calm, depending on the person and circumstances. Spiritual gifts are not necessarily exercised in crisis. Many are manifested in a growing process of openness to the Spirit.

Finally, personal experience is not necessarily individual or selfish. Some of the most intensely personal and meaningful charismatic experiences occur amidst the fellowship of other members of the body of Christ.

Danger and Opportunity   Like other powerful movements in the church's history, the charismatic renewal has its peculiar dangers. The rushing stream not only waters the countryside but also throws debris on the riverbanks. Edward O'Connor notes, "The Pentecostal movement, even though it seems to be the work of the Holy Spirit in its root and principal impulse, is also a complex mélange of human energies that in part correspond to the Spirit's plans, but in part deviate from it, conflict with it and counterfeit it."[20] Any good gift of God can be used for the wrong motives or in mistaken ways.

O'Connor describes two major errors of what he terms "charismania." The first is the mentality which views the charismatic as the principal, if not the sole, criterion of spiritual excellence. It identifies spiritual growth with abundant exercise of the charisms, especially the most spectacular. It forgets that love is the major measure of Christian spirituality. To counteract this attitude we need to stress that spiritual gifts are not goals in themselves but a means of building up the body of Christ in love. While the miraculous charisms have long been suppressed, they should not now be overemphasized. There is rich spiritual life in many Christians who do not exercise extraordinary gifts.

A second form of charismania expects charismatic activity to take the place of the ordinary exercise of human abilities and the normal activities of church life. While some Christians make the mistake of programming the Spirit *out* of certain charisms today, others try to program him *into* a predictable pattern of gifts. Some people seem to want their entire lives to be guided by heavenly messages and all sickness to be healed miraculously. Others see theological study and sermon preparation replaced by prophetic utterance, and church ministers replaced by charismatic leadership.

Christ is not building his church of charisms, but of people, with all their faculties of mind and will and emotions. The Scripture makes provision for overseers (bishops or guardians) and deacons (1 Tim. 3) for orderly ministry and governance. The Holy Spirit, sovereign over human nature and church organization, often works beyond as well as through our planning and programs. Nevertheless, it is in the well-built fireplace that we should expect the sometimes unpredictable fire of his activity.

The cure for charismania is not to deny or disparage certain misused charisms. Paul's prescription for the Corinthians was understanding of the nature and purpose of charisms. He did not advocate surgery, the amputation of errant members, but therapy for training in their proper use. No spiritual gift can be depreciated without slighting the Giver.

For centuries the church has suffered from an operational gap between biblical teaching about spiritual gifts and their actual use in the Christian community. Today this gap is being closed by raising charismatic experience to the level taught and lived in the New Testament. Across the entire denominational spectrum, at home and abroad,[21] many congregations are coming to know in a new way both the Scriptures and the power of God with respect to the charisms. This widespread activity of the Holy Spirit presents exciting possibilities for learning new lessons. The key is realizing the relationship between expectation and experience.

On many occasions Jesus connected healing with the faith of those healed. "According to your faith will it be done to you" (Mt. 9:29). On one occasion the people of his home town took offense because he was merely the carpenter's son. "And he did not do many miracles there because of their lack of faith" (Mt. 13:58). As Clark Pinnock observes, "Christ makes himself experientially present in proportion to the faith of the community. There *are* degrees of faith according to the New Testament."[22] Where the expectation is limited, so will be the experience, whether in prayer or evangelism or spiritual gifts.

Expectancy is a key element of the charismatic renewal. All Christians have the same Lord, the same Spirit and all exercise some spiritual gifts. The difference is mainly one of expectancy, of faith for the full range of charisms for the church's worship, service and mission. With this expectancy comes the Spirit's manifestation of these gifts today as in New Testament times.

15
Baptism in the Spirit

If you want to polarize a discussion just ask: "What do you think about the baptism in the Spirit?" One may immediately give witness to a remarkable change in his life through this recent experience. Another is likely to object that the baptism in the Spirit took place when she became a Christian. Others will stiffen as they brace themselves for sparks in an atmosphere as charged as if someone had broached the question of predestination and free will.

The issues in this subject are more complex than they appear after the first burst of pyrotechnics. They involve principles of biblical interpretation as well as current perceptions of the Holy Spirit's activity. Interaction between the two can clarify the New Testament use of the phrase "baptize in the Spirit" and our experience of it today.[1]

A Second Experience? Chapter five sketched the classical Pentecostal doctrine of the baptism in the Holy Spirit, which understands it as a full reception of the Holy Spirit "distinct from and subsequent to" conversion, a second experience to be sought by all Christians. The initial physical evidence of this Spirit-baptism is speaking in tongues, and its result is power for witness and service through exercising the full range of spiritual gifts found in the New Testament. Pentecostals not only teach this doctrine, they experience it.

Early Neo-Pentecostalism in the 1960s held much the same view of the baptism in the Spirit. Dennis Bennett, for example, describes this second experience in the Christian life: "The Holy Spirit comes to live in us when we receive Jesus, and are born again of the Spirit. The baptism in the Holy Spirit is the *pouring out* of the Spirit."[2] He explains it is receiving the Holy Spirit in the sense of making him welcome, so that Jesus can baptize the believer with his refreshing and renewing power. Bennett does not prescribe a list of conditions for this baptism. The requirement is simply making sure one has received the Lord Jesus as Savior, renouncing false teachings in modern cults and asking in faith. Speaking in tongues is to be expected and exercised as the scriptural sign of this experience.

Bennett's interpretation of Scripture to support this view follows the reasoning of classical Pentecostalism (see chap. 5, pp. 56ff.): as Jesus was first *conceived* by the Holy Spirit, then anointed or *baptized* in the Spirit, and as the first disciples also first *received* the new life in the Spirit (Jn. 20:22) and then were *baptized* in the Spirit (Acts 2), so all Christians in succeeding generations should have this same double experience. Bennett sees this pattern repeated at Samaria, Caesarea and Ephesus as well as in the life of Paul.

Though support for the baptism in the Spirit as a distinct second experience subsequent to conversion is largely based on events in the Acts, one of Paul's statements is also used as evidence: "For we were all baptized by one Spirit into one body . . . and we were all given the one Spirit to drink" (1 Cor. 12:13). Here Bennett sees two separate events: spiritual baptism into Christ at conversion, followed by "the baptism with the Holy Spirit, in which the now indwelling Holy Spirit poured forth to manifest Jesus to the world through the life of the believer."[3]

This interpretation of the baptism in the Spirit in Luke-

Acts and Paul has significant weaknesses. We are ready now to see both the element of truth in Pentecostal understanding of the baptism in the Spirit and the points at which it misses the mark.

Principles of Interpretation   We have noted that Luke and Paul each has his own perspective and purpose in writing. If we are to interpret correctly, each biblical author must be allowed to present his message in his own way.

A word or phrase can be used in several different ways. Paul, for example, in his letter to the Romans, has four different meanings for *flesh*.[4] In a given passage, therefore, the meaning of a word must be determined largely on the basis of context and usage. This principle undergirds all literary interpretation. If the connotation of a word is imposed from the outside, there is no control—the passage can be made to yield whatever meaning the interpreter wishes. Much of the misunderstanding and debate over the baptism in the Spirit results from neglecting this principle.

Also, an event or experience may have several dimensions of meaning described by different terms. Often, however, our understanding of a complex event is arbitrarily narrowed by equating it with just one of these descriptions. For example, the Scripture teaches that in his death Christ is the victor over sin and Satan and he is our example, as well as our substitute and representative. No one term adequately explains the atonement.

Finally, words are not ends in themselves. They are signs pointing to ideas. Sometimes a sign becomes blurred as it is weathered by storms of controversy. When it no longer serves to communicate, it should be replaced, at least for purposes of discussion, by a synonym which is clearer and less laden with emotional overtones.

The phrase "baptism in the Spirit" does not occur in the New Testament. It is taken from "baptize with (in) the Spirit" which occurs seven times. First used by John the Baptist and recorded in each of the four Gospels, this phrase then appears twice as a quotation in Acts. These six occurrences refer to the experience of the disciples at Pentecost. The phrase is used once by Paul to describe the incorporation of the Corinthian believers into the body of Christ.

Given these various contexts, a study of baptism in the Spirit must consider the possibility of more than one meaning. We should not presuppose that the phrase is used identically by Luke and Paul, especially since it is used to describe two complex events—the experience of the disciples at Pentecost and the conversion of unbelievers at Corinth.

The Gift My Father Promised   The crowds who came out to hear John the Baptist expected the messianic age to be marked by renewed activity of the Spirit. John declares that the Messiah will baptize them with the Spirit. However, he does not explain the nature of this experience or exactly what will happen.

This phrase next appears on the lips of Jesus as he gives final instructions to his disciples before the ascension. He repeats John's statement and calls the baptism "the gift my Father promised" (Acts 1:4). On two other occasions Jesus explains the meaning of this event. The disciples will be clothed with power from on high to be his witnesses from Jerusalem to the ends of the earth (Lk. 24:49; Acts 1:8). The Lord will provide his church with the power of the Spirit to carry out its commission.

Luke briefly reports the coming of the Spirit. The facts are comparatively few: time and place; a sound like wind and the appearance of fire; the disciples speaking in other tongues and the pilgrims amazed to hear them declare the wonders of God in their own languages. Any witness standing nearby could have described this much. But Luke has a theological interpretation of this event: he teaches that the disciples were "filled with the Holy Spirit" (Acts 2:4). (Others had a different interpretation: "They have had too much wine.") Luke coins his own term for this experience and uses it consistently throughout the rest of Acts.

Peter also has an explanation, especially for those who think the disciples are drunk. This is the fulfillment of Joel's prophecy for the New Age: "In the last days, God says, I will pour out my Spirit on all people. Your sons and daughters will prophesy" (Acts 2:17). Significantly, Peter does *not* quote Ezekiel's prophecy, "A new heart I will give you. . . . And I will put my spirit within you, and cause you to walk in my statutes and be careful to observe my ordinances" (Ezek. 36:26-27). While this inward cleansing activity of the Spirit for a new life and righteous living also takes place in the New Age, Peter does not give this explanation. The immediate result of the Spirit's being poured out is not moral living but prophetic activity for powerful witness, as Jesus promised.

Later on, through Peter's preaching, the Holy Spirit was also poured out on the Gentiles; they spoke in tongues and praised God. In his report to the apostles in Jerusalem Peter declared: "The Holy Spirit came on them as he had come on us at the beginning. Then I remembered what the Lord had said, 'John baptized with water, but you will be baptized with the Holy Spirit.' " (Acts 11:15-16). Cornelius and his friends had the same prophetic experience of the Spirit that the disciples had when they began their ministry.

This brief summary shows that Luke's narrative is more than descriptive. Luke writes from the perspective of one seeking to emphasize the role of the Spirit in bringing the New Age. His purpose is to teach the meaning of the Spirit's activity at Pentecost. Luke does not leave his readers to guess the significance of Jesus' baptizing the disciples in the Spirit. He explains their experience in the words of Joel, Jesus and Peter, all of whom agree that it involves the prophetic activity of the Spirit.[5] To this witness he adds his own by calling it a "filling with the Spirit," the term he consistently uses to describe the Spirit's prophetic activity. Luke's teaching is clear: at Pentecost baptism in the Spirit empowered the disciples for witness.

The phrase "baptize with the Spirit" is also used once by Paul (see pp. 136ff.) in 1 Corinthians 12. He is discussing the use of spiritual gifts in the Christian community. His purpose is to teach the unity in Christ which undergirds their diversity. After listing a wide variety of spiritual gifts, he emphasizes that the body is a unit. "So it is with Christ. For we were all baptized by [in] one Spirit into one body—whether Jews or Greeks, slave or free—and we were all given the one Spirit to drink" (1 Cor. 12:12-13).

The context is the beginning of the Christian life, for which Paul also uses other terms for the Spirit's activity: *regenerating*, *sealing* and *sanctifying* (Tit. 3:5; Eph. 1:13; Rom. 15:16). Here he describes this beginning as being baptized in the Spirit into the body of Christ.

It is now clear that Paul's connotation and use of "baptize in the Spirit" is entirely different from Luke's. According to Luke's teaching, the baptism in the Spirit for the disciples was an empowering for prophetic witness. According to Paul, the baptism in the Spirit for the Corinthians was their incorporation into the body of Christ. Luke's context is the unfolding of redemptive history and the mission of the church, while Paul's is the experience of individual believers when they become members of Christ's body. This distinction—the two meanings of baptize in the Spirit—helps clarify the significance of Pentecost for the church today.

The Main Issue   Pentecostalism and traditional theology, both Protestant and Roman Catholic, are at loggerheads over the meaning of the baptism in the Spirit. They start with different passages of Scripture. Each position is correct in its basic interpretation but wrong in the inference made and the use to which the passage is put.

The Pentecostals begin with Acts 2 and the disciples' experience of the baptism in the Spirit. They rightly read Luke's message as outlined above. The baptizing is a pouring out, a filling, a clothing with power from on high, for witness. The action of the Holy Spirit equips the disciples for their mission.

But the Pentecostal view errs in interpreting this event as a definitive second experience distinct from and subsequent to conversion. As we have seen (pp. 95, 108), this baptism in the Spirit should not be understood as a milestone in the disciples' individual spiritual pilgrimage. This is neither the intent nor the context of Luke's teaching. From Luke's theological perspective it is a sign, not of the disciples' inner experience, but of the coming of the New Age in God's plan of redemptive history. Furthermore, the record does not indicate that the disciples' experience of baptism in the Spirit at Pentecost was unique. Luke describes it as a "filling with the Spirit" which was frequently repeated. Each time the result was the same—a prophetic activity of the Spirit.

The attempt to find a second experience of the Spirit in 1 Corinthians 12:13 misreads Paul's statement. The first clause reads "baptized by [in or with] the Spirit," and "given the one Spirit to drink" is another way of describing this same experience, not a second one. Also, Paul twice declares that *all*, not just a certain group, had this experience. Furthermore, the sealing of the Spirit (in Eph. 1:13) occurs at conversion and not subsequently. The Pentecostal (and evangelical "deeper life") doctrine of the baptism in the Spirit as a distinct second experience[6] is not taught in the New Testament letters.

Now then, what can be said about the traditional theological view of baptism in the Spirit? It correctly interprets Paul's use of the term in 1 Corinthians 12:13 to mean an action of the Spirit at the beginning of the Christian life when the believer is incorporated into the body of Christ. But it incorrectly insists that this must also be the meaning in Acts 2. This assertion overlooks two significant facts.

First, the basic meaning of "baptize" is to immerse or wash. It does not always convey the idea of initiation. Because of this connotation of a cleansing bath (as a symbol or sign of spiritual cleansing from sin, Tit. 3:5), baptism was an appropriate rite to use for Christian initiation. But this does not exhaust the meaning of the term. Even in ordinary language baptism is "any experience or ordeal that initiates, tests or purifies."[7] To insist that "baptism" always implies initiation is to fail to recognize the different meanings a word can convey.

The second error of the conventional theological method we have already noted, namely, that Paul's writing is considered didactic and therefore normative for doctrine, while Luke's is labeled descriptive, as if he were simply illustrating principles taught elsewhere. As a result, the meaning of baptism in the Spirit at Pentecost is derived from Paul's definition of the term, even though his context and usage are not Luke's. Unfortunately, this procedure muffles Luke's distinctive teaching on the Holy Spirit. It strips Luke of his identity as a theologian by reading his writing as if it were Paul's.[8]

Even granting the distinction between didactic and descriptive, Luke's interpretation of baptism in the Spirit (as a prophetic and serving activity, not an initiatory action of salvation) stands. The explicit interpretations of Jesus, Joel and Peter confirm Luke's own: baptism in the Spirit in Acts 2 is a pouring out and filling with the Spirit to empower the disciples' witness.

In their concern to pinpoint the beginning of the New Age and the church at Pentecost, many scholars blur the difference between the disciples' prophetic baptism in the Spirit and the initial reception of the Spirit by the three thousand who responded to Peter's message. Systematic theology, being averse to loose ends, tends to cut off whatever cannot be neatly packaged. By whatever means the unique experience of the disciples who bridged the old and new ages is made to fit a doctrine of the church, care should be taken not to put into Luke's mouth words that make him teach what he does not intend.[9]

When each writer is allowed to speak for himself, the different meanings of baptize in the Spirit become clear. For Paul it is a once and for all action in the Spirit at conversion incorporating the individual into the body of Christ.[10] For Luke, it describes the enduement with power for effective witness and service which, after Pentecost, was frequently repeated. The former is inward and relational to Christ and his body; the latter is outward and functional in the mission of the church.[11]

The relationship between Acts 2 and 1 Corinthians 12 is well summed up by Clark Pinnock:

"Baptism" is a flexible metaphor, not a technical term. Luke seems to regard it as synonymous with "fullness" (Acts 2:4; cf. 11-16). Therefore, so long as we recognize conversion as truly a baptism in the Spirit, there is no reason why we cannot use "baptism" to refer to subsequent fillings of the Spirit as well. This later experience, or experiences, should not be tied in with the tight "second blessing" schema, but should be seen as an actualization of what we have already received in the initial charismatic experience, which is conversion.[12]

A Question of Labels   The church often faces the problem of the medicine bottle and its label. It is possible for a person's experience of God to be better than his doctrinal explanation of it. Unfortunately, the reverse can also be true. Orthodox theology is often affirmed with little Christian character and service. Good medicine may be incorrectly labeled, while an accurate label can adorn an empty bottle.

Today thousands of Christians in the charismatic renewal witness to a profound, life-changing experience which they call the baptism in the Spirit.[13] They testify that as a result they know Jesus Christ as their Lord in a more personal and practical way. They have a new love for the Word of God which they read diligently and apply. Their prayers, formerly long on petition, now feature worship and praise. They have a love for other Christians which transcends denominational barriers, and a sense of belonging to each other in the body of Christ. Equally important is a more effective witness to non-Christian friends.

These Christians share a new understanding of the nature and purpose of spiritual gifts as manifestations of the Spirit's power within the fellowship to build the body of Christ. Many, although not all, pray in tongues in their private devotions. More basic is an openness and expectancy for the full range of charisms, each a manifestation of the Spirit according to his will and the need of the occasion.

How are these experiences to be assessed and what about their theological explanation? First, the test of Scripture shows that these are dimensions of Christian experience both taught and practiced in the New Testament. Second, except for the exercise of certain spiritual gifts, they characterized the renewals sketched in chapter five: the Wesleyan transformation of England and the holiness and evangelical deeper life movements in the United States. Still, the explanation of the baptism in the Spirit as the requisite second stage of Christian experience does not have the biblical support it claims.

Nevertheless, the experiences of these Christians in the charismatic renewal can no more be discounted for this reason than can the revivals of Wesley, Finney and Torrey who also taught the necessity of a second experience, although their explanations had a somewhat different theological shape. The medicine is powerful even though the label is incorrect.

What, then, is the biblical description for this evident, powerful working of the Holy Spirit? For many this life-changing experience is their conversion, the beginning of personal faith in Jesus Christ. For others it is a rededication or a full commitment to his lordship. For still others it is a new openness to the Spirit's manifestations of power in worship, witness and service.[14] This wide a range of experiences also occurs in evangelistic revivals under the label of "decision for Christ." A theology of Christian growth must have room for crises and dramatic workings of the Spirit as well as for the slower maturing of his fruit called sanctification.

In recent years Protestant and Roman Catholic theologians

involved in the charismatic renewal have struggled with this question of labels. During the 1960s the movement was called Neo-Pentecostalism, and many early groups owed much to the encouragement of classical Pentecostals. But their doctrine of the baptism in the Spirit proved unacceptable in formulating a theology of charismatic renewal.

The Malines conference in May 1974 differentiated between the theological and experiential meanings of the baptism in the Spirit. While in the first sense every member of the church has been baptized in the Spirit, there is an experiential sense which Catholics usually mean by the term.

> *It refers to the moment or the growth process in virtue of which the Spirit, given during the celebration of initiation, comes to conscious experience.... There are no special classes of Spirit-bearers, no separate groups of Spirit-filled believers. Fullness of life in the Spirit, participation in the abundant life of the Spirit, is a common possession of the whole Church, although not appropriated in equal measure by all.*[15]

Although biblical, this twofold use of the phrase is confusing. For this reason some leaders prefer to speak of the "release of the Spirit."

Presbyterian theologian Rodman Williams describes this baptizing or filling with the Holy Spirit as a new dimension of his activity. It is not an aspect of sanctification, but "the actualization of a dynamic whereby the whole person is energized to fulfill new possibilities ... a dynamic movement of the Holy Spirit which results in a new sense of God's presence and power."[16] He emphasizes that this action occurs through Christ since it is he who baptizes with the Spirit.

Further study and experience are necessary to do full justice to both the Scriptures and the power of God with respect to the charismatic renewal. While this brief consideration of a difficult subject leaves questions unanswered, at least it clarifies several points. The New Testament does not present *the* baptism in the Spirit which must refer *either* to the beginning of the Christian life *or* to subsequent experiences. Paul teaches *a* Spirit-baptism into the body of Christ which also involves regeneration, sealing and indwelling by the Spirit. This is part and parcel of becoming a Christian because "if anyone does not have the Spirit of Christ, he does not belong to Christ" (Rom. 8:9). Luke teaches *a* baptism in the Spirit which is a pouring out and a filling of the Spirit to endue with power for witness and service. From his perspective it is neither the first nor the second stage of salvation in the life of the individual.[17] Rather it is a repeated filling with the Spirit which manifests his presence as a sign of the New Age. Paul also teaches a repeated filling with the Spirit, although his characteristic language is "charism or manifestation of the Spirit."

Both Luke and Paul teach a direct working of the Spirit through the believer, different from regeneration and sanctification, for prophetic witness, worship and service. (Compare chap. 18, pp. 226ff.) Pentecostalism recaptured for the church the dynamic, charismatic activity of the Spirit. But it became entrenched in a theological position defending the need for a second experience "distinct from and subsequent to" conversion. Opposed to this doctrine, as well as the contemporary relevance of many spiritual gifts, traditional theology dug in behind Paul's definition of baptism in the Spirit. So the battle has been waged from these fixed positions with little movement on either side.

Military strategists often prepare to refight the last war. Unfortunately for them, the next conflict usually brings new battle lines, new weapons. World War 2 opened with the impregnable French Maginot Line facing an equally strong Siegfried Line. Each army was safe behind its ramparts but unable to advance. Suddenly the German panzer divisions moved swiftly around these fixed positions and rolled into Paris without a pitched battle. The Maginot Line remained impregnable, but unfortunately for the French its powerful guns were in the wrong place pointing in the wrong direction.

Theologians are also prone to refight earlier wars. Their

lines and weapons, protecting territory already won, are often ill prepared to take new ground. For decades Pentecostal and traditional theologies of the baptism in the Spirit faced each other along one major doctrinal battle line. Then suddenly the Holy Spirit moved around these fixed positions to infiltrate charismatic renewal behind the lines in mainline Protestant and Roman Catholic churches.

This fluid situation is confusing to many; much theological debate continues to cling to false dichotomies and categories. It is not clear how some of the doctrinal tensions will be resolved. But a continuing search of the Scriptures and openness to the creative activity of our sovereign Lord should reveal more of his strategy for the church's mission today.

16
Prophecy and Tongues

Are you reading this chapter first? If so, you have company since in the popular mind the charismatic renewal is usually equated with speaking in tongues. Since the early 1960s the press has featured this element, even dubbing it the "tongues movement." Thrust into the limelight, this controversial charism all too often takes center stage in discussion of the charismatic renewal. While it has a place in the cast of spiritual gifts, speaking in tongues does not deserve the role of hero (or villain) often assigned to it.

In both the New Testament and the early centuries of the church, speaking in tongues is linked with prophecy. At Pentecost it takes the form of prophecy as the disciples declare the wonders of God in the diverse languages of the pilgrims. For Paul gifts of inspired speech play a special role in building the body of Christ. Both prophecy and speaking in tongues continued long after the first century, although their use gradually waned along with other charisms.

The following pages scan the historical evidence for these two gifts. We shall then consider the use of prophecy and tongues today in the light of biblical teaching and conflicting views of their nature and purpose.

Faith of the Fathers   The Apostolic Fathers, who had direct
contact with Paul or a disciple, often combined these two
charisms in the single category of prophecy.[1] One reason for
combining them may have been to avoid giving ammunition
to those who were attacking Christians for alleged irrational
behavior. Nevertheless, Irenaeus (ca. A.D. 130-200) reported
contemporary practice of both gifts. "In like manner we do
hear many brethren in the church, who possess prophetic
gifts, and those who through the Spirit speak all kinds of languages, and bring to light for the general benefit the hidden
things of men and declare the mysteries of God."[2]

Writing voluminously around A.D. 225, Tertullian commented specifically on speaking in tongues as well as prophecy.

> *Let Marcion then exhibit, as gifts of his God, some prophets, such
> as have not spoken by human sense, but with the Spirit of God, such
> as have both predicted things to come, and have made manifest the
> secrets of the heart (1 Cor. 14:25); let him produce a psalm, a
> vision, a prayer—only let it be by the Spirit, in an ecstasy, that is in
> a rapture, whenever an interpretation of tongues has occurred to
> him.*[3]

As late as the fourth century, Cyril of Jerusalem thought it
possible that his candidates for baptism might receive the gift
of prophecy.[4] But by this time these gifts were no longer con-
tinuously exercised in the church. Some explanation had to be
found for their general disappearance. Augustine, who set
the mold of Western Christianity for seven hundred years,
formulated the doctrine that speaking in tongues was a special
gift for evangelism in the apostolic period, after which it
passed away. The need for prophecy and tongues as a way for
the Spirit to speak through men was decreasingly valued by
a church that was turning to fixed forms of worship.

A further development inhibited the exercise of tongues
in the Western church. It gradually came to be considered
an evidence of demon possession. Around the year 1000 a
book of public services reflected this view in its section on

Exorcism of the Possessed: "Signs of possession are the following: ability to speak with some facility in a strange tongue or to understand it when spoken by another; the faculty of divulging future and hidden events; display of powers which are beyond the subject's age and natural condition."[5]

This official church policy, which persisted for many centuries, may be a reason that speaking in tongues was seldom mentioned during this period. This fear of demonic influence persists and is reflected in the influential writing of Ronald Knox: "To speak with tongues you had never learned was, and is, a recognized symptom in cases of alleged diabolical possession."[6]

Nevertheless, the exercise of prophecy and speaking in tongues did not disappear entirely. They recurred in certain renewal movements characterized by the manifestation of varied charisms such as healings, inspired preaching and miracles. One was the ascetic movement which swept through Egypt and Asia Minor during the fourth to sixth centuries. Another renewal involving charismatic activity comprised the Cistercian, Franciscan and Dominican movements in France and Italy in the twelfth and thirteenth centuries.[7]

Isolated occurrences of prophecy and tongues have been discovered in more recent centuries.[8] Speaking in tongues has varied from rhythmic syllables unrelated to any ordinary language to speaking in living or dead or subliminal languages. No wonder this phenomenon gives rise to widely differing evaluations. These will be explored after a consideration of prophecy.

They Shall Prophesy In both Old and New Testaments, prophecy is an immediate communication of God's word to his people through human lips. It reveals God's redemptive purpose in a specific situation, whether present or future, and calls for responsible action. The prophet should speak *only* and *all* God's message, however unpopular it may be. Because there is always the danger of false prophecy, a message must be tested for harmony with prior revelation.[9]

In the New Age, as foretold by Joel and fulfilled at Pentecost, prophecy becomes widespread, no longer confined to a few select individuals. Young and old, men and women, slaves and free now prophesy. This reality is both reflected and guided by Paul's teaching in 1 Corinthians 14. He recognizes that all believers have the potential for exercising this charism and gives instructions for its proper use. They limit the number of prophecies in one meeting and provide for the message to be tested by others who may exercise the gift of discernment.

The teaching of both Luke and Paul confirms Joel's anticipation. Our study of the context and usage of prophecy in their writings revealed several functions of this charism: its first and most specialized use involved the "apostles and prophets" who constituted the foundation of the church. Through them the Holy Spirit revealed the mystery of Christ (Eph. 2:20; 3:5). As witnesses of the resurrection they prophesied and wrote most of the books of the New Testament. Both their experience and mission were unique and unrepeatable.

Second, prophecy is useful for edifying and encouraging the church. Paul expected any of the congregation, men and women, to prophesy on a given occasion (1 Cor. 11:4, 5; 14:26, 31). They do not have equal authority with him; their message must be tested. While it is not destined to become sacred Scripture, such prophecy has value to build up the body of Christ and therefore is needed by the church in *every* generation (see chap. 13, pp. 157ff.).

Peter, one of the twelve apostles, also recognizes this more general exercise of prophecy. Writing from Rome to five distant churches in Asia Minor, he instructs the believers in their use of charisms.

Above all, love each other deeply, because love covers over a multitude of sins. Offer hospitality to one another without grumbling. Each one should use whatever spiritual gift he has received to serve

*others, faithfully administering God's grace in its various forms.
If anyone speaks, he should do it as one speaking the very words of
God. If anyone serves, he should do it with the strength God provides, so that in all things God may be praised through Jesus Christ.
(1 Pet. 4:8-11)*

This passage is similar to Romans 12:6-8. Peter lists hospitality, prophecy and service as charisms without any distinction
between "supernatural and natural," temporary and permanent. He defines prophecy as speaking the very words of God.
Peter does not water down its value because it may come
through anyone in these congregations far from Jerusalem
and Rome. His brief teaching on spiritual gifts here remarkably confirms Paul's, even to his strong concern for the motivation of love and the praise of God through Jesus Christ.

A third function of prophecy in the early church is related to the foregoing. It appears as the continuing ministry
of a relatively few persons. "These were called 'prophets'—
not because the gift of prophesying was confined to them, but
presumably because their inspiration was more regular and
frequent."[10] Examples are Agabus, Judas and Silas, and Philip's four daughters. They conducted their ministry alone or
in groups, in one congregation or throughout a region (Acts
11:27-28; 13:1; 15:32; 21:9). Prophets delivered special messages and had unusual knowledge (Acts 21:10-11; 1 Cor.
13:2). While distinct from teachers who expounded a doctrine, their function seems to be related to the gift of teaching
(Acts 13:1).

Prophets, then and now, face a formidable challenge from
their counterfeits which are predicted in the New Testament.
So their messages must be tested by the revelation God has
already given in Scripture. The first letter of John is a study
in discernment as it turns the searchlight on a person's conduct, motivation and teaching.

The church today often has confidence in the gift of teaching but a fear of prophecy, sometimes well justified. The individual with an open Bible appears more objective and trust-

worthy than one who prophesies. But a survey of the many false cults and sects whose teachers claim biblical authority shows how unwarranted this sense of confidence can be. Any gift can be abused; the greater the potential for good, the more harm in its misuse. The message of teaching as well as prophecy must be tested. Does it agree with the overall biblical revelation, honor Jesus Christ as Lord, speak the truth in love and build the Christian community?

In the early church, prophecy served a continuing purpose beyond providing new revelation. Through this charism the Holy Spirit gave encouragement, comfort, admonition and guidance to the community. The apostles had confidence that if the Spirit manifested this gift he would provide the means to safeguard its exercise, including the companion charism of discernment.

Prophecy is reappearing in the church today. Fear of its misuse should not quench the benefit intended by the Holy Spirit when it is properly used within the body of Christ.[11]

Speaking in Tongues   Our study of Acts and 1 Corinthians showed the different kinds of speaking in tongues. At Pentecost the disciples were filled with the Spirit and spoke "in other tongues" so that the visitors from other countries heard them "declaring the wonders of God in our own tongues" (Acts 2:4, 11). To the perplexed crowd Peter gave the explanation. This was a manifestation of the prophetic outpouring of the Spirit promised by Joel.

At Caesarea the Gentiles were suddenly heard "speaking in tongues and praising God" (10:46). At Ephesus the twelve disciples "spoke in tongues and prophesied" (19:6). In the latter two cases there is no indication of recognizable foreign languages. The speaking in tongues can either *be* the praise and prophecy or *accompany* it. In Acts this manifestation of the Spirit takes no standard form.

Paul writes about "different kinds of tongues" (1 Cor. 12:10). His teaching about the need for interpretation in public worship implies that such speaking is not a recognizable foreign language. Otherwise why should unbelievers think that the speaker is out of his mind (14:23)? This is hardly the usual reaction in a cosmopolitan culture to hearing a foreign language one doesn't understand! Paul also describes a private use of tongues in prayer which is nonrational; that is, it does not use the mind as in ordinary prayer (14:14).

Luke and Paul mention a variety of speaking in tongues. This charism cannot be reduced to one model for all occurrences.[12] It serves several purposes. As a form of prophecy it is an evidence of the Spirit's activity in the New Age empowering the church for witness. With the companion gift of interpretation in public worship it strengthens the body of Christ. And in private devotions it edifies the individual.

Neither Luke nor Paul teaches that speaking in tongues is a sign of the individual's inner spiritual development. In the Acts it is often *one* evidence of the Spirit's outpouring, of which there are also others. But it cannot be taken as *the* sign of a second inner experience of baptism in the Spirit.[13] Paul presents this charism as one of many which builds the body, not as a mark of spiritual maturity (or immaturity).

Of all the spiritual gifts, speaking in tongues stirs the greatest anxiety and controversy both inside and outside the church. Why is it the burr under the saddle of the charismatic renewal? The answer lies in psychological as well as theological reactions. First we should understand the cultural conditioning which lies at the heart of current opposition to speaking in tongues.

Cultural Perspectives   In our scientific culture the charge of emotionalism is the kiss of death—except in sports, love and war. The rationalism of Western thought stirs suspicion of anything considered irrational. To the general public, speaking in tongues is usually associated with psychological instability. It certainly is not a socially acceptable way of behaving.

Several evaluations of the phenomenon have contributed

to this popular attitude.[14] The comparative religion perspective views Christianity as a variant of the common religious experience of mankind. Other religions also have conversion, sacrifice, rituals, prayer and glossolalia (speaking in tongues). It is noted that both the ancient world and some cultures today have ecstatic experiences involving a frenzy in which the participants moan, groan, wail and dance. Christian glossolalia, therefore, is considered simply one version of this primitive experience and without religious value.

> *Words and sounds which are without connection and meaning to men are uttered in ecstasy. The phenomenon is well known to students of the psychology of primitive and emotional types of religion. Such outbursts were known in the Hellenistic mystical religions of the time, and some parallels are also found in Judaism.*[15]

In chapter eight, however, we noted that the Greek word *glōssa* literally means "tongue" or "language." There is no linguistic basis for translating it "ecstasy." Nor can it be assumed that the Christian expression resembled the pagan form. Paul clearly considered it to be a meaningful manifestation of the Holy Spirit controlled by the individual. He also expected that in public worship it would be interpreted, an element not found in other religions either ancient or modern.

A second evaluation of speaking in tongues grants the essential difference between Christian and pagan forms but still links the former with strong religious emotionalism: "Students of the psychology of religion have noted [glossolalia], and describe it in terms of the release of strong emotion which cannot find satisfying expression in more normal ways ... [it is] an innocuous way of letting off superfluous spiritual steam."[16] Here the basic experience is confused with the atmosphere in which it sometimes occurs. Speaking in tongues *can* occur with strong emotion, as can ordinary prayer and preaching. It can also take place in a calm and quiet manner.

After years of study and direct observation, Kilian McDonnell concludes: "It has not been demonstrated that glossolalia as a psychological phenomenon is related in any immediately direct manner to personality variables. . . . Emotional instability does not seem to characterize the Pentecostal-charismatic community."[17] Nevertheless, the customary connection of speaking in tongues with emotionalism by reputed authorities has forged an iron-bound prejudice in the public mind.

A third view of speaking in tongues links this activity with unbalanced mental states; it is considered a result of psychological disturbance. George Cutten's standard treatise contends that glossolalia is related to schizophrenia and hysteria.[18] While other writers do not go this far, they consider those who speak in tongues to be "uncommonly disturbed." During the 1960s many Christian opponents of glossolalia uncritically echoed this secular view to support their position.

In its report of 1970 a United Presbyterian Special Committee observed:

Most of the so-called scientific studies and evaluations are based upon psychological models which either (a) assume at the outset that such states are pathological, or (b) have been prepared subjectively without following normally accepted controls, so as to make them almost meaningless from a research standpoint. . . . The most current evidence available indicates no justification for making a sweeping generalization that participants in the (charismatic) movement are maladjusted individuals, emotionally unstable, or emotionally deprived.[19]

The report also observes that many judgments have been made about the charismatic experience by persons with only superficial knowledge of the phenomena.

The Presbyterian Special Committee noted that it will be a tragic day for the church if psychological norms become the criteria by which the truth and value of Christian experience is judged. "Psychological insight has enriched, deepened and humbled our knowledge of ourselves beyond measure; but, when it is asked for a decisive answer to the question of whether a man has or has not experienced the living Christ it is an aborted and inappropriate use of the science."[20]

A fourth view is more favorable to Christian speaking in tongues but still casts a cloud over those who exercise this gift. John Kildahl's research completed in 1971 showed that, "On any broad criteria of emotional well-being, the tongues speakers and non-tongues speakers were about the same."[21] He also concluded that a profound sense of trust in an authority figure is necessary for beginning to speak in tongues. "Without complete submission to the leader, speaking in tongues was not initiated. . . . There were no loners among the tongues-speakers."[22] This conclusion influenced church commissions in the early 1970s and is still frequently quoted.

Kilian McDonnell evaluates Kildahl's book and finds that it fails to pass the test of scientific writing.[23] The data are not presented in a professional way, and the author takes no note of readily available studies, some far more extensive than his own, which do not support his interpretation. One of them reported that a fourth of the persons interviewed began to speak in tongues while alone, that is, without anyone present to instruct, encourage and coach.[24] The rapidly growing charismatic renewal witnesses thousands of Christians beginning to speak in tongues without the influence of Kildahl's benevolent authority figure.

A fifth view links speaking in tongues with demonic influence. It is believed that a desire to be open to the Spirit also opens the personality to the intrusion of evil powers. While demonic influence is possible in tongues-speaking, as it is in other activities by Christians, no study to date has produced such evidence. Furthermore, the Bible pictures Satan as a clever enemy—not the red devil with recognizable horns and hoofs. We underestimate his ingenuity if we suppose that his greatest deception comes through the spiritual gift least acceptable to our culture, rather than through those of knowledge and teaching which are so highly esteemed and even idolized.

A Foreign Language?   When speaking in tongues attracted

widespread attention in the 1960s it naturally came under scientific scrutiny. Linguistic experts made recordings, analyzed the sounds and compared them with a variety of known languages. Could these utterances possibly qualify as "real languages"?

In 1972 William Samarin wrote a comprehensive report of speaking in tongues based on a wide range of published material and his personal investigation. His approach was both linguistic and sociological. He recognized that a valid study required knowing who the speakers are and how they use tongues. He did not start with the common prejudice that they are abnormal. Although a Christian, Samarin described his approach as "secular." He searched for an answer to the question "Why do people speak in tongues?" He scientifically analyzed the words themselves apart from whatever religious meaning they might have for the speaker.

Regarding the question of real language, Samarin concludes: "In spite of superficial similarities, glossolalia is fundamentally *not* language. All specimens of glossolalia that have ever been studied have produced no features that would even suggest that they reflect some kind of communicative system . . . [Glossolalia is a] simplified form of extemporaneous pseudolanguage."[25]

This scientific conclusion can be a surprise and disappointment to those who believe that their tongues-speaking is a miraculously-given real language, just as it may please those who do not believe in the validity of this experience. But both reactions are premature. Even if true, this conclusion is irrelevant to the meaning and purpose of speaking in tongues. It is still a means of expression that can be used by the Holy Spirit for the edification of the speaker in private and the Christian community in public, when accompanied by interpretation. A scientific description can no more explain away the spiritual significance of speaking in tongues than it can conversion, prayer and Christian community. All charisms involve divine initiative in the midst of thoroughly human activity.

Tongues is essentially a prayer gift, not miraculously imparted to the Christian, but nonetheless inspired by the Spirit. George Montague views it not as a language but as preconceptual prayer.[26] It is a means of praying with wordless sounds beyond conceptual language, of expressing oneself to God in nonrational speech.

If tongues are not normally a real language, is there ever an occasion when such speaking is a recognized foreign language? Samarin realizes that an authentic case would be miraculous and concludes: "Contrary to common belief, it has never been scientifically demonstrated that xenoglossia occurs among Pentecostals; people just do not talk languages they are unfamiliar with."[27]

This scientific statement does not take into account a possible miraculous work of the Holy Spirit. By its very nature a miracle is a unique historical event and cannot be reproduced in the laboratory. It is verified by credible witnesses rather than by scientific demonstration under controlled conditions. The Holy Spirit is not known for command performances so that his work can be made scientifically acceptable. The scientist has a right to study religious phenomena, but if he recognizes the limitations of his method he will refrain from pronouncing what people can or cannot do by the power of the Spirit. Speaking in tongues as a recognizable foreign language, while infrequent, has been verified by a number of reliable witnesses.[28]

The scientific method can analyze, measure and label the words, but it is not qualified to evaluate the dimension of meaning for the speaker's relationship to God. The scientist can accurately analyze the bread and wine of communion or the water of baptism, comparing it molecule for molecule with any bakery bread, table wine or tap water. But this method cannot measure the religious meaning of these elements. Scientific analysis is good as far as it can go, but the question of meaning, values and purpose in human experience goes much further.

Tongues Today   Before concluding with a look at the use of speaking in tongues today, one fact should be noted. Most commentaries paint a picture of this charism along the following lines: at Corinth it was an emotional, sensational experience similar to the ecstasy of the pagan religions. The Christians had an exaggerated respect for this gift which they considered of the highest value. Misuse of tongues was the greatest problem in the church. Paul considers it of least value since it appears last on some of his lists. At best he begrudgingly commands that it not be forbidden.[29]

These assertions do not have the verse references one would expect in commentaries otherwise well documented. Our exposition (chaps. 10-13) has noted that Paul's statements do not support these conjectures. Significantly, these opinions come from a culture for which speaking in tongues is both intellectually and socially unacceptable. Since in every generation Christianity is influenced by its environment, is it not possible that this spiritual gift is far more a problem for the modern church than it was for the Corinthians? The first eleven chapters of 1 Corinthians indicate that for Paul other issues were of much greater concern (see p. 158).

One perplexing question deserves an answer. What is the purpose of speaking in tongues, a nonrational speech which cannot be understood without interpretation? While the complete answer may not be known, several points can be made in response. Many in the charismatic renewal do not consider speaking in tongues as the initial evidence of the baptism in the Spirit. It often begins, either alone or in a group, when the Holy Spirit is breaking through in a new way. This response to God's initiative is accompanied by a profound sense of his presence and a new openness to his love and power. Tongues provides a means for extended praise and thanksgiving.[30]

For some it is a highly emotional experience, perhaps like their conversion; for others it is quiet and calm like other milestones in their Christian lives. Once a person starts praying in tongues he can initiate and stop it at will, just like ordinary prayer. Many autobiographical sketches show the wide variety of initial experiences and meaning for the individuals involved.

Speaking in tongues is also a rebuke to our rationalistic age whose intellectual pride infects even the church. The mind, one of God's great gifts, is idolized at the expense of other dimensions of human nature. A skeptical age accepts only what it can logically analyze and scientifically explain. How much better we feel when we know that the Bible is scientifically reliable; *now* we can be confident that it is the Word of God! The resurgence of speaking in tongues with interpretation can be a sign that "the foolishness of God is wiser than man's wisdom" (1 Cor. 1:25).

The private use of tongues serves not so much as a charism for building the body as to strengthen the individual's relationship with God. Christians who pray in tongues find it an expression of Romans 8:26. Here Paul comments that on occasion we cannot find words to express our deepest concern. "The Spirit helps us in our weakness. We do not know how we ought to pray, but the Spirit himself intercedes for us with groans that words cannot express." Is it the Spirit or the believer who groans? Many commentators think it must be the believer since it is he who does not know how to pray as he ought.[31]

While it is not certain that Paul here is referring to speaking in tongues, the principle is the same. Through its exercise—beyond the capacity of his intellect—a Christian can continue expressing his concerns when he no longer knows what to say. Private prayer in tongues can strengthen worship and praise for which words seem to fail even sooner than in petition.

Another use of tongues involves singing in the Spirit, a spontaneous melodic expression of worship. It occurs in both private and congregational prayer. The participants go beyond ordinary speech into a transcendent language of praise as they improvise the music to express their joy.

Contemporary singing in the Spirit has brought a redis-covery of jubilation, the spontaneous overflowing of joy prev-alent in the church from the fourth to the ninth centuries.[32] This wordless praying and singing aloud, a vital dimension of Christian worship, was largely lost in the following cen-turies of growing formalism. Through the current charismat-ic renewal this mode of praise is being recaptured by the church. Many modern Christians are learning to appreciate not only St. Augustine's mind, which guided Western thought for a thousand years, but also his heart, which ex-claimed: "Rejoice and speak. If you cannot express your joy, jubilate; jubilation expresses your joy if you cannot speak; it cannot be a silent joy."[33]

This pattern, including prophecy, interpreted tongues and singing in the Spirit in public worship, has come to life in hundreds of charismatic fellowships which expect the Holy Spirit to manifest these charisms and guard against their mis-use. This renewal, like others in the past, challenges theologi-cal traditions and organizational structures. How ready are the fireplaces to undergo the necessary remodeling to accom-modate the newly kindled fire?

17
Healing

Pain and suffering are the lowest common denominator of human existence. Sickness is no respecter of persons. It crosses all boundaries of age and class, race and religion as it paves the way for man's last enemy, death.

Christians are often asked, "If God is both good and almighty, why does he allow so much suffering?" In the face of human anguish, no other question puts us more on the defensive. We grope for an adequate answer knowing that "He jests at scars who never felt a wound."

In this chapter we shall not reason why and how sickness has arrived. Our approach is not philosophical. Rather we put the question another way: "Given the suffering of human existence, is there any evidence that God cares and is willing to help?" This is a practical approach which takes us directly to Jesus Christ, his commission to the church and its responsibility today for a ministry of healing.

New Testament Healing We may never understand *why* God allows evil and suffering. But we know that he cares about it and has acted at great cost to himself. The heart of the gospel is not the inspiring idea "God is love," but saving action—

"God so loved the world that he gave his one and only Son" (Jn. 3:16).

God has revealed to us who he is, who we are and his purpose for us in redemptive action and prophetic message. Jesus Christ is the great Act and Word of God.

In Jesus Christ, God became fully human, suffered with us and finally died for us. Word and act are partners in his mission of revelation and redemption. We have seen that Jesus' ministry had two foci—preaching and healing. His healing demonstrated God's concern for the total person, his desire that people become both holy and whole. Peter testified to Cornelius how "God anointed Jesus of Nazareth with the Holy Spirit and power, and how he went around doing good and healing all who were under the power of the devil" (Acts 10:38). Our Lord's healing ministry not only showed his compassion, but also demonstrated the coming of the kingdom in power over the evil forces which cause sin, disease and death.

Jesus in turn commissioned his disciples with this twofold ministry. "He sent them out to preach the kingdom of God and to heal the sick" (Lk. 9:2; see 10:9). When they returned with joy, Jesus said, "I saw Satan fall like lightning from heaven. I have given you authority to trample on snakes and scorpions, and to overcome all the power of the enemy; nothing will harm you" (Lk. 10:18-19; see Mk. 16:17-18).

The record in Acts shows that this preaching and healing ministry continued in the early church. Peter healed a lame man at the temple gate and then declared the gospel to the crowd which gathered (Acts. 3:1-16). Paul spoke boldly at Ephesus for two years where he healed the sick and those possessed by evil spirits (Acts 19:8-12). Through the Holy Spirit powerful words and acts spearheaded the Christian mission.

The charisms at Corinth included "gifts of healings" (1 Cor. 12:9). The healing ministry was not limited to the apostles, and Paul gives no indication that it would soon end. Like the other gifts, various kinds of healing are needed in every generation to build the body of Christ.

James instructed readers scattered throughout the empire how to take spiritual initiative when sickness strikes:

Is any one of you sick? He should call the elders of the church to pray over him and anoint him with oil in the name of the Lord. And the prayer offered in faith will make the sick person well; the Lord will raise him up. If he has sinned, he will be forgiven. Therefore, confess your sins to each other and pray for each other so that you may be healed. The prayer of a righteous man is powerful and effective. (Jas. 5:14-16)

It is significant that James connects physical and spiritual healing. In recent years we have learned much about the effects of attitudes and emotions on physical well-being; bitterness and resentment not only fracture interpersonal relationships but also undermine health.

Some suggest that since the Greeks used oil as medication, this is what James had in mind. While a medical house call seems scientifically more respectable than a visit for prayer, the text does not support this conjecture. Anointing in the name of the Lord was a familiar religious act and James explicitly says it is the believing prayer that heals.

The New Testament also reports a number of situations where immediate physical healing did *not* take place. Paul writes that Epaphroditus was ill, apparently for some time, and almost died although he was eventually restored to health (Phil. 2:25-30). Timothy had recurring stomach trouble for which Paul recommended the use of wine (1 Tim. 5:23). The apostle himself had a disability which he called a "thorn in the flesh." While we cannot be sure of its nature, we do know that it was not healed at the time he wrote, even though he had earnestly prayed to this end. But the very fact that three times Paul "pleaded with the Lord to take it away" (2 Cor. 12:8) demonstrated his expectancy of healing and perseverance in prayer for that result.

The New Testament attributes sin, physical, psychological

and spiritual illness, and death to Satan.[1] "The reason the Son of God appeared was to destroy the devil's work" (1 Jn. 3:8). Through his life, death and resurrection Jesus defeated Satan and hamstrung his domination over mankind. The early church looked to the risen Christ for freedom from sin and sickness, not as a right to be demanded but as a gift to be received. The body has a value of its own. It is not just a house for the soul. This understanding of human life and God's salvation in Christ made healing an integral part of the church's message and mission.

The Church's Record   During the second and third centuries the church experienced vital growth throughout the Roman Empire. Healing was not only practiced, but also comprised part of the doctrinal teaching given to all new converts. Before long, however, some began to emphasize the mind or soul at the expense of the body, concentrating on the "spiritual" part of man as most valuable. But the church stood firm in its conviction that salvation involves the total person. Most writers of this period had witnessed some instance of healing. Evelyn Frost has gathered writings from the period A.D. 100-250 which show a continuation of the healing practices described in the New Testament.[2]

Irenaeus (ca. A.D. 180), who lived in Gaul (France), attested the range of healings found in the Gospels and Acts, noting that often these miracles led to conversion. He contrasted Christian healing with the weakness of the heretics of his time.[3]

Around A.D. 210 Tertullian reported several kinds of healing.[4] And Origen who was martyred around A.D. 253, wrote:

There are still preserved among Christians traces of that Holy Spirit which appeared in the form of a dove. They expel evil spirits, and perform many cures, and foresee certain events. We too have seen many persons freed from grievous calamities, and from distractions of mind, and madness, and countless other ills, which could be cured neither by men nor devils.[5]

The healing ministry continued, but the fire was beginning to die. Around A.D. 250, Cyprian noted that the church had become soft and flabby. He expressed concern about Christians being "eager about our patrimony and our gain, seeking to satisfy our pride, yielding ourselves wholly to emulation and to strife."[6] He believed that the persecution by Decius was God's judgment on the moral laxity and division in the church.

The records show that far from ending with the apostolic era, the healing ministry reported in the New Testament continued in the church for almost three centuries.

Constantine's Edict of Milan in A.D. 313 marked the beginning of a new era for the church. Persecution ceased, Christianity became the established religion, worship became more structured and nominal Christianity was the rule. Not surprisingly the exercise of many spiritual gifts waned.

Nevertheless, the Eastern church continued its healing ministry under the leadership of four outstanding bishops. Basil the Great (ca. 330-379), who had some medical training, founded a large hospital outside Caesarea—the first public institution devoted to caring for the sick. He also believed in and practiced healing through prayer. Gregory of Nyssa (fl. 379-94) developed a theology of healing in his book *The Making of Man* based on the healing miracles of Christ.

In the West, however, Augustine taught that the extraordinary charisms were designed only for the first century. His early writings stated that Christians no longer are to expect the gift of healing. Toward the end of his life, however, events in his own diocese caused him to change his mind; his theology was challenged by the power of God through remarkable healings in his parish. In 424, as *The City of God* was nearing completion, Augustine described in one of the final sections the miracles that were taking place:

Once I realized how many miracles were occurring in our own day and which were so like the miracles of old and also how wrong it would be to allow the memory of these marvels of divine power to perish from among our people. It is only two years ago that the keeping of records was begun here in Hippo, and already, at this writing, we have nearly seventy attested miracles.[7]

Augustine not only witnessed miraculous healings, but on at least one occasion he laid hands on a sick man who departed well. His greatness is seen not only in the brilliance of his mind, but also in his willingness to change it in the light of new evidence.

Nevertheless, with the fall of the Roman Empire and the coming of the Middle Ages the spiritual fire died down, to blaze again only through occasional reform and renewal.[8] Miracles of healing became associated with outstanding individuals. By the thirteenth century the practice of prayer for the sick and anointing with oil, instructed by James, had withered to "last rites" for the dying rather than healing for the sick. Concern for the whole man in *this* life, so evident in the first three centuries, had given way to making sure that his soul was saved for eternity.

While the Protestant Reformation changed many aspects of church life, it perpetuated this view of healing: in biblical times God worked in the ordinary world with miracles and healings; but once the saving work of Christ and the canon of Scripture were completed, they were no longer necessary. Faith in Christ secured salvation of the soul in the spiritual world, and the indwelling Spirit provided the power to obey the biblical rules established for living in the physical world.

Luther shared this view and repeatedly affirmed that the "real miracles" were not visible ones. But like Augustine, he lived to witness and participate in the healings he had long disparaged. Toward the end of his life he saw his friend Melanchthon brought back from the brink of death through his own prayers. Five years later, in 1545, shortly before he died, Luther wrote instructions for a healing service based on the letter of James, stating, "This is what we do, and that we have been accustomed to do, for a cabinetmaker here was similarly afflicted with madness and we cured him by prayer in Christ's name."[9]

Unfortunately, Luther didn't integrate these experiences into his theology. One cannot help wondering how different the church's healing ministry would have been if three giants of the faith—Augustine, Aquinas and Luther—had come to appreciate it early in their ministry and had built into their teaching the place spiritual gifts occupied during the first three centuries.

Sickness came to be viewed as a specific punishment given by God for man's own good. This teaching appears in the Office of the Visitation of the Sick, written by the Church of England in the sixteenth century and still in operation. The minister declares that God is the Lord of life and death and then proclaims: "Wherefore, whatsoever your sickness is, know you certainly that it is God's visitation."[10] He then urges the sufferer, no matter how ill, to concentrate on his sins and repent.

The church had now arrived at the other end of the scale. In the New Testament it is Satan who sends sickness, while the risen Christ heals through the power of the Spirit. Now the church assures the sufferer that it is God who has certainly sent the sickness. The minister visits not to anoint for healing, but to insure salvation of the soul.

While the church may provide hospitals and doctors, and encourage the sufferer *in* his sickness, it is not expected to have a ministry through spiritual gifts and anointing with prayer to deliver him *from* it.

As the twentieth century dawned, no major church accepted or approved a theology affirming the direct healing activity of God through gifts of the Spirit. No wonder that most Christians believe that God is directly responsible for sickness, having sent it as punishment to bring the sinner to repentance or as a cross to produce greater patience in the saint.

Healing Renewed   Nevertheless, the ministry of healing did not disappear completely. It continued, for example, in parts of the Roman Catholic church and in the ministry of several well-known Protestant leaders. In the United States A. J. Gordon, a Baptist minister in Boston, published his *Ministry of Healing* in 1882. He describes the history of healing and gives examples from his own ministry. He notes that "the most powerful effect of such experiences is upon the subjects themselves, in the marked consecration and extraordinary anointing which almost invariably attend them."[11]

A. B. Simpson, who founded the Christian and Missionary Alliance in 1877, wrote *The Gospel of Healing*[12] as a result of his study of Scripture and his own ministry. Andrew Murray of South Africa also taught: "The pardon of sin and the healing of sickness complete one another."[13]

Early in the 1900s the new Pentecostal movement revived the healing ministry of the church. Gifts of healing, as well as the other charisms, were exercised. Less well known was a stream of healing which flowed in the Episcopal church.

A pioneer effort launched in 1906 showed that there need be no conflict between healing with and without medicine; one doesn't have to choose between modern medical science and gifts of healing. Elwood Worcester, rector of Emmanuel Church in Boston, and Dr. Samuel McComb worked with patients who had disorders of the nervous system. As the treatment progressed, it was always continued in close cooperation with a medical doctor. Worcester accepted manic-depressive cases (which at that time almost all physicians considered hopeless) and many suicide-bound applicants, not one of which took his own life. For twenty-five years the "Immanuel Movement" brought healing to thousands, although it lost momentum after the death of its founder.

In 1910 Henry Wilson, an Episcopal minister in Ashville, N. C., founded the Order of the Nazarene to foster a ministry of healing. This movement, which became inactive with his retirement in 1929, inspired John Banks to devote the last thirty years of his ministry to healing. He founded the interdenominational Order of St. Luke the Physician in 1947, comprising clergy and laity committed to a ministry of healing. During the next decade the order spread to hundreds of churches in the United States and abroad.

Since World War 2 the healing ministry in America has moved in two main streams. The first flowed from classical Pentecostal churches, but soon spread far beyond its banks to become an independent movement. Many individualistic leaders established their own organizations and followings. As the fires moved out of the fireplace, independent of ecclesiastical authority, they ranged across the spectrum from genuine to counterfeit. The latter brought the activities of the "faith healers" into disrepute.

This movement has been documented by David Harrell.[14] It crested in the late 1950s and rapidly subsided as the charismatic renewal in the historic Protestant and Roman Catholic churches gained strength in the 1960s. Nevertheless, several respected leaders in this movement such as Oral Roberts and Kathryn Kuhlman continued their healing ministries.

The second stream has flowed more steadily within the established churches. Unlike the independent revivalistic ministry, which often features the miraculous as the high point of the meeting, these services emphasize prayer for the whole person. Immediate healings are expected but not demanded. It is recognized that healing is often needed in more than one dimension and sometimes comes gradually.

Among the pioneers in this ministry are Alfred Price, Agnes Sanford, Don Gross and, more recently, Francis MacNutt and Michael Scanlan. Their teaching and healing services are usually held within the context of the local church with its clergy and congregation. Gifts of healing with other charisms are manifested to strengthen various dimensions of corporate life and service.

All healing ministries cannot be dismissed as a "freak phenomenon of the faith healers" on the sectarian fringe.[15] Like other ministries and gifts, healing can be misunderstood and misused so as to become a point of controversy and division.

But when properly exercised it mends personal relationships as well as individuals.

Principles of Healing   The church's healing ministry is based on the example of her Lord and his commission to the disciples. Jesus demonstrated his concern to make people both holy and whole. Then he sent his disciples to do the same. After the first few centuries the church betrayed this trust in failing to heal as well as preach. But in recent years it has begun to recover this vital dimension of its ministry.

This recovery is due in part to our rediscovery of the biblical view of man as a total person. Just as sin affects every dimension of our existence, so salvation is meant to restore the health of the whole person. The entire fulfillment of God's purpose will never be achieved amid the evil of this life. Complete spiritual, emotional and physical healing will come only in the resurrection. Nevertheless, until then the church has a message and mission for the total person.

Modern medicine has come to realize the strong relationship between physical and emotional illness. Dr. Charles Mayo estimates that the spiritual and psychological factor in disease varies from 65 per cent to 75 per cent.[16] No longer can the church settle for custody of the spirit and leave the rest to medicine and psychiatry, as if a person were compartmentalized. Increasingly, Christians involved in the healing ministry are dealing with the whole person to provide the appropriate means of aid whether through prayer or counseling or medicine or all three.[17]

One difficulty is the question of terminology. "Faith" healing starts with two strikes against it: the unsavory reputation of the so-called faith healers and the fact that faith is exercised by all who are engaged in healing activities from prayer to surgery. "Divine" healing implies that only charismatic healing comes from God, when in reality every means of healing is his gift.

Since we are considering charisms of healing we shall use

the term "spiritual," not because the healing is limited to a person's spirit but to indicate a direct action by the Holy Spirit. Paul writes about "gifts of healings." Since God is concerned for the whole person, ministry is needed in varied dimensions. An individual's physical illness may be due to emotional stresses. An ulcer or depression is often traced to a strained relationship at home or at work.

It is sobering to realize that a person can be physically healed and yet fail to fulfill God's purpose in this blessing. On one occasion ten lepers met Jesus and called for help. He sent them to the temple for checking by the priests and on the way they were healed. Only one returned to thank him. Jesus asked, "Were not all ten cleansed? Where are the other nine? Was no one found to return and give praise to God except this foreigner?" (Lk. 17:17-18). Only the Samaritan was healed in *spirit* as well as body.

This holistic approach bridges the modern gulf between "supernatural" and "natural," which implies that God is to be thanked for healing through prayer, but science gets the credit for penicillin. Furthermore, "spiritual healing," because it recognizes the need for emotional, physical and spiritual health, goes beyond the narrow focus on sudden, miraculous physical healings as the major, if not only, demonstration of the Spirit's power. The prevalent failure of the church is to expect too little of healing charisms, but the remedy is hardly to demand a certain dramatic kind of healing. Christian concern for the whole person welcomes any means by which God chooses to exert his healing power.

Several contemporary examples will help clarify what it means to take initiative in prayer while expecting manifestations of the Spirit's healing power.

The Practice of Healing   In 1942 Alfred Price became rector of St. Stephen's Church in Philadelphia. The congregation had dwindled to the place where the vestry considered closing this inner-city church with a suburban membership. As a seminary student Price had been deeply impressed with Christ's healing ministry. He decided to demonstrate it in this impossible situation amid alcoholism, prostitution, drug addiction and illness of many kinds. So he announced a public service of spiritual healing each Thursday at noon.

About twenty attended the first service. At the end, after a long, nerve-wracking silence, several came forward for prayer. This weekly meeting, augmented by a second service at 5:30 P.M., has continued ever since. The healing ministry has been undergirded by a prayer fellowship of people healed in the church and disciplined to devote half an hour at a scheduled time for intercessory prayer. Members include doctors and nurses, clergy and congregation.

Alfred Price writes that over a thirty-year period, "I have been privileged to share in an amazing way in the mighty acts of God. I have seen people healed at the altar of my church from colds to cancer, earache to epilepsy, arthritis to chronic alcoholism, mental depression to mental derangement."[18] Nothing is promised, guaranteed or charged, but much is expected. These services have inspired hundreds of ministers in many denominations to start a similar ministry.

Another recent pioneer in spiritual healing is Agnes Sanford who exercises a gift of "healing of the memories." She came to understand how many people, often Christians for a long time, are scarred by resentment, anger and frustration from wounds in the past. Through sensitive listening and prayer these deep hurts can be healed and the person delivered from present pain.[19] During the 1950s Edgar and Agnes Sanford founded the School for Pastoral Care for ministers and laypeople interested in a healing ministry.

In recent years Fr. Francis MacNutt has become one of the foremost Roman Catholic leaders in the healing ministry. His initial interest was spurred by Alfred Price, and his participation in a School of Pastoral Care in 1967 led him to launch a healing ministry. "I would no longer have to tell people whose sicknesses were disintegrating their personalities that their illness was a God-sent cross, but I would hold up the hope that God wanted them well, even when medical science could not help."[20]

Francis MacNutt has developed a remarkable healing and teaching ministry. In no way does he disparage the need for physicians and nurses, psychiatrists and pharmacists. He advocates a team effort to cure the sick through every possible means. His recent book *Healing* discusses the nature and practice of spiritual healing in the various dimensions of spiritual, emotional and physical illness. He describes the different kinds of prayer each requires.

Two Dangers As the practice of healing increases, several dangers should be recognized. One is the teaching that healing is the Christian's right to be claimed on the basis of Isaiah 53:5.

> But he was wounded for our transgressions,
>   he was bruised for our iniquities;
> upon him was the chastisement that made us whole,
>   and with his stripes we are healed.

Some teach that since Christ has borne our physical as well as our spiritual sickness, Christians must "lay claim" to their healing in both realms. On this basis they are instructed to exercise faith for immediate healing and continue to claim it even though the symptoms of the sickness persist. Concern about persistence of symptoms is considered a lack of faith. In fact, the sufferer is often told that it takes more faith to keep his healing than to gain it in the first place.

The damage done by this view takes its toll in several ways. Wrestling with the problem of continuing symptoms builds an increasing burden of guilt and perplexity. "Am I really healed, and if so, why do the symptoms persist? If not, where did my faith break down so that I lost my healing? Should I visit the doctor?" Meanwhile the symptoms may worsen as the disease continues unchecked, until at last a desperation visit is made to the doctor whose medical assistance may be too late. When the sufferer finally takes this step he is sometimes made to feel like a defector from the faith, denying the "healing" God has already given. To the continuing pain is added a crushing burden of guilt. What is supposed to be a gift of grace becomes a religion of works in the guise of a misnamed faith. No wonder that doctors to whom such a sufferer finally comes have harsh words for "faith healing."

While the ultimate purpose of salvation is to make us whole, the context and parallelism of Isaiah 53:5 focus on atonement for sin. Furthermore, the New Testament does not teach that immediate healing of any sickness is the Christian's right or that it requires more faith to keep one's healing than to receive it. God is surely on the side of health; but difficulties, which we often do not understand, hinder both wholeness and holiness. Furthermore, the Scripture makes it clear that when a person is miraculously healed, the symptoms disappear and everyone knows it. The paralytic arose, picked up his mat and carried it out; the formerly violent Gerasene demoniac sat quietly, clothed and in his right mind. There is no indication that they had to exercise faith to "keep their healing."

While the ministry of spiritual healing encounters difficulties and suffers from misuse, the other side of the coin should be seen. What are the perils of *not* practicing it? First, there is the danger of not exercising the full ministry our Lord desires for his church. Second is the risk of denying Christian love to the sick by failing to do all we can for their healing through believing prayer. Third is the danger of weakening our witness to a secular world which worships human achievement. It is hardly impressed by arguments in support of biblical miracles two thousand years ago given by those who do not expect them today. In the end the popular belief is reinforced: it is God who sends sickness for punishment and strengthening character, while modern science cures disease and restores health.

Is It God's Will?   Many people have no objection to spiritual healing but hesitate to pray for it because they have legitimate questions which are unanswered. They ask, "Is is God's will?" The answer to this important question is twofold. First, Jesus Christ came to make people whole. The Greek word *sōzō* means "heal" as well as "save." The healing power of the Great Physician extends to all dimensions of a person's complex being. While God's purpose in a specific case is often not known in advance, the New Testament encourages us to pray for whatever healing we need.

The second answer lies in our instinctive reaction when illness comes. What happens when a mother is awakened in the night by the cries of her child with an earache and high temperature? Does she pray, "Lord, show me whether it is your will for Billy to recover. If so, I will call the doctor"? No! Her unhesitating reach for the phone to get medical help shows the mother's confidence that God wants her to act so as to bring about her child's healing.

Why, then, do we waver in seeking *spiritual* therapy? Our doubting reflects the church's long-held double standard for healing. A Christian should no more hesitate to pray for healing than a doctor hesitates to begin appropriate medical treatment. Neither can promise precise results in advance; both are responsible to act in faith and leave the results to God.

But what about Paul's much-discussed "thorn in my flesh" (2 Cor. 12:7)? Since he does not tell us, we cannot assume physical illness. Knowing that God is on the side of health, Paul did not accept this difficulty passively; he prayed three times that it would be removed. Paul continued in prayer until he was told that he would have to bear it and why. His example is a model of expectant persevering prayer for healing which does not demand a certain result.

Another question asks, "If God desires people to be well, why is there so much sickness?" No one sensitive to human suffering offers a pat answer. But the problem also appears in other areas. Peter writes that God wants everyone to come to repentance (2 Pet. 3:9). Paul teaches that the will of God is our sanctification (1 Thess. 4:3). Then why are so many unrepentant and lacking holiness of life? Even though we do not have answers to these questions, we should continue to preach the gospel, call for holy living and pray for healing.

A healing ministry can also be inhibited by a fear of failure. If we pray for healing and it doesn't happen, won't the person's faith be undermined? This fear must be faced. The issue is how we define failure. Don Gross concludes from his extensive experience with spiritual healing:

> *Disappointments can come when detailed predictions of healing fail to materialize, and the way to overcome such disappointments is to wait and see, openmindedly just what God will do. We can increase faith, hope and expectancy by concentrating on what God* has *done, on His* promises, *in a clear visualization of the healing we desire, and by thanking Him for the healing he is giving in His perfect way.*[21]

Our responsibility is expectantly to obey his instructions for healing, then trust God. Only let us not hold God responsible for not healing before we have done our part.

Here also medical doctors provide a parallel. None has a perfect record. Yet they have the faith and courage to act with the best resources at hand. Sometimes the treatment or surgery doesn't work and the patient dies. But physicians do not give up (nor do we), disillusioned with the practice of medicine. Cannot the church act with the same faith, drawing on the spiritual resources of the Lord? The answer to fear of disappointment is not to minimize expectancy lest God let us down, but to maximize expectant prayer and thereby demonstrate the love of Christ for the sick.

Today the church is beginning to rediscover its ministry of spiritual healing. After such long neglect much remains to be learned through trial and error about its practice. In every great renewal painful remodeling of the fireplace is necessary for the new fire to burn well within its structure. It is heartening to witness new Christian initiatives in prayer and faith to heal the whole person with all the resources God makes available. Such healing can be a sign of the great compassion of Christ which brings people to God.[22]

Yet much sickness persists and death still comes prematurely. We are reminded that perfect healing will take place only with the resurrection body in the presence of the Lord. Nevertheless the church has a ministry of preaching and healing until that day arrives.

No modern scholar has done more than C. S. Lewis to counter objections to Christianity and explain its truth to the modern mind. His *Problem of Pain* has proved valuable to many perplexed by suffering. In his preface Lewis writes that his only purpose was to solve the *intellectual* problem raised by suffering.

> *Nor have I anything to offer my readers except my conviction that when pain is to be borne, a little courage helps more than much knowledge, and a little human sympathy more than courage, and the least tincture of the love of God more than all.*[23]

May the day soon come when the church of Jesus Christ matches the knowledge of God it imparts through preaching with the love of God it shares through its ministry of healing.

18
The Challenge
of Renewal

Long ago there was an innkeeper by the name of Procrustes. He offered only one bed of fixed length on which all travelers were forced to lie. Procrustes cut off the feet of those who were too long and stretched the bodies that were too short. The result each time was an exact fit to the bed.

The emissaries of church renewal often suffer the same fate as the travelers in this Greek myth. On arrival they find a bed of tradition with theological legs, organizational frame and cultural mattress upon which they must lie. Unacceptable experiences are labeled enthusiastic and cut off. Unfamiliar teachings are branded heretical and stretched to fit. The price of lodging is adjustment to the status quo. Only when the bearers of renewal have enough strength to redesign the bed is there significant change.

Every major renewal challenges traditional thought and practice. Otherwise it would not be needed. The charismatic renewal is no exception. Its discovery of biblical teaching about the Holy Spirit, long overlooked or misunderstood, raises profound questions.

The Western church has long neglected the role of the Holy Spirit, especially in the body of Christ.[1] The charismatic renewal reveals areas of the Spirit's activity which the church has overlooked in developing its theology. It is no wonder, then, that this dynamic movement challenges some accepted theological categories.

Charisms and the Christian Traditionally, spiritual gifts have been defined basically as abilities, possessed by the individual, expressing the believer's spiritual growth as a dimension of sanctification. The charismatic renewal challenges this view. Charisms need to be appreciated as a distinct, dynamic manifestation of the Holy Spirit through the Christian for strengthening the body of Christ.

Both Protestant and Roman Catholic doctrines deal with the Holy Spirit's work in creation, revelation, the Incarnation, regeneration and sanctification, and final redemption. But none of these categories adequately expresses the charismatic activity of the Spirit. The New Testament has many terms for becoming and maturing as a Christian. Traditional theology focuses them in justification/regeneration and sanctification. It identifies the baptism in the Spirit with the former and the Spirit's filling with the latter. But our study of Luke and Paul shows that the fit is not this neat.

For more than a century evangelical, revival and Pentecostal movements have challenged this interpretation of the baptism and filling with the Spirit. They point to the book of Acts where mature believers had further fillings which empowered their worship, witness and service. These manifestations of the Holy Spirit are found also in Romans 12 and 1 Corinthians 12 where they are called spiritual gifts.[2] Neither Luke nor Paul considers the filling of the Spirit a dimension of sanctification. The exercise of these gifts is not a sign of individual spiritual maturity.

Hendrikus Berkhof calls this filling activity a "third gift" of the Spirit, different from justification/regeneration and sanctification. He believes the Pentecostals are basically right in seeing a work of the Holy Spirit beyond that which is recognized by the major denominations, even though he cannot accept their theological interpretation of this experience. He stresses that this third gift is not *another stage* of spiritual experience; it belongs with the others and forms a unity with them.

Being filled with the Spirit equips the individual *at every stage* of the Christian life to be an instrument of the Spirit in the church and the world. This activity is not the same as the development of spiritual maturity—Christlike character and moral living. The *gifts* of the Spirit are different from the *fruit*. Berkhof writes:

> *The filling by the Spirit means that the justified and sanctified are now turned, so to speak, inside out. In Acts they are turned primarily to the world; in Paul to the total body of Christ; but this is merely a difference in situation and emphasis.*[3]

After centuries of neglect, the significance of this dimension of the Spirit's action needs much more reflection. Yet two points are clear. First, it is not an additional experience "beyond Christ." If justification is Christ's righteousness *for* us and sanctification is his life being formed *in* us, then filling with the Spirit and exercising spiritual gifts is Christ's work *through* us as members of his body in witness and service.

Second, while charisms are not primarily for individual use, in a unique way they mark the individuality of the Christian as a member of the body. Justification and sanctification (or holy living evident as fruit of the Spirit) have the same characteristics for all. But each member of the body functions differently. In a wonderful way this dimension of the Spirit's activity affirms the uniqueness of the believer even while he is functioning as a member of the body united with others. "In filling us, he [the Spirit] occupies our individuality, the special mark which I and I alone bear, a special contribution which I have to make to the whole of life. He takes it up for the whole kingdom of God."[4]

If charismatic activity is the *Spirit's* action through a believer, what is the exact nature of a charism? Three main answers vie for recognition. The traditional view, as we have said, sees a spiritual gift as an ability, talent, capacity or faculty with which a person is endowed, similar to an aptitude for art or music.[5] This gift is a possession which the individual develops and continues to use. A charism is therefore considered to be the activation or heightening of a natural ability.

Many in the Pentecostal-charismatic movement counter that "a natural gift is not a charism."[6] Rather, the spiritual gift is a supernatural power entirely different from a natural ability. A third view transcends this natural-vs.-supernatural debate. It emphasizes *function* rather than *faculty*. In other words, a charism is neither a natural ability nor a new impartation which a person *possesses*, but a new functioning of what God has already given, activated and exercised by the power of the Spirit. Arnold Bittlinger defines a charism as "a gracious manifestation of the Holy Spirit, working in and through but going beyond, the believer's natural ability for the common good of the people of God."[7] The charism is a gift because that ability has a new function and power. In its exercise the unity of the divine and the human should be recognized.[8]

In 1 Corinthians 12:7 Paul does not define a spiritual gift in terms of static individual possession, but dynamic corporate action. The gift itself is a "manifestation of the Spirit . . . given for the common good."

Gifts for the Body While these insights are valuable for understanding the charismatic activity of the Spirit in the individual, this is not the primary concern in the New Testament. Luke's perspective on filling with the Spirit does not focus on the inner life, but on the external consequences—the growth of the church. Nor in Paul's teaching do charisms correspond to individual maturity. His one standard for judging their value is whether they build up the body of Christ.

When spiritual gifts are considered primarily as an aspect of individual sanctification, the key question is: "What is my gift and how shall I discover and use it?" When they are understood primarily as a function of the body, a much different question emerges: "How does the Spirit desire to manifest his gifts through members of the body to strengthen its life and mission in the world?" This focus on the community rather than the individual places the exercise of spiritual gifts primarily in the arena of ecclesiology (the doctrine of the church) and secondarily in the context of individual Christian growth.

The heart of the charismatic renewal is not the question of speaking in tongues or even baptism in the Spirit (about which there is marked difference of opinion even within the renewal). Rather it is commitment to the full range of charisms as manifestations of the Holy Spirit to meet the needs of the Christian community. The charismatic renewal affirms the New Testament teaching that all of these spiritual gifts are essential to the life and mission of the church. It expects these charisms and witnesses to their presence today.

This statement affirms several realities. Spiritual gifts for today are not limited to the so-called natural or nonmiraculous. Neither is the exercise of certain gifts confined to a few church officers. Nor are the charisms individual possessions for private use. Rather, *all* the gifts are to be exercised *throughout the body*, as the Holy Spirit manifests them, for strengthening the Christian *community*.

This shift in focus, from individual sanctification to corporate worship and witness, challenges the prevalent institutional model of the church. Howard Snyder notes that

> *the contemporary church in its institutional form makes little room for spontaneous spiritual gifts. Worse yet, too often it does not need spiritual gifts in order to function more or less successfully. When the local church is structured after an institutional rather than a charismatic model, spiritual gifts are replaced by aptitude, education and technique, and thus become superfluous.*[9]

We have seen how the Western church has both "desupernaturalized" and "institutionalized" spiritual gifts. With the miraculous charisms relegated to the first century and the remaining significant gifts assigned to church offices, what was left for the congregation? Of more than twenty charisms in nine New Testament lists, barely half a dozen—such as serving, contribution and showing hospitality—remained for the "laity." No wonder spiritual gifts came to be identified with individual abilities and natural talents.

Now, however, the full range of charisms is being manifested throughout the membership of the body, often by persons without theological education or church office. This situation is forcing theological reflection on the relationship of charismatic activity to the structure and functioning of the church.

The two major Presbyterian churches in the United States have studied the charismatic renewal and have issued reports (1970 and 1971) which evaluate biblical teaching and current emphasis on spiritual gifts in the light of the Westminster Confession of Faith. The reports express concern for the relationship of these gifts to the Word and sacraments in which the grace of the covenant is dispensed and administered. One report recognizes that "though baptism is a channel of God's grace, this grace is not automatically efficacious. Accordingly, there may be special need in the Reformed tradition to lay stress on later occasions . . . on which God's grace may also be appropriated."[10]

Lutheran theologians are also wrestling with the relationship of the charisms to the sacraments. In its evaluation of the charismatic renewal, the 1974 report of the Lutheran Church in America recognizes that "the Lutheran zeal to preserve sacramental objectivity [baptism is God's act] may have led to an undue focusing on the rite itself with a corresponding neglect of the paradigmatic function of baptism [a pattern for the Christian life]."[11] The report urges understanding the charismatic experience in a manner consonant with the Scriptures and traditional Lutheran theology and offers positive pastoral guidelines.

Unlike Neo-Pentecostalism in the mainline Protestant

churches, the Roman Catholic renewal has involved theologians from the beginning. Their reflections on the theological meaning of the renewal, especially in the light of the Second Vatican Council, has produced an extensive literature. In a recent work Donald Gelpi notes that many Catholic prayer groups present Spirit-baptism as a renewal of one's confirmation. He summarizes the doctrinal stance of Vatican II on gifts of the Holy Spirit and then discusses the relationship of charism to sacrament and to hierarchy. Gelpi explores the interaction between "charismatic" gifts of the members and "hierarchical" gifts, such as teaching, expressed by an official church leader. He shows how they can supplement each other and concludes that "sacraments and hierarchy are in the last analysis unintelligible apart from a theology of charism."[12]

Across a broad spectrum of churches many theologians have passed from questioning *whether* the charismatic renewal has a valid place in their community to exploring *how* it can give deeper meaning to the confessions and canons to which they are committed. For them the charismatic renewal has largely changed from a suspected outsider threatening the church, to a valued member of the family making its own contribution to the worship, witness and service of the Christian community.

Church Programs   While the theologians ponder these issues, local churches face immediate questions about how to accommodate the charismatic renewal. This time, unlike seventy years ago, the fire has been allowed to remain in the fireplace. What does this imply for existing programs, and how can tensions between the old and the new be handled?

It is understandable that during the 1960s the charismatic model appeared largely in fellowship groups outside existing church programs. The members usually remained active in their own congregations, even those hostile to the renewal. But in weekly "prayer and praise services" in homes Christians from a variety of denominations gathered to learn more about the nature and exercise of spiritual gifts. These weekly meetings are still the strength of the charismatic renewal.

In recent years, however, many churches have found ways for this expression to take place within their program. Sunday evening or a weeknight is devoted to this model of worship and witness to supplement the traditional services.[13] As with any revival, there should be the opportunity to remodel the fireplace gradually, welcoming the new while maintaining the best of the old.

Yet several major barriers inhibit the growth of charismatic activity in a church, even where there is no theological opposition. First is a lack of expectancy. The Scriptures consistently link expectancy and faith with the work of God in our lives— whether in prayer or evangelism, missionary concern or spiritual gifts. That is why Paul instructed the Corinthians (despite their difficulties with certain charisms), "Eagerly desire spiritual gifts" (1 Cor. 14:1). Where little is expected, usually little happens.

Second is the fear of misuse. Like evangelism and teaching, charisms such as prophecy, tongues and healing are often abused. The resulting damage inhibits many from exercising them. Yet the growing use of these unfamiliar gifts shows that they may be expected and can be properly exercised.

There is also a deeper fear of the unknown, of what we cannot predict and control. A technological age, abounding with prepackaged, controlled programs guaranteeing results, makes it difficult even in church programs to trust God himself to work in unexpected ways. We are secure with familiar forms. Remodeling the fireplace, though necessary, can be painful.

Despite these barriers progress is being made. Successful experiments in the integration of a charismatic community with a congregation or parish have been reported.[14] New forms of community, such as extended families, are taking shape.[15] While much pioneering remains, and each church has its own set of opportunities and difficulties, basic approaches have been worked out for those who are ready to move ahead.

The Question of Division The charismatic renewal is often charged with being divisive. This serious criticism must be considered carefully. It raises questions about the nature of revivals, biblical truth and the cause of division.

Every revival by its nature becomes an occasion for division. Reflecting judgment on current ways of thinking and acting, it calls for change. Some welcome the call while others reject it. The response is always mixed, just as it was in biblical times.

According to the Scriptures, truth involves more than the mind; since it is a revelation from God, it calls for a response of the heart and will. Biblical truth calls for decision and so divides those who respond positively from the others who react negatively. Simeon declared that Jesus would cause the "falling and rising of many," and Jesus himself said he would bring division even in families (Lk. 2:34; Mt. 10:34-36).

We should realize that it is people, not the truth, who cause division. Any truth can become an occasion for division if people consider it worth dividing over. A difference of opinion does not necessarily cause division. The important issue is not *that* we disagree, but *what* we disagree about and *how* we handle our disagreement. Every church has basic truths accepted by all, and others about which members agree to disagree. Augustine urged a constructive approach to this problem: "In essentials, unity; in nonessentials, diversity; in all things, charity."

Often the difficulty involves terminology and faulty communication. Some object to the term "charismatic" Christians as inaccurate and divisive since all believers are charismatic in the sense of exercising some charism.[16] This is true. Is not every Christian also a disciple, witness and steward of his possessions? But if all Christians are everything the New Testament calls them, why is not the church today the powerful force it was in the first century?

The reality is that not all Christians are fully committed to the Lordship of Jesus Christ, nor do all effectively witness to him or live sacrificially in our materialistic culture. Hence the need for discipleship seminars, evangelism workshops and training in stewardship. Likewise, the charismatic renewal recognizes that not all Christians expect the full range of spiritual gifts in the church today. The witness of many, formerly unconcerned or opposed but now expectant, confirms this.

God has broken through traditional theologies and structures to work in new ways. People who rediscover biblical truths long lost or denied often tend to overemphasize them. Yet gifts such as prophecy, healings and speaking in tongues sometimes need to be stressed. While set in a cast, the muscles of a broken arm or leg atrophy because of inactivity. When the cast is removed, that limb is especially exercised, not because it is more important than others, but because the weak member must be strengthened. The charismatic renewal at times reaffirms certain gifts long denied so that the *full range* of charisms can be exercised. It wants the church to be enriched in Christ in every way, not lacking any spiritual gift and kept strong until the end (1 Cor. 1:5-8).

Ardent advocates of renewal should beware of the tendency toward an individualism that leads to independence of authority. When confronted by indifference or opposition within the church, they may be tempted to take the fire out into the middle of the floor, to go it alone and make their own fellowship. This separatism further fractures the church which is already tragically broken into hundreds of denominations and sects. It is more often a sign of rugged American individualism and unwillingness to cooperate than a directive from the Lord.

Spiritual gifts such as evangelism, prophecy and healing, to mention a few, are not given to individuals for building a personal following. The history of the evangelistic and healing movements in recent decades shows that the greatest danger of misusing spiritual gifts arises when leaders operate independently of the discipline and correction of local church authority. In the long run fire outside the fireplace either dies out through individualism or constructs a hearth more authoritarian than the one it left.

On the other hand, the custodians of the fireplace are responsible to forestall division by being open to change in programs and nonessential points of theology. Christian leaders need to guard against an unwillingness to hear divergent interpretations of Scripture which seem to question their authority. Too easily they can mistake their traditions for the Word of God and resist any change that threatens their security.

Nevertheless, it is heartening to note how mature and sensitive leadership can prevent unnecessary division. Hundreds of churches today witness to the loving unity possible amid marked diversity of perspective among its members regarding spiritual gifts. The healthiest manifestations of charismatic renewal occur in such local churches (as Paul instructed in 1 Corinthians), where they build the body of Christ.

The charismatic renewal does not settle historic theological differences about the nature and organization of the church with its ordinances or sacraments. It does not call for a standard design of fireplace—only for sufficient changes so that the Holy Spirit can work creatively. The renewal recognizes that the Holy Spirit is sovereign and free. He blows when, where and how he wills, retaining the initiative at every moment in the community's life.

Each church is challenged to recognize and receive this creativity according to its own situation. The charismatic renewal was not initiated by human planning and it provides no blueprint for the future. It does not yet give answers to some of the profound questions it raises. They will be discovered only through a continuing desire to know more of the Scriptures and the power of God.

Blow on the Coal of the Heart Finally, the charismatic renewal challenges our post-Christian secular culture which has substituted the sovereignty of man for that of God. It is ironic that even while the "God is dead" movement of the 1960s was enjoying its brief popularity, the Holy Spirit was working unnoticed to demonstrate that he is very much alive. To an age proud of its power to control the forces of nature and society, God is speaking not only with words but with powerful and miraculous actions.

The last decade has witnessed an unexpected rise of the occult and the activity of evil spirits capturing the attention of millions. Is it surprising that this movement should be matched by an equally unexpected and more powerful activity of the Holy Spirit?

The Lord is renewing his church by many means. One of them is the charismatic renewal which was not humanly conceived, planned and organized. Its demonstration of the creative and often unpredictable power of the Holy Spirit witnesses to the sovereignty of God in history and in the church of Christ.

For many years unbelievers have criticized, and concerned believers have wept over, the ineffectiveness of today's church. Archibald MacLeish concludes his play *J.B.* with these words:

Blow on the coal of the heart.
The candles in churches are out.
The lights have gone out in the sky.
Blow on the coal of the heart
And we'll see by and by . . .
We'll see where we are.
The wit won't burn and the wet soul smoulders.
Blow on the coal of the heart and we'll know . . .
We'll know. . . .[17]

According to our Lord Jesus Christ, the Holy Spirit is like the wind blowing wherever it pleases (Jn. 3:8). Today the Spirit is blowing on the coal of the heart in unexpected ways. Smoldering souls are beginning to flame, and in a new way we see and know the love and power of God.

Appendixes

Appendix A
The Impartation
of the Spirit
in the Gospel of John

While this study concentrates on Luke's Gospel, a comprehensive discussion must take note of the impartation of the Holy Spirit before the ascension as recorded in John 20. First we briefly consider John's perspective.

While John has a different theological emphasis than Luke, both writers strongly link the Spirit to Jesus. In one sentence John conveys a wealth of meaning as he reports the words of the Baptist: "The one who sent me to baptize with water told me, 'The man on whom you see the Spirit come down and remain is he who will baptize with the Holy Spirit' " (Jn. 1:33). The phrase "come down and remain" parallels Luke's description of Jesus as the Bearer of the Spirit, while the promise of baptism indicates that Jesus will also be the Giver of the Spirit.[1]

John again links the Spirit and Jesus in the latter's great invitation at the Feast of Tabernacles.

"If a man is thirsty, let him come to me and drink. Whoever believes in me, as the Scripture has said, streams of living water will flow from within him." By this he meant the Spirit, whom those who believed in him were later to receive. Up to that time the Spirit had not been given, since Jesus had not yet been glorified. (Jn. 7:37-39)

Only after his ascension will Jesus pour out the Spirit in all his fullness so that believers can be filled to overflowing.[2]

John also connects the Holy Spirit with mission. In chapter 16 the Spirit is promised to guide the disciples into all truth and to convict the world of sin, righteousness and judgment. In fact, the upper room discourse, with its dominant theme of continuity between the ministries of Jesus and the Spirit, is, in this respect, John's preview of the Acts.

The strongest link between Jesus and the Spirit and mission comes after the resurrection in words to the disciples gathered in fear behind locked doors.

Jesus came and stood among them and said, "Peace be with you!" After he said this, he showed them his hands and side. The disciples were overjoyed when they saw the Lord.

Again Jesus said, "Peace be with you! As the Father has sent me, I am sending you." And with that he breathed on them and said, "Receive the Holy Spirit." (Jn. 20:19-22)

The proper interpretation of this passage must lie within the framework of John's purpose, taking what he means to teach, no more and no less. It has long been recognized that the intent and style of the fourth Gospel is different from the first three. While securely anchored in history, John's narrative cannot be neatly dovetailed with Luke's as if they were moving along the same linear track.[3] This account in chapter 20 should not be viewed as filling a gap in Luke's sequence and interpreted within his framework. In his Gospel, John teaches the unity of the final decisive events in Jesus' ministry: death, resurrection, ascension and gift of the Spirit. He records this fourth event of the cluster in the context of the commission given to the disciples by the risen Lord.

Some interpreters consider this impartation of the Holy Spirit to be the disciples' regeneration. Thus the baptism with the Spirit fifty days later is a second and distinct work of grace in their spiritual lives. Other interpreters, concerned to preserve Pentecost for the initial reception of the Spirit, take Jesus' words as the promise of a future event.

The first view reads too much into this event. John's purpose here is not to deal with the inner life of the disciples, the stages of their spiritual development. The immediate context is their mission in the world and responsibility in connection with the forgiveness of sins (20:21b, 23). The meaning for the disciples lies in the link between Jesus and the Spirit. The Lord demonstrates to them that the coming of the Spirit is something *he* does for them, just as he has promised. "As Augustine observes, the Lord showed that the Spirit was not the Spirit of the Father only but also his own."[4]

The second view fails to do justice to the clear reading of the text. All three verbs are in the present tense. Jesus says, "Peace be with you. . . . I am sending you. . . . Receive the Holy Spirit." The last verb cannot be made to mean, "You *will receive* the Holy Spirit." Furthermore, John records that Jesus breathed on them; an impartation actually took place.[5] The problem of reading too much into a text is hardly solved by taking too little from it!

So we understand this event, in the light of John's purpose, as a real impartation of the Spirit. The author does not answer *our* question as to exactly what happened in the disciples' spiritual experience. He does show, however, that the Spirit's coming is the gift of the risen Lord to the disciples in the context of the commission they receive—to go, preach and forgive sins.

In the upper room discourse before his death Jesus had said in effect, "I am going. You are staying, but you will not be alone. I have a mission for you, but you cannot perform it in your own wisdom and strength. I will send the Spirit as your comforter, teacher and guide. Through him I will complete my teaching, and through you he will fulfill the mission of the church." Now, after his death and resurrection, the Lord communicates this reality to his disciples in both words and action. Before his departure, he graciously gives them, not only their mission, but also the experience of the Spirit they need until his full coming with power at Pentecost.

Appendix B
Notes on
New Testament
Gift Lists

The New Testament has nine lists of gifts, eight of which appear in the writings of Paul. Of the latter, six consist of charisms (Rom. 12:6-8; 1 Cor. 12:8-10; 13:1-3; 13:8; 14:6; 14:26); one comprises gifted individuals (Eph. 4:11); and one has both categories (1 Cor. 12:28). Peter's list consists of charisms (1 Pet. 4:9-11).

It is commonly assumed that the biblical writers provide an order of rank, so that the relative value of a gift can be determined by its place on a list. Thus, prophecy and wisdom are to be considered most important because they often appear first, while speaking in tongues is the least of the charisms because it comes last (Rom. 12:6-8; 1 Cor. 12:8-10). But this assumption is valid only if the context and usage show that the author *intends* to list the gifts in order of rank. Otherwise such an evaluation by a commentator reflects his own view more than that of the biblical writer. The following brief analysis examines the way spiritual gifts are listed and how their order may be properly understood.

Ephesians 4:11 Apostles, prophets, evangelists, pastors, teachers.

In Ephesians Paul stresses the importance of the founding role played by the first apostles and prophets in the church (Eph. 2:20; 3:5). Evangelists then preach the gospel and bring others into the Christian community. Pastors and teachers provide the ongoing nurture and guidance needed by the new converts as well as the older believers. The list of gifted individuals in Ephesians 4:11 seems to indicate something of a chronological order in the initial establishment of the church and subsequent Christian communities. There is no evidence, however, that Paul considers evangelists more important than pastors in any absolute sense or that the teachers are of least importance because they are listed last.

Romans 12:6-8 Prophesying, serving, teaching, encouraging, contributing, leading, showing mercy.

Prophecy is prominent in Paul's teaching and appears early on most of his lists. The other gifts show no order of rank. Mercy, for example, can hardly be considered least important just because it comes last. It appears that this list is a random selection of charisms of speech and action illustrating the diverse functions of members in the same body.

1 Corinthians 12:8-10 Wisdom, knowledge; faith, healings, miracles; prophecy, discerning of spirits; speaking in tongues, interpretation of tongues.

Wisdom and knowledge are involved in the most serious problem at Corinth, to which Paul devotes most of the first four chapters. The next three are charisms of action which are not prominent in this letter. The last two pairs involve inspired speech and figure prominently in Paul's instruction in 1 Corinthians 14.

The three groups do not evidence an absolute order of rank. Within each group the first word appears to be key: *wisdom* involves knowledge; *faith* is basic to healings and miracles; speaking in tongues with interpretation is a form of *prophecy*. If there is an order, it seems to be one of degree of misuse, since this is a problem-oriented letter. First and last place on a list or in a sentence can be positions of emphasis. Both wisdom (first) and tongues (last) were being misused at Corinth.

1 Corinthians 12:28 First apostles, second prophets, third teachers, then miracles, then gifts of healings, helpful deeds, administrations, different kinds of tongues.

The ranking of gifted individuals is obvious; this is the only list in which Paul assigns an explicit order of importance. The five charisms appear to be a random sample of action and speech, three appearing in 1 Corinthians 12:8-10 and two similar to the gifts in Romans 12.

Notice that only the *gifted individuals* are explicitly ranked. It is not clear why, among the *charisms*, miracles and healings come first. As valuable as they are, these two are not necessarily the most important for every occasion. Here also the pattern is a random illustration of diversity, rather than an order of rank.

This same illustration of diversity is evident in the four brief lists of 1 Corinthians 13 and 14.

13:1-3	*13:8*	*14:6*	*14:26*
tongues	prophecies	revelation	instruction
prophecy	tongues	knowledge	revelation
knowledge	knowledge	prophecy	tongues
faith		teaching	interpretation

Most of these charisms involve speech and knowledge, which are important in building up the body. Since the context in chapter 14 is public worship, this focus on gifts of speech is understandable. In these four brief lists, the same gifts do not appear in any consistent order. Sometimes, for example, tongues is first, sometimes it appears second or third. It is evident that Paul does not intend to teach the relative value of spiritual gifts by the place they occupy on a list.

1 Peter 4:9-11 Hospitality, prophecy, service.

Hospitality without grumbling, speaking the very words of God and serving with the strength God provides are all charisms. The context of this list and the order of the gifts show no intent to assign value according to place. Like Paul, Peter uses a random sample to illustrate his teaching that the gifts should be used in love "to serve others, faithfully administering God's grace in its various forms" (4:10).

Conclusion   Our study of these lists of charisms shows that Paul consistently selects and orders gifts randomly in order to illustrate diversity, rather than to indicate rank. Where there appears to be a logical order, it must be understood in the context of the passage and not made an absolute for all occasions. This pattern is consistent with Paul's doctrine of the body wherein each member serves a meaningful function according to the needs of the community, not according to a hierarchical ladder of status.

Every charism, as a manifestation of the Spirit for the common good, is valuable as it strengthens the body in its own way at the right time. No one member or gift is most important at all times; this prominence belongs only to the Head. It is not surprising, therefore, that attempts to rank a gift according to its place on the list are subjective at best. For example, scholars who give the lowest value to speaking in tongues because it appears last in 1 Corinthians 12, fail to draw the same conclusion about teaching in Ephesians 4:11.

Furthermore, these lists provide no basis for the frequently used categories of *natural* and *supernatural*, *permanent* and *temporary*, *ordinary* and *spectacular*, *normal* and *abnormal*, *usual* and *unusual*. These categories, derived largely from experience, are imposed upon the text. The last two distinctions are statistical terms based on the status quo. They reflect the current experience of the church more than the standard of biblical teaching on which our doctrine and practice of spiritual gifts should be based.

The charismatic renewal calls for a return to the New Testament model of the church in which members of the body exercise the full range of charisms for worship, witness and service.

Notes
& Indexes

Notes

Chapter 1 *(pp. 13-18)*

[1]Mark Gerzon, *The Whole World Is Watching* (New York: Paper Back Library, 1970), p. 37.

[2]Kenneth G. Howkins, *The Challenge of Religious Studies* (Downers Grove, IL: InterVarsity Press, 1973), p. 18.

Chapter 2 *(pp. 19-28)*

[1]*Trinity* (Christmastide 1962-63), pp. 3ff.

[2]Charles H. Troutman, *Speaking in Tongues*, Memorandum No. 22: Members of IVCF Staff, 2 Apr. 1963, p. 1.

[3]Ibid., p. 1.

[4]Ibid., p. 3.

[5]Clarence T. Shedd, *Two Centuries of Student Christian Movements* (New York: Association Press, 1923). "Great causes are first incarnated by prophetic individuals and then shared by creative groups if they are rightly to affect humanity's upward march.... Universities have always been breeding places for such groups" (p. 20).

Chapter 3 *(pp. 29-38)*

[1]Subsequently, his account was published: John Randall, *In God's Providence: The Birth of a Catholic Charismatic Parish* (Locust Valley, NY: Living Flame Press, 1973).

[2]Ralph Martin, *The Spirit and the Church* (New York: Paulist Press, 1976), pp. 33f.

[3]Randall, p. 6.

[4]Ibid., p. 11.

[5]Michael Harper, *A New Way of Living* (Plainfield, NJ: Logos International, 1973). See also W. Graham Pulkingham, *They Left Their Nets* (New York: Morehouse-Barlow, 1973).

[6]*The Providence Sunday Journal,* 9 Dec. 1973, pp. F-1, 4.

[7]Randall, p. 52.

[8]John Randall, "The Parish and the Charismatic Renewal," *New Covenant,* Nov. 1976, p. 22.

Chapter 4 (pp. 39-52)

[1]Klaude Kendrick, *The Promise Fulfilled: A History of the Modern Pentecostal Movement* (Springfield, MO: Gospel Publishing House, 1961), p. 47. A survey of Parham's life and theology appears on pp. 37-64.

[2]Stanley H. Frodsham, *With Signs Following* (Springfield, MO: Gospel Publishing House, 1946). She wrote of her experience: "As hands were laid upon my head the Holy Spirit fell on me, and I began to speak in tongues, glorifying God. I talked several languages. It was as though rivers of living water were proceeding from my innermost being" (p. 20).

[3]John Thomas Nichol, *The Pentecostals* (Plainfield, NJ: Logos International, 1966), p. 28.

[4]Vinson Synan, *The Holiness-Pentecostal Movement in the United States* (Grand Rapids: Eerdmans, 1971), p. 97, chaps. 1-4.

[5]Frank Bartleman, *How Pentecost Came to Los Angeles: As It Was in the Beginning* (Los Angeles: Privately printed, 1925), pp. 44-58.

[6]Walter J. Hollenweger, *The Pentecostals* (Minneapolis: Augsburg Publishing House, 1972), pp. 63-65. See Nils Bloch-Hoell, *The Pentecostal Movement: Its Origin, Development and Distinctive Character* (London: Allen and Unwin, 1964) and Donald Gee, *Wind and Flame* (Nottingham: Assemblies of God Pub. House, 1967).

[7]William W. Menzies, *Anointed to Serve* (Springfield, MO: Gospel Publishing House, 1971), p. 72.

[8]Frank Mead, *Handbook of Denominations in the United States,* 6th ed. (Nashville: Abingdon Press, 1975), pp. 209-14. Eleven Pentecostal bodies are listed.

[9]Nichol, chap. 12.

[10]Steve Durasoff, *Bright Wind of the Spirit: Pentecostalism Today* (Englewood Cliffs, NJ: Prentice-Hall, 1972), pp. 145ff.

[11]Henry Pitt Van Dusen, "The Third Force in Christendom," *Life,* 9 June 1958, p. 124.

[12]David J. Du Plessis, *The Spirit Bade Me Go* (Oakland: Privately published, 1963), pp. 13-14.

[13]*Trinity,* Vol. 1, No. 2, 1961-62, pp. 6-7.

[14]Dennis J. Bennett, *Nine O'Clock in the Morning* (Plainfield, NJ: Logos International, 1970), pp. 66ff.

[15]Larry Christenson, *The Charismatic Renewal Among Lutherans* (Minneapolis: Lutheran Charismatic Renewal Services, 1976), p. 30.

[16]Robert Walker, "Church on the Mountaintop," *Christian Life,* Vol. 25,

No. 3, July, 1963, p. 31.

[17]Richard Quebedeaux, *The New Charismatics* (Garden City, NJ: Doubleday, 1976). Chap. 6 contrasts the development of the charismatic renewal with that of early Pentecostalism. See also Kilian McDonnell, *Charismatic Renewal and the Churches* (New York: Seabury Press, 1976), pp. 41-78.

[18]*Report of the Special Committee on the Work of the Holy Spirit* (Philadelphia: The United Presbyterian Church of the United States of America, Office of the General Assembly, 1970). *The Person and Work of the Holy Spirit, with Special Reference to "the Baptism of the Holy Spirit."* Paper prepared by the Permanent Theological Committee of the Presbyterian Church in the United States. Recommended to the churches for study by the General Assembly in 1971.

[19]Erling Jorstad, *Bold in the Spirit: Lutheran Charismatic Renewal in America Today* (Minneapolis: Augsburg Publishing House, 1974), pp. 30-31.

[20]*The Charismatic Movement and Lutheran Theology*, A Report of the Commission on Theology and Church Relations of the Lutheran Church-Missouri Synod, Jan. 1972. *The Charismatic Movement in the Lutheran Church in America* (Board of Publications, LCA, 1974).

[21]*National Courier*, 3 Sept. 1976, p. 14.

[22]Ralph Martin, pp. 24ff.

[23]Kevin and Dorothy Ranaghan, *Catholic Pentecostals* (New York: Corliss Press, 1969), p. 22.

[24]Edward D. O'Connor, *The Pentecostal Movement in the Catholic Church* (Notre Dame: Ave Maria Press, 1971), pp. 61ff.

[25]"New Era for the Church?" *Logos Journal*, March/April, 1977.

[26]Martin, pp. 105-07.

[27]Kilian McDonnell, ed., *Theological and Pastoral Orientations on the Catholic Charismatic Renewal* (Notre Dame: Word of Life, 1974). This document was prepared at Malines, Belgium, May 21-26, 1974. "The Literature of the Catholic Charismatic Renewal 1967-74," in *Perspectives on Charismatic Renewal* ed. Edward D. O'Connor (Notre Dame: University of Notre Dame Press, 1975), pp. 145-84.

Chapter 5 *(pp. 53-62)*

[1]The Greek preposition *en* has a variety of translations. Baptism is said to be *with*, *in* or *of* the Spirit. Though *with* is more common in NT translations and in early Pentecostal terminology, the word *in* is more common today and will be used exclusively in the last section of this book.

[2]John Telford, ed., *The Letters of the Rev. John Wesley* (London: Epworth Press, 1931), pp. 221-22.

[3]Timothy L. Smith, *Revivalism and Social Reform* (New York: Abingdon Press, 1957). For an account of Wesley's influence on Finney see pp. 103-05.

4Synan, pp. 50ff.

5William E. Boardman, *The Higher Christian Life* (Boston: Henry Hoyt, 1859), p. 47.

6Frederick Dale Bruner, *A Theology of the Holy Spirit* (Grand Rapids: Eerdmans, 1970). Pages 335-41 present excerpts from the teaching of R. A. Torrey, Andrew Murray, A. J. Gordon and F. B. Meyer on the nature of this second experience and the conditions for its reception.

7R. A. Torrey, *The Holy Spirit* (New York: Fleming H. Revell, 1927), pp. 112, 119.

8Albert B. Simpson, *The Holy Spirit, or Power from on High* (New York: Christian Alliance Publishing House, 1895), pp. 31-37.

9Ralph M. Riggs, *The Spirit Himself* (Springfield, MO: Gospel Publishing House, 1949), pp. 59-61, 95.

10In most respects Pentecostal theology coincides squarely with evangelical Protestant theology (Donald Grey Barnhouse, "Finding Fellowship with Pentecostals," *Eternity*, Apr. 1958, pp. 8-10). The early Pentecostals did not think they were creating new doctrines. They believed in the authority of Scripture; the deity, atoning death and resurrection of Christ; regeneration by the Holy Spirit and justification by faith; and the personal return of Jesus Christ. They also accepted the emphasis on divine healing taught by Baptist A. J. Gordon and Presbyterian A. B. Simpson. After reviewing the doctrinal position of his group in England, Pentecostal historian Donald Gee writes, "In all this it will be seen that Assemblies of God are entirely one with every true evangelical section of the Christian Church" (*The Story of the Great Revival*, London: Assemblies of God Pub. House, n.d., p. 7).

11Ernest Williams, *Systematic Theology* (Springfield, MO: Gospel Publishing House, 1953), III, 47.

12Ibid., II, 26.

13Donald Gee, *Pentecost*, No. 45 (Sept. 1958). See also Riggs, chap. 12, "The Baptism in the Spirit: How to Receive It." He urges Christians to obey, ask and believe.

14Lewi Pethrus, *The Wind Bloweth Where It Listeth* (Chicago: Philadelphia Book Concern, 1945), p. 51.

15For example, Charles Finney emphasized total obedience; Andrew Murray specified absolute surrender and prayer; F. B. Meyer prescribed confession, surrender and faith; R. A. Torrey taught seven steps including the preceding. See Bruner, op. cit., pp. 332-34.

16George H. Williams and Edith Waldvogel, "A History of Speaking in Tongues and Related Gifts," in *The Charismatic Movement*, ed. Michael P. Hamilton (Grand Rapids: Eerdmans, 1975), pp. 85-87, 96-97.

17Riggs, p. 89.

[18]Synan, p. 145.

[19]Menzies, pp. 124-30.

Chapter 6 *(pp. 65-76)*

[1]Numbers 11:24-29; Judges 3:10; 1 Samuel 10:6; Nehemiah 9:20; Isaiah 59:21; Ezekiel 2:2; Micah 3:8.

[2]E. Earle Ellis, *The Gospel of Luke* (London: Oliphants, 1974). "In rearranging their materials without regard for chronological sequence, the Gospel writers follow a common literary practice." His "orderly account" (1:3) is designed to suit his theological and literary purpose.

[3]James D. G. Dunn, *Baptism in the Holy Spirit* (London, SCM Press, 1970). "It is not so much that Jesus became what he was not before, but that history became what it was not before; and Jesus as the one who effects these changes of history from within history, is himself affected by them" (p. 124).

[4]Gerhard Kittel and Gerhard Friedrich, eds., *Theological Dictionary of the New Testament,* Vol. VI (Grand Rapids: Eerdmans, 1968), p. 400.

[5]Strictly speaking, his ministry has three elements: preaching, teaching and healing.

[6]William F. Arndt and F. Wilbur Gingrich, *A Greek-English Lexicon of the New Testament* (Chicago: University of Chicago Press, 1959), pp. 805-06.

[7]In 1899 Abraham Kuyper wrote, "The Church has never sufficiently confessed the influence of the Holy Spirit exerted upon the work of Christ. The general impression is that the work of the Holy Spirit begins when the work of the Mediator on earth is finished, as tho until that time the Holy Spirit celebrated His divine day of rest." *The Work of the Holy Spirit* (Grand Rapids: Eerdmans, 1956), p. 97.

[8]Henry Bettenson, *Documents of the Christian Church* (New York: Oxford University Press, 1947), p. 49.

[9]The New Testament teaches that Jesus is the God-Man and the persons of the Trinity are coequal. Luke describes the relationship of the Spirit to Jesus functionally in his humanity and earthly ministry. See Thomas A. Smail, *Reflected Glory: The Spirit in Christ and Christians* (Grand Rapids: Eerdmans, 1976), "Behold the Man."

[10]John Owen, *The Holy Spirit* (Grand Rapids: Kregel Publications, 1960), p. 96.

[11]John Haughy, *The Conspiracy of God, the Holy Spirit in Men* (New York: Doubleday, 1973), pp. 5, 7.

[12]Kuyper, p. 100. "He was guided, impelled, animated, and supported by the Holy Spirit at every step of His Messianic ministry." See also Owen, p. 99.

[13]James D. G. Dunn, *Jesus and the Spirit* (London: SCM Press, 1975), p. 89.

[14]Hendrikus Berkhof, *The Doctrine of the Holy Spirit* (Richmond: John Knox

Press, 1967), p. 19.

Chapter 7 *(pp. 77-84)*

[1]Alfred Plummer, *The Gospel According to St. Luke* (Edinburgh: T & T Clark, 1922), p. 95.

[2]Michael Green, *I Believe in the Holy Spirit* (Grand Rapids: Eerdmans, 1975), p. 38.

[3]Owen, pp. 86, 76. "We are taught to pray that God would give his Holy Spirit to us, that through his assistance we may live to God, in that holy obedience which he requires at our hands. . . . The Apostle Paul, in all his most solemn prayers for the churches in his days, makes this his chief petition for them, that God would give to them and increase in them the gifts and graces of the Spirit. Eph. i.17; iii.16."

[4]Isaiah's prophecy, quoted by Jesus (Lk. 4:18-19), indicates that when the Spirit comes on a person he anoints for *service*.

[5]Dunn, *Baptism in the Holy Spirit*, p. 41.

Chapter 8 *(pp. 85-96)*

[1]F. W. Foakes-Jackson, *The Acts of the Apostles* (London: Hodder and Stoughton, 1931). "Galilean believers could be understood, and the fact that every man heard them in his own tongue may be explained as allegorical of the future diffusion of the gospel to all nations" (p. 82).

[2]E. M. Blaiklock, *The Acts of the Apostles* (London: Tyndale Press, 1959). "It seems reasonable, mainly on the grounds that such a miracle would serve no immediately practicable purpose, to reject the view that foreign languages were spoken by those who had no knowledge of them" (p. 57).

[3]Kuyper, p. 138. "In the midst of the Babeldom of the nations, on the day of Pentecost the one pure and mighty human language was revealed which one day all will speak, and all the brothers and sisters from all nations and tongues will understand" (p. 138). Cf. Richard Rackham, *The Acts of the Apostles* (London: Methuen & Co., 1906), p. 21.

[4]F. F. Bruce, "The Acts of the Apostles," in *The New Bible Commentary*, ed. D. Guthrie and J. A. Motyer (Grand Rapids: Eerdmans, 1970). "The disciples were heard praising God in languages and dialects different from their native Galilean Aramaic, but recognizable by visitors to the feast as those which some of them spoke" (p. 975).

[5]Arndt and Gingrich, "Acts 2:4 may mean either *speak with different* (even other than their own) *tongues* or *speak in foreign languages*" (p. 315).

[6]Bruner, p. 163.

[7]F. F. Bruce, *Commentary on the Book of Acts* (Grand Rapids: Eerdmans, 1955). The author notes that the early apostles' preaching regularly falls into four parts: "(1) the announcement that the age of fulfillment has arrived; (2) a rehearsal of the ministry, death and triumph of Jesus; (3) citation of Old Testament scriptures whose fulfillment in these events

prove Jesus to be the Messiah; (4) a call to repentance" (p. 69).

[8]See Paul's declaration in Acts 20:21. Repentance and faith are two sides of the same coin. The individual turns away from sin to God and believes in Jesus Christ.

[9]Dunn, *Baptism in the Holy Spirit*, p. 91.

[10]These observations do not exhaust the meaning of Pentecost for the church; they simply explain Luke's interpretation. Additional significance may be gained from other writers, but their teaching is brought to, not derived from, Acts 2. Care must be exercised not to "put words in Luke's mouth."

[11]Roger Stronstad, *The Charismatic Theology of St. Luke* (unpublished paper), p. 36. The author lists the phenomena associated with eight of the nine occurrences in Acts. Six have the nature of prophecy and witness.

[12]For example, Peter in Acts 2:4; 4:8; 4:31. "Luke's use of the aorist indicative for seven of the nine references confirms the potentially repetitive character of being filled with the Spirit. . . . This contrasts with the ingressive aorist which would give the meaning '*became* filled with the Holy Spirit.' " (Stronstad, p. 37.)

[13]This subject will be considered further in chapter 15. Here it should be noted that *Luke* does not teach that Pentecost marks for the disciples either the *initial* experience of regeneration and incorporation into Christ or a necessary *second* experience of the Spirit for spiritual maturity.

[14]Charles H. Talbert, *Literary Patterns, Theological Themes and the Genre of Luke-Acts*, Society of Biblical Literature Monograph Series, 20 (Missoula MT: Scholars Press, 1974), p. 16. See also John R. W. Stott, *Baptism and Fullness: The Work of the Holy Spirit Today* (Downers Grove, IL: InterVarsity Press, 1976), pp. 48-50.

[15]Gordon D. Fee, "Hermeneutics and Historical Precedent—A Major Problem in Pentecostal Hermeneutics," in *Perspectives on the New Pentecostalism*, ed., Russell P. Spittler (Grand Rapids: Baker Book House, 1976). "In Acts, as well as in the Pauline churches (cf. 1 Thess. 5:19-21; 1 Cor. 12—14), a charismatic dimension was a normal phenomenon in the reception of the Spirit. . . . Contemporary Christians may—on the basis of the New Testament pattern—still expect such a dimension of life in the Spirit" (p. 131).

Chapter 9 *(pp. 97-109)*

[1]Dunn, *Baptism in the Holy Spirit*, p. 66. This statement seems to be a redefinition of what constitutes a Christian (cf. Rom. 3:21-24; 5:1-2; 8:1; 10:9). In chapter 5 "The Riddle of Samaria" the author analyzes five possible solutions to the problem.

[2]Bruce, *Commentary on the Book of Acts*. "The context leaves us in no doubt that their reception of the Spirit was attended by external manifestations

such as had marked His descent on the earliest disciples at Pentecost" (p. 181).

[3]The Greek *elambanon* is in the imperfect tense and may be translated "began to receive," implying repeated manifestations rather than a once and for all action.

[4]Bruner (op. cit.) stresses the need for Peter and John to see with their own eyes and be involved with their hands in "the impartation of the gift of God (v. 20), merited by nothing, least of all by race or prior religion" (p. 176).

[5]Some interpreters see here the beginning of the rite of confirmation. Cf. R. B. Rackham, *The Acts of the Apostles* (London: Methuen & Co., 1906), p. 117. Contra Bruce, *Commentary on the Book of Acts*, p. 182.

[6]Green, p. 138.

[7]Stronstad. "The temporal separation between belief and the reception of the Spirit . . . poses no theological inconsistency or contradiction. The problem is with the presupposition of the commentators and is not with Luke's narrative" (p. 49).

[8]Riggs, p. 110.

[9]Dunn, *Baptism in the Holy Spirit*, pp. 74ff.

[10]When Peter had to defend his visit later at Jerusalem, he reported that "the Holy Spirit came on them as he had come on us at the beginning" (11:15) and links this event with the promised baptism with the Spirit. Both received "the same gift" (11:17) of the Spirit even though their conversion experiences were markedly different.

[11]Here Luke does not use the adjective "other" tongues (2:4) or indicate that they were recognizable foreign languages, as at Pentecost. The tongues at Caesarea served a different purpose, although they were likewise a prophetic utterance.

[12]Pentecostal writers hold that while the pouring out of the Spirit immediately followed conversion, it was still a second act of grace. "Could we not even consider that this visitation was God's ideal, His perfect pattern: believe Christ, receive the Holy Spirit in immediate succession?" Riggs, p. 111. This view is valid only if other passages show that Luke teaches a Spirit-baptism subsequent to conversion.

[13]Moses had exclaimed, "Would that all the LORD's people were prophets, that the LORD would put his spirit upon them" (Num. 11:29). Luke reports also that Philip the evangelist had "four unmarried daughters who had the gift of prophecy" (21:9).

[14]The KJV translation "Have ye received the Holy Ghost since ye believed" is inaccurate. The Greek tenses indicate neither a time interval between these events, nor a gradual process, but a definite act at that moment.

[15]Donald Gee, *God's Great Gift: Seven Talks Together About the Holy Spirit*

(Springfield, MO: Gospel Publishing House, n.d.), p. 7. Pentecostal interpreters hold that the twelve were already Christians; as a result of Paul's
teaching they moved into fuller obedience and received the baptism with
the Spirit.

[16]Dunn, *Baptism in the Spirit,* p. 85ff.

[17]Bruce, *Commentary on the Book of Acts,* p. 387.

[18]Anthony Hoekema, *Holy Spirit Baptism* (Grand Rapids: Eerdmans, 1972),
p. 23f.

[19]For example, most of the commands in "didactic" Leviticus, as well as
the experiences in "descriptive" Exodus are not intended for Christians
today, although both have instructive value. Likewise, some of Paul's explicit instructions to the churches of his day are not necessarily for us.

[20]The apostolic preaching reflects this conviction. Peter's message of "good
news" to Cornelius is largely "what happened throughout Judea" in the
actions of Jesus (Acts 10:36-39). Jesus' actions themselves teach much
about God's character and purpose.

[21]*Webster's New World Dictionary* (New York: World Publishing Co., 1951),
p. 407.

[22]Fee, p. 126.

[23]I. Howard Marshall, *Luke: Historian and Theologian* (Grand Rapids: Zon-
dervan, 1970), p. 45. See also Ellis, pp. 9-10.

[24]Fee, pp. 130-31.

Chapter 10 (pp. 113-24)

[1]Owen, p. 89. See Smail, *Reflected Glory,* pp. 24-36.

[2]Berkhof, p. 68. For justification, compare Romans 3:23-24; 5:1. For
sanctification, Romans 15:16; Ephesians 5:26.

[3]Paul uses "sealing" with the Holy Spirit, for example, as a metaphor for
salvation. This seal is a guarantee (Eph. 1:13-14), a mark identifying us as
God's possessions (Eph. 4:30), and a deposit (2 Cor. 1:21-22). It also serves
to "endue with power from heaven" according to Arndt and Gingrich,
p. 804. The KJV translates Ephesians 1:13 "after that ye believed, ye were
sealed," implying that the sealing comes subsequent to conversion, thus
supporting the Pentecostal view that "sealing" is another term for the
baptism in the Spirit. But the correct translation is "when ye believed."
Sealing takes place at conversion.

[4]Dunn, *Jesus and the Spirit,* p. 205. He notes three other elements of grace:
(1) It is a dynamic concept, an act of God; (2) all grace is one grace of God;
(3) it is always God's action, not something we possess.

[5]Scholars are divided on whether verse 21 goes with this sentence or begins a new section. While Paul uses the participle "submitting," its connection with the preceding three is tenuous. Both NIV and RSV start the
new paragraph with verse 21.

6F. F. Bruce, *The Epistle to the Ephesians* (London: Pickering & Inglis, 1961), p. 111.

7Arndt and Gingrich, p. 887.

8Romans 12:6-8; 1 Corinthians 12:8-10; Ephesians 4:11. 1 Corinthians 12:28 combines elements of the last two. Several other shorter lists appear in 1 Corinthians 13—14. An analysis of these lists appears in Appendix B.

9See chap. 14 for a discussion of this question.

10After the first few centuries spiritual gifts of prophecy and teaching were identified with offices in the church. John Calvin considered these as appointed offices of minister, deacon and elder. *The Epistles of Paul the Apostle to the Romans and to the Thessalonians*, trans. Ross Mackenzie (Grand Rapids: Eerdmans, 1961), p. 269. C. K. Barrett observes: "It is, however, quite impossible to regard this as a list of ministers. The present list should be compared with that of 1 Corinthians 12:5ff., rather than that of 1 Corinthians 12:28. *To Paul, the Spirit suggests primarily function and activity, rather than office.*" *The Epistle to the Romans* (London: Adam and Charles Black, 1973), p. 237.

11The Greek word *apostoloi* is translated "messengers" in the RSV and "representatives" in the NIV. See also 1 Corinthians 15:5-7; Philippians 2:25. Arnold Bittlinger notes four possible groups of apostles in the NT and describes the characteristics of an apostle in *Gifts and Ministries* (Grand Rapids: Eerdmans, 1973), pp. 51ff.

12Bittlinger, op. cit., p. 24.

Chapter 11 (pp. 125-38)

1C. K. Barrett, *A Commentary on the First Epistle to the Corinthians* (London: Adam and Charles Black, 1968), p. 38. Cf. Archibald Robertson and Alfred Plummer, *A Critical and Exegetical Commentary on the first Epistle of St. Paul to the Corinthians* (Edinburgh: T & T Clark, 1911), p. 5.

2Arndt and Gingrich, p. 685. See E. Earle Ellis, *Prophecy and Hermeneutic* (Tubingen: J. C. B. Mohr, 1977), " 'Spiritual Gifts' in the Pauline Community," pp. 21-42.

3Arnold Bittlinger, *Gifts and Graces* (London: Hodder and Stoughton, 1967), pp. 16-18. The author discusses several possible interpretations of this puzzling expression.

4Donald Bridge and David Phypers, *Spiritual Gifts and the Church* (Downers Grove, IL: InterVarsity Press, 1974). An explanation of these Greek words appears on pp. 21-23.

5Charles Hodge, *Commentary on the First Epistle to the Corinthians* (Grand Rapids: Eerdmans, 1950. "The principle of classification is not discernible. It is better to take the classification as we find it. . . . The Scriptures are much more like a work of nature than a work of art; much more like a landscape than a building" (pp. 244-45).

258

[6]Dunn, *Jesus and the Spirit*, p. 221.

[7]E. Earle Ellis, "*Wisdom* and *Knowledge* in 1 Corinthians," *Tyndale Bulletin* 25 (1974), pp. 96-97.

[8]Siegfried Grossman, *Charisma: The Gifts of the Spirit* (Wheaton: Key Publishers, 1971), p. 70.

[9]James Moffatt, *The First Epistle of Paul to the Corinthians* (London: Hodder and Stoughton, 1959). "Such marvelous results of faith are not the prerogative of apostles, but spiritual functions open to any member of the church who had the gift" (p. 182).

[10]Dunn, *Jesus and the Spirit*, p. 229.

[11]Ibid., p. 234.

[12]Werner Meyer, quoted by Bittlinger, *Gifts and Graces*, p. 99.

[13]*Webster's New World Dictionary*, p. 459.

[14]Stott, pp. 38-43. The author notes four parts in every kind of baptism: subject, object, element and purpose. Here the Holy Spirit is not the subject, but the element.

[15]Here the KJV accurately shows the difference between the two groups (individuals and spiritual gifts) which is obscured by the RSV, NIV and NEB.

[16]Moffatt, p. 190. "The order is not strictly one of importance any more than above (vv. 8-10). . . . When Orientals enumerated several things or persons they often spoke of the first three especially (e.g., Gen. 32:19; Mt. 22:25)."

Chapter 12 (pp. 139-48)

[1]Barrett, *The First Epistle to the Corinthians*, p. 297.

[2]Arndt and Gingrich, p. 848.

[3]Hodge, p. 264.

[4]Although usually translated "and," *kai* sometimes has the meaning of "but" (Acts 16:7).

[5]Robertson and Plummer, *A Critical and Exegetical Commentary on the First Epistle of St. Paul to the Corinthians*, p. 289.

[6]Frederik W. Grosheide, *Commentary on the First Epistle to the Corinthians* (London: Marshall, Morgan and Scott, 1954), p. 303.

[7]Merrill F. Unger, *The Baptism and Gifts of the Holy Spirit* (Chicago: Moody Press, 1974). "The question of the permanency of certain gifts is *the* subject of the chapter, not, as popularly supposed, the topic of love . . . the gifts of prophecy, tongues, and knowledge would no longer be needed and no longer manifested when the finished written revelation of God has arrived" (p. 143).

[8]S. Lewis Johnson, *The Wycliffe Bible Commentary*, ed. C. F. Pfeiffer and E. F. Harrison (Chicago: Moody Press, 1962). "*That which is perfect* cannot be a reference to the completion of the canon of Scripture" (p. 1252).

[9]Robertson and Plummer, p. 297.

[10]Some interpreters equate "talking like a child" with "speaking in tongues," making this gift a symptom of immaturity which will soon pass away. This subjective interpretation misuses Paul's metaphor by arbitrarily taking one part literally. It is also inconsistent with the legitimate role he gives to tongues in 1 Corinthians 14.

[11]Hodge, p. 275. "Certain it is that there will always be room even in heaven for confidence in God, and for hope of the ever advancing and enjoying blessedness of the redeemed."

[12]Krister Stendahl, "The New Testament Evidence," in *The Charismatic Movement*, ed. M. P. Hamilton (Grand Rapids: Eerdmans, 1975), p. 51.

Chapter 13 (pp. 149-59)

[1]The word translated "spiritual gifts," *pneumatika*, may refer especially to the "prophetic-type" gifts considered in this chapter. E. Earle Ellis, "Christ and Spirit in 1 Corinthians," in *Christ and Spirit in the New Testament*, ed. B. Lindars and S. S. Smalley (Cambridge: The University Press, 1973), p. 274. Cf. Romans 1:11; 1 Corinthians 14:37.

[2]Hodge, pp. 293f.

[3]Stendahl, pp. 52-53, 59.

[4]Robertson and Plummer, p. 312.

[5]Arndt and Gingrich, p. 29.

[6]Green, p. 168. "Because of its non-ethical and sub-personal character, the apostle was most unwilling to concur with the Corinthians' estimate of it as the best and most valuable of the gifts of the Spirit."

[7]H. E. Dana and Julius Mantey, *A Manual Grammar of the Greek New Testament* (New York: The Macmillan Company, 1955). "A prohibition in the present imperative demands that action then in progress be stopped" (p. 301). The common assertion that here Paul gives grudging assent to the use of tongues is unsupported by the text.

[8]Howard M. Ervin, *These Are Not Drunken as Ye Suppose* (Plainfield, NJ: Logos International, 1968), chap. 24.

[9]Dunn, *Jesus and the Spirit*, p. 341.

Chapter 14 (pp. 163-76)

[1]Justin Martyr quoted in James W. Jones, *Filled with New Wine* (New York: Harper & Row, 1974), p. 56.

[2]Irenaeus, *Against Heresies*, V, vi, 1, in *The Ante-Nicene Fathers* (Grand Rapids: Eerdmans, 1973), I, 531.

[3]Tertullian, *A Treatise of the Soul*, ix, *The Ante-Nicene Fathers*, III, 188.

[4]Novatian, *Treatise Concerning the Trinity*, XXIX, *The Ante-Nicene Fathers*, V, 641.

[5]Hilary of Poitiers, *On the Trinity*, II, XXXIV, NPF, 2nd series, IX, 61.

[6]Morton T. Kelsey, *Tongue Speaking* (Garden City, NJ: Doubleday, 1964),

pp. 41ff.

7Athanasios F. S. Emmert, "Charismatic Developments in the Eastern Orthodox Church," in *Perspectives on the New Pentecostalism*, ed. Russell P. Spittler (Grand Rapids: Baker Book House, 1976), p. 40.

8John Calvin, *The Institutes of the Christian Religion*, trans. F. L. Battles (Philadelphia: Westminster Press, 1960), p. 1467.

9Owen, p. 86.

10Hodge, pp. 262f.

11John F. Walvoord, *The Doctrine of the Holy Spirit* (Dallas: Dallas Theological Seminary, 1943), pp. 190-91. Of fifteen New Testament gifts, he identifies seven as temporary for the apostolic world: apostleship, prophecy, miracles, healing, tongues, interpreting tongues and discerning spirits (p. 185). The author's reasoning starts with experience, assuming these gifts disappeared with the apostolic era.

12Quoted in Michael Harper, *As at the Beginning* (Plainfield, NJ: Logos International, 1971), pp. 17-18.

13The categories of "natural" and "supernatural" events are products of Western philosophical thought which views the former as explainable by modern science, while the latter are attributed to divine action. This distinction has produced a "God of the Gaps" needed only to account for what we cannot yet explain. This understanding of God and his creation is a far cry from the biblical view. The Bible distinguishes between regular, recurring events and miracles, which are unusual, unexpected and often (though not always) unexplainable. The writers do not, however, consider the former as "natural" in the sense of happening apart from God's action. They see God active in all events—whether rain or resurrection or invading armies—as he constantly works in nature and history. Spiritual gifts may be called "*supra*natural," that is, *beyond* or *above* the ordinary, but not *super*natural, "occurring outside the normal experience or knowledge of man." Cf. Smail, pp. 15-16; Psa. 65:9-13; Jer. 5:24.

14Kuyper, p. 187. "These are the ordinary offices embracing the care of the spiritual and temporal affairs of the Church." Note that Paul does provide for such offices in the church (1 Tim. 3), but he does not assign the charismatic functions to them.

15For example, the NIV translates 1 Corinthians 12:8, "the ability to speak with wisdom . . . the ability to speak with knowledge," and so on, when the Greek simply says, "a word of wisdom . . . a word of knowledge."

16Robert H. Culpepper, *Evaluating the Charismatic Movement* (Valley Forge, PA: Judson Press, 1977). "The gifts are not static, but are evidences of the Spirit coming to expression through various members of the body. A charism has the character of an event" (p. 87).

17The relationship between individual abilities and charismatic manifestatations will be considered in chap. 18.

[18] McDonnell, *Theological and Pastoral Orientations on the Catholic Charismatic Renewal*, p. 21.

[19] William G. MacDonald, "Pentecostal Theology; A Classical Viewpoint," in Spittler. "Does this holy experience result in an experience-centered theology? Hardly. The better way to label it is this: Christ-centered, experience-certified theology" (p. 64).

[20] O'Connor, *The Pentecostal Movement in the Catholic Church*, p. 221f.

[21] David Howard, *By the Power of the Spirit* (Downers Grove, IL: InterVarsity Press, 1973), pp. 53f.

[22] Clark H. Pinnock, "An Evangelical Theology of the Charismatic Renewal," (unpublished paper), p. 11.

Chapter 15 (pp. 177-89)

[1] The Greek preposition *en* can be translated either "in" or "with." Most modern versions translate the *en pneumati* of John's promise, baptize "with the Spirit." Early Pentecostals frequently spoke of baptism *with* the Spirit. In the current charismatic renewal the phrase "baptism in the Spirit" is common and will be used in these last chapters.

[2] Dennis and Rita Bennett, *The Holy Spirit and You* (Plainfield, NJ: Logos International, 1971), p. 36. "Speaking in tongues is what happens when and as you are baptized in the Spirit. . . . If you want the free and full outpouring that is the baptism in the Holy Spirit, you must expect it to happen as in the Scripture" (pp. 64-65).

[3] Ibid., pp. 23f.

[4] Flesh: Romans 1:3 and 4:1; 3:20; 2:28; 7:5 and 8:1. A fifth meaning appears in 2 Cor. 5:16; see Arndt and Gingrich, p. 751.

[5] Stronstad, p. 32.

[6] Riggs, pp. 79ff. Torrey, *The Holy Spirit*, pp. 107ff.

[7] *Webster's New World Dictionary*, p. 116. cf. Mark 7:4.

[8] James Barr, *The Semantics of Biblical Language* (London: Oxford University Press, 1961). He calls this procedure an "illegitimate identity transfer."

[9] "It is so common in high calibre books on the Spirit by Dunn, Bruner, and now Green, to 'harmonize' Paul and Luke so that Luke gets painted with Paul's brush. If you read Luke by himself, and listen to him, it seems rather clear that the outpouring of the Spirit he has in mind is not brought into relation to *salvation*, as it is in Paul, but in relation to *service* and *witness*." Clark Pinnock, HIS, June 1976, p. 21. See also Dunn, *Baptism in the Spirit*, pp. 49ff.

[10] Herbert Schneider, "Baptism in the Holy Spirit in the New Testament" in *The Holy Spirit and Power: The Catholic Charismatic Renewal*, ed. Kilian McDonnell (Garden City: Doubleday & Company, 1975), pp. 43ff. Pre-

occupation with the phrase *baptism in the Spirit* is ironic and unfortunate: Paul uses it only once. It is just one of many phrases he employs to describe the Spirit's activity. Schneider analyzes these phrases for the gift of the Spirit in their contexts of life, hope, sonship and the like. They "refer in one way or another to the event that makes a man a Christian ... the beginning of a new relationship of an individual with God" (pp. 44-45).

[11]*The Person and Work of the Holy Spirit. With Special Reference to "the Baptism of the Holy Spirit,"* a paper of the Permanent Theological Committee of the Presbyterian Church in the United States commended by the General Assembly in 1971 to the churches for study. " 'Baptism with the Holy Spirit,' as the book of Acts portrays it, is a phrase which refers most often to the empowering of those who believe to share in the mission of Jesus Christ. The significance of 'baptism with the Spirit' is also represented in terms such as 'outpouring,' 'falling upon,' 'filling' and 'receiving,' being for the most part attempts to depict the action of God whereby believers are enabled to give expression to the gospel through extraordinary praise, powerful witness and boldness of action. Accordingly, those who speak of such a 'baptism with the Spirit' and who give evidence of this special empowering work of the Spirit, can claim scriptural support" (pp. 10, 14).

[12]Clark Pinnock, "The New Pentecostalism: Reflections of an Observer," in Spittler, p. 186. Reformed theologian Charles Hodge recognized this flexibility of the phrase. "Any communication of the Holy Spirit is called a baptism because the Spirit is said to be poured out and those upon whom he is poured out, whether in his regenerating, sanctifying or inspiring influences, are said to be baptized." *An Exposition of the First Epistle to the Corinthians*, p. 254.

[13]Cf. J. Rodman Williams, "A Profile of the Charismatic Movement," *Christianity Today*, 28 Feb. 1975, pp. 9f. Leon Joseph Cardinal Suenens, "Come, Holy Spirit," *New Covenant*, Oct. 1973, pp. 7-8; also, see report on a theological conference on the charismatic renewal at Notre Dame, pp. 13-14.

[14]Donald L. Gelpi, S. J., *Pentecostalism, A Theological Viewpoint* (New York: Paulist Press, 1971), pp. 178-83.

[15]McDonnell, ed., *Theological and Pastoral Orientations on the Catholic Charismatic Renewal*, pp. 12, 30. See also Leon Joseph Cardinal Suenens, *A New Pentecost?*, pp. 80f. "We are concerned with a new coming of the Spirit already present, of an 'outpouring' which does not come from outside, but springs up from within ... an action of the Spirit which releases and frees life and interior energies."

[16]J. Rodman Williams, *The Pentecostal Reality* (Plainfield, NJ: Logos Inter-

national, 1971), pp. 12, 14.

[17]Luke doesn't trace the inner experience of those disciples who began to follow Jesus in the old era. Only John reports that they received the Spirit from Jesus before the Ascension.

Chapter 16 *(pp. 191-205)*

[1]Kelsey, pp. 34f.

[2]Irenaeus, *Against Heresies*, V, vi, 1, *The Ante-Nicene Fathers*, I, 531.

[3]Tertullian, quoted in Kelsey, pp. 37-38.

[4]Cyril of Jerusalem, *Catechetical Lectures* 16:12; 17:37, quoted in Green, p. 172.

[5]Philip Weller, trans. and ed., *The Roman Ritual* (Milwaukee: The Bruce Publishing Company, 1952), II, 169.

[6]Ronald A. Knox, *Enthusiasm: A Chapter in the History of Religion* (Oxford: The Clarendon Press, 1950), p. 551. Nevertheless, the church honored tongue-speaking as an evidence of piety in canonizing several illustrious people. See Stanley M. Burgess, "Medieval Examples of Charismatic Piety in the Roman Catholic Church," in Spittler, pp. 15-26.

[7]Bruce Yocum, *Prophecy* (Ann Arbor: Word of Life, 1976), pp. 22ff.

[8]Williams and Waldvogel, "A History of Speaking in Tongues and Related Gifts."

[9]Deut. 13:1-5; 18:20-22; 1 Cor. 14:27; 1 Jn. 4:1-6. See John Murray, *The Epistle to the Romans* (Grand Rapids: Eerdmans, 1956), II, pp. 123ff.

[10]E. Earle Ellis, "The Role of the Christian Prophet in the Acts," *Apostolic History in the Gospel*, ed. W. W. Gasque and R. P. Martin (London: Paternoster, 1970), pp. 55f., 62f.

[11]Donald Gee, *Spiritual Gifts in the Work of the Ministry Today* (Springfield, MO: Gospel Publishing House, 1963), chapter 3 "Prophetical Ministry." See Bruce Yocum, "What Is a Prophet?" *New Wine*, Jan. 1977, pp. 4-9, 14.

[12]Hodge takes Pentecost as the model and assumes that speaking in tongues in 1 Corinthians must also be foreign languages. *An Exposition to the First Epistle to the Corinthians*, pp. 279ff. On the other hand Kuyper (pp. 134ff.) takes Paul's charism as standard so that the tongues at Pentecost could not have been foreign languages.

[13]Many Neo-Pentecostalists hold this view. Howard M. Ervin, *These Are Not Drunken As Ye Suppose*. All "spoke with tongues as the initial evidence of their baptism infilling with the Holy Spirit" (pp. 105, 109). See Larry Christenson, *Speaking in Tongues* (Minneapolis: Bethany Fellowship, 1972), chap. 2. The author notes that Scripture does not teach that speaking in tongues is the only valid evidence of Spirit-baptism. "But in showing us the pattern, Scripture gives us no consistent suggestion of any other" (p. 54). He presents this charism as "sign," "gift" and "ministry."

[14]Malcolm Cornwell, C. P., *The Gift o, Tongues Today* (Pecos, NM: Dove Publications, 1975). An excellent brief summary of current authors and publications on tongues.

[15]*The Interpreter's Bible* (New York: Abingdon Press, 1953), X, 155.

[16]Ibid., p. 155.

[17]McDonnell, *Charismatic Renewal and the Churches*, pp. 152-53.

[18]George Barton Cutten, *Speaking in Tongues: Historically and Psychologically Considered* (New Haven: Yale University Press, 1927).

[19]*Report of the Special Committee on the Work of the Holy Spirit* (Philadelphia: Office of the General Assembly, 1970), p. 11.

[20]Ibid., p. 15. Early in the neo-Pentecostal movement, speaking in tongues gained new credibility through the influential book by John L. Sherrill, *They Speak with Other Tongues* (New York: McGraw-Hill, 1964). See pp. 85-97.

[21]John P. Kildahl, *The Psychology of Speaking in Tongues* (New York: Harper and Row, 1972), p. 47.

[22]Ibid., p. 50. "It is our thesis that hypnotizability constitutes the sine qua non of the glossolalia experience" (p. 54). The research example consisted of twenty persons.

[23]McDonnell, *Charismatic Renewal and the Churches*, pp. 134-38. The author thoroughly reviews and evaluates twentieth-century research on the psychological aspects of speaking in tongues. "With the exception of Vivier most of the psychological studies reviewed in this book are seriously defective in research design" (p. 150).

[24]Luther P. Gerlach and Virginia H. Hine, *People, Power, Change: Movements of Social Transformation* (Indianapolis: Bobbs-Merrill, 1970), p. 113.

[25]William J. Samarin, *Tongues of Men and Angels* (New York: The Macmillan Company, 1972), p. 227.

[26]George Montague, *The Spirit and His Gifts* (New York: Paulist Press, 1974), pp. 18-29. Kilian McDonnell writes, "Speaking or praying in tongues is to prayer what abstract painting is to art. Just as good abstract art is not color and form without order or discipline, but is a non-objective expression of deep feelings and convictions, so also tongues" (*Charismatic Renewal and the Churches*, p. 9).

[27]Samarin, p. 221.

[28]Dennis J. Bennett, "The Gifts of the Holy Spirit," in *The Charismatic Movement*, ed. Michael Hamilton (Grand Rapids: Eerdmans, 1975), pp. 25ff.

[29]For example, Bruner, *A Theology of the Holy Spirit*, p. 293, disparages "tongue-words" in favor of "the cooler words of wisdom and knowledge" and declares that in 1 Corinthians 12—14 "we are face to face with the spiritual problem *par excellence* in Corinth."

[30]Simon Tugwell, *Did You Receive the Spirit* (New York: Paulist Press, 1972). The author describes tongues as "a gift of praise and thanksgiving, and these are the hallmark of the messianic age in which we live" (p. 65). See J. Massingberd Ford, *Baptism of the Spirit* (Techny, IL: Divine Word Publishers, 1971). "For the individual the gift of tongues can be a gateway towards another spiritual dimension" (p. 112)

[31]John Calvin, *The Epistles of Paul the Apostle to the Romans and to the Thessalonians.* "The Spirit, therefore, must prescribe the manner of our praying. Paul calls the groans into which we break forth by the impulse of the Spirit *unutterable*, because they far exceed the capacity of our intellect. The Spirit of God is said to *intercede*, not because He in fact humbles Himself as a suppliant to pray or groan, but because He stirs up in our hearts the prayers which it is proper for us to address to God" (p. 78). See Stendhal, *The Charismatic Movement*, pp. 58ff.

[32]Eddie Ensley, *Sounds of Wonder* (New York: Paulist Press, 1977). The author describes the different types of jubilation, beginning with Augustine, and traces its history in the following centuries. "The tradition of jubilation and other forms of expressive prayer gives a new conceptual framework for understanding glossolalia. . . . A profound identity between New Testament, traditional and present day glossolalia emerges. All three are a wordless vocalized entrance into the mystery of God's love" (pp. 125, 119).

[33]Ibid., p. 8. "What is jubilation? Joy that cannot be expressed in words; yet the voice expresses what is conceived within and cannot be explained verbally; this is jubilation" (Augustine on Ps. 94:4).

Chapter 17 (pp. 207-23)

[1]Sin: 1 John 3:8; physical illness: Luke 13:16; spiritual or psychological illness: Mark 3:22-23; death: Hebrews 2:14.

[2]Evelyn Frost, *Christian Healing* (London: A. R. Mowbray, 1949), pp. 64-70.

[3]Morton T. Kelsey, *Healing and Christianity* (New York: Harper & Row, 1973), pp. 150-51.

[4]Tertullian, *Ad Scapulam*, iv., *The Ante-Nicene Fathers* "And how men of rank (to say nothing of common people) have been delivered from devils and healed of diseases! Even Severus himself, father of Antonine (the Emperor), was graciously mindful of the Christians. For he sought out the Christian Proculus . . . and in gratitude for his once having cured him by anointing, he kept him in his palace till the day of his death."

[5]Origen, *Against Celsus,* I, xlvi, in *The Ante-Nicene Fathers,* III, 24.

[6]Cyprian, *Epistle* 6, 1 and 4, *The Ante-Nicene Fathers.*

[7]Saint Augustine, *The City of God* XII, 8, trans. Walsh and Honan (New York: Fathers of the Church, 1954), p. 445.

[8]Kelsey, *Healing and Christianity*, pp. 184f. This comprehensive history

traces the record from biblical times until the present.

9W. J. Koolman, *By Faith Alone: The Life of Martin Luther*, trans. Bertram Woolf (London: Lutterworth Press, 1954), p. 192.

10Kelsey, *Healing and Christianity*, pp. 16f.

11A. J. Gordon, *The Ministry of Healing*, 2d ed. (Harrisburg: Christian Publications, 1961), p. 206.

12A. B. Simpson, *The Gospel of Healing* (Harrisburg: Christian Publications, 1915).

13Andrew Murray, *Divine Healing* (Plainfield, NJ: Logos International, 1974), p. 2.

14David Edwin Harrell, Jr., *All Things Are Possible* (Bloomington: Indiana University Press, 1975).

15Wade H. Boggs, Jr., *Faith Healing and the Christian Faith* (Richmond: John Knox Press, 1956). The author attributes the "small amount of blundering success" of faith healers to their power of suggestion. "In using their accidental discovery of the psychosomatic principle, they are no more and no less effective than non-religious practitioners or even charlatans" (p. 25).

16Cited in Eugene Selzer, "Sacraments and Healing," *Hospital Progress*, No. 54 (Oct. 1973), p. 10.

17Michael Scanlan, *Inner Healing* (New York: Paulist Press, 1974), pp. 5f.

18Alfred W. Price, *Ambassadors of God's Healing and an Adventure in the Church's Healing Ministry* (Irvington: Luke's Press, n.d.), p. 77.

19Agnes Sanford, *The Healing Gifts of the Spirit* (Philadelphia: J. B. Lippincott, 1966).

20Francis MacNutt, *Healing* (Notre Dame: Ave Maria Press, 1974), pp. 13-14. "The healing acts of Jesus were themselves the message that he had come to set men free; they were not just to prove that his message was true. In a very basic sense, his medium was his message."

21Don H. Gross, *The Case for Spiritual Healing* (New York: Thomas Nelson & Sons, 1958), pp. 208-09.

22MacNutt, *Healing*. "My own experience leads me to the conclusion that healing is the most convincing demonstration to most people that God is *with us*—that he is not 'out there' beyond the reach of human compassion" (p. 24).

23C. S. Lewis, *The Problem of Pain* (New York: Macmillan, 1962), p. 10.

Chapter 18 (pp. 225-36)

1For example, in three volumes with 2260 pages published in 1871, Charles Hodge devotes 13 pages to the Holy Spirit. *Systematic Theology* (Grand Rapids: Eerdmans, 1946). Augustus Strong gives barely 10 of 1056 pages to the Holy Spirit. *Systematic Theology* (Philadelphia: Judson Press, 1951). Neither deals with the subject of spiritual gifts.

[2]The link between Luke and Paul is not the "baptism in the Spirit" (which they use differently), but "filled with the Spirit" which results in manifestations of his power (e.g., Acts 2:4, 8; 4:8, 31; 7:55; Eph. 5:18-19). While Paul does not use the "filling" terminology in Romans 12 and 1 Corinthians 12, but rather "charisms" or "spiritual gifts," these manifestations of the Spirit's activity are similar to those in Acts.

[3]Berkhof, p. 89.

[4]Ibid., p. 90.

[5]"1 Corinthians," *The Interpreter's Bible*, Vol. 10 (Nashville: Abingdon, 1955). "It is as legitimate in Paul's view to desire and develop a gift for prophecy, or for healing, or for the interpretation of Christian truth and experience, as to develop one's gift for music or art or science. One might add that it is a Christian duty to develop any power or capacity with which we have been endowed" (p. 165).

[6]"The Charismatic Movement within the Church of Scotland," Report of the Panel on Doctrine, May 1974, p. 17. See Howard M. Ervin, *These Are Not Drunken As Ye Suppose*. "These charisms are 'supernatural' manifestations of the Holy Spirit. They are not 'natural' talents" (p. 122).

[7]Bittlinger, *Gifts and Ministries*, p. 18. A German Lutheran, the author explores the relationship between charisms and the ministries of Ephesians 4:11.

[8]Yet the gifted person who has a continuing ministry such as teaching should have certain natural abilities for study and communication. The relationship between the free manifestations of the Spirit in a charismatic fellowship and the exercise of ministries, including church leadership, needs further study.

[9]Howard A. Snyder, *The Problem of Wineskins* (Downers Grove, IL: InterVarsity Press, 1975), p. 130. "The urgent need today is that spiritual gifts be seen and understood in the context of ecclesiology, as in the New Testament. A biblical understanding of spiritual gifts is absolutely essential for a biblical conception of the church" (p. 137).

[10]*The Person and Work of the Holy Spirit* (The Presbyterian Church in the United States, 1971), p. 14. John Haughy expresses concern that the charismatic renewal not be made "a distinct spirituality," but rather renew all spiritualities in the church. "The Domestication of the Holy Spirit," *Catholic Charismatic*, March/April 1976, pp. 8-11.

[11]*The Charismatic Movement in the Lutheran Church in America* (Board of Publications, L.C.A., 1974), p. 6.

[12]Donald L. Gelpi, "Pentecostal Theology: A Roman Catholic Viewpoint," in Spittler, p. 103.

[13]Erling Jorstad, ed., *The Holy Spirit in Today's Church* (Nashville: Abingdon, 1973), pp. 29-48.

[14]Michael Harper, *A New Way of Living* (Plainfield, NJ: Logos International, 1973); John Randall, *In God's Providence* (Locust Valley, NY: Living Flame Press, 1973); George Martin, *Parish Renewal: A Charismatic Approach* (Ann Arbor: Word of Life, 1976)

[15]See bibliography for books giving suggestions and guidelines for integrating a charismatic community with an existing congregation. James W. Jones, *Filled with New Wine*, pp. 91-114. Jones shows the crucial importance of community (*koinonia*) in manifesting both fruit and gifts of the Spirit.

[16]Recognizing the truth of this statement, we have not used the term "charismatic Christian" in this book.

[17]Archibald MacLeish, *J.B.* (Boston: Houghton Mifflin, 1958), p. 153.

Appendix A (pp. 239-41)

[1]John also declares in this passage the twofold role of suffering Servant and messianic Son: "Look, the Lamb of God, who takes away the sin of the world! . . . I have seen and I testify that this is the Son of God" (Jn. 1:29, 34).

[2]Stott, *Baptism and Fullness*, pp. 52-54.

[3]Dunn, *Baptism in the Holy Spirit*, p. 175.

[4]B. F. Westcott, *The Gospel According to St. John* (London: John Murray, 1903), p. 295.

[5]F. F. Bruce, *Commentary on the Book of Acts*, p. 32. Bruce notes that Jesus' action should be translated "he breathed into them" and notes the allusion to Genesis 2:7 where the Septuagint uses the same verb to describe the Creator's "breathing into" Adam's nostrils the breath of life. Westcott (op. cit., p. 295) also makes this point and adds: "To regard the words and acts as a promise and a symbol of the future gift is wholly arbitrary and unnatural."

Author Index

This index can be used as a bibliography. Turn to the page(s) listed below which follow an author's name. On these pages a footnote number will be found. This number refers to a footnote (pp. 249-69) containing the title and all bibliographic data of a book by that author.

Stott, John, *94, 136, 240*
Stronstad, Roger, *93, 101, 181*
Strong, Augustus, *225*
Suenens, Cardinal, *51, 185, 187*
Synan, Vinson, *41, 54, 60*
Talbert, Charles, *94*
Telford, John, *54*

Tertullian, *164, 192, 210*
Torrey, R. A., *55, 59, 183*
Troutman, Charles, *27*
Tugwell, Simon, *203*
Unger, Merrill, *145*
Van Dusen, Henry, *43*
Walker, Robert, *46*
Walvoord, John, *167*
Weller, Philip, *193*
Wesley, John, *17, 54, 59, 167-68, 186*

Westcott, B. F., *241*
Wilkerson, David, *33, 48-49*
Wilkerson, Donald, *33*
Williams, Ernest, *56-57*
Williams, George and Wald-vogel, Edith, *59, 193*
Williams, Rodman, *185*
Yocum, Bruce, *193, 196*

Subject Index

Antioch, *104*
Apostle, *113, 121-22, 138, 194, 243*
Azusa Street Mission, *41-42, 53*
Baptism (baptize), *77-78, 184;* water, *69, 77, 81, 90-91, 99, 103, 192, 230;* fire, *69, 77-78*
Baptism (baptize) in (with) the Spirit, biblical *53, 56, 69, 77-78, 81, 136;* contemporary, *33, 50, 178, 226, 229;* Pentecostal, *40ff., 53ff., 177ff.;* requirements for, *58ff., 178*
Basil the Great, *211*
Bethel Bible College, *40-41, 53*
Body of Christ, *118 ff., 129, 136, 145, 170-71, 182, 225ff., 246*
Bosworth, F. F., *60-61*
Caesarea, *57, 101, 178, 196*
Catholic Charismatic, 51, 230
Charismatic Renewal, *16ff., 163-64, 187, 199, 225ff., 236;* history (see also Pentecostalism), *39-52;* Episcopal, *44-45;* Lutheran, *45 ff., 230;* Presbyterian, *46-47, 230;* Roman Catholic, *29ff., 38, 231;* Yale University, *20ff., 26-27*
Charisms, see Spiritual Gifts
Church, biblical, *13, 88, 91ff., 95, 97ff., 104, 122, 125ff., 137, 170-71;* historical, *164ff., 167, 192-93, 210ff.;* contemporary, *13-14, 225ff.*
Community, *50, 91, 231-32;* extended families, *35-36, 232*
Corinth, *125ff., 149ff., 244*
Cornelius, *57, 60, 102-03, 181, 208*
Cursillo Movement, *32-33, 47-48*
Discernment of spirits, *134, 165, 196, 244*
Division, *68, 126, 211, 215*
Duquesne Weekend, *47ff.*
Eastern Orthodoxy, *166*
Ephesus, *57, 60, 101, 104-05, 125, 178, 196, 208*
Evangelism (evangelist), *121-22, 243-44*
Faith, *90 (n. 8). 109;* gift of, *132, 142-43, 244-45*

Finney, Charles, *40, 54, 186*
Fire, *77-78, 86, 211-12*
Fireplace, *15-16, 27, 43, 164, 174, 205, 215, 222, 231-32*
Francis of Assisi, *17*
Fruit of the Spirit, *117-18, 141-42, 173*
Full Gospel Business Men's Fellowship International, *43, 47*
Glossolalia (see also Tongues, speaking in), *135, 198, 201*
Gordon, A. J., *55, 214*
Healing, by Jesus, *72ff., 208;* gifts of, *132-33, 138, 169, 208, 244-45;* historical, *164-65, 167, 210ff.;* contemporary, *23, 213ff.*
Hilary of Poitiers, *65*
Holiness Movement, *40, 55, 186*
Holy Spirit, baptism (see also Baptism in the Spirit), filled with, *57, 86ff., 98, 108-09, 115ff., 181, 183, 184, 226-27;* full of, *71, 98-99, 109, 185;* gift of, *57, 58, 81, 90, 94, 103;* gifts of, see Spiritual Gifts; and Jesus, *70ff., 74ff., 80ff., 93, 239ff.;* in the New Age, *65ff., 69ff.;* power of, *71, 80, 85ff., 93, 100, 106;* promise of, *80, 81, 90, 93;* receiving, *57, 90, 99-100, 103, 105, 108;* sealing with, *114 (n. 3), 182*
Inter-Varsity Christian Fellowship, *14, 19, 25ff.*
Irving, Edward, *59*
Jerusalem, *66, 68, 73, 80-83, 85ff., 97ff., 104ff.*
Jesus Christ, conception of, *66-67, 178;* baptism of, *69ff.,* anointing, *57, 61, 70ff., 178, 208, 239;* mission of, *72, 208;* death of, *70, 78, 80, 90, 93, 208, 240;* resurrection of, *90, 93, 240;* ascension and exaltation of, *81ff., 90, 92, 98, 240*
Jesus Movement, *14*
John the Apostle, *97ff., 108, 171, 239ff.*
John the Baptist, *66-67, 69, 179-80, 239*
Judea, *73, 82*
Justification, *114, 226-27*
Keswick Movement, *55*

other books on the Holy Spirit from InterVarsity Press: